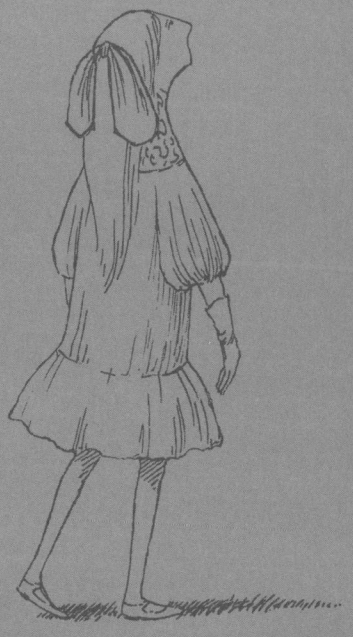

ELEGANT ENIGMAS

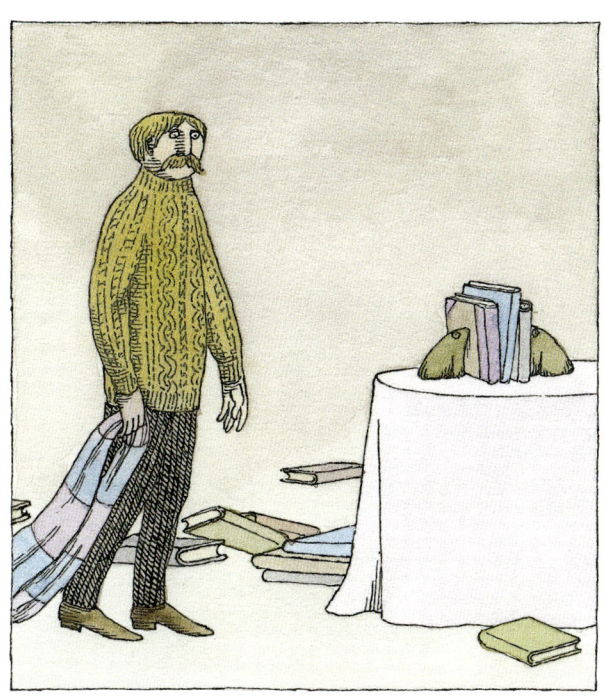

The helpful thought for which you look
Is written somewhere in a book.

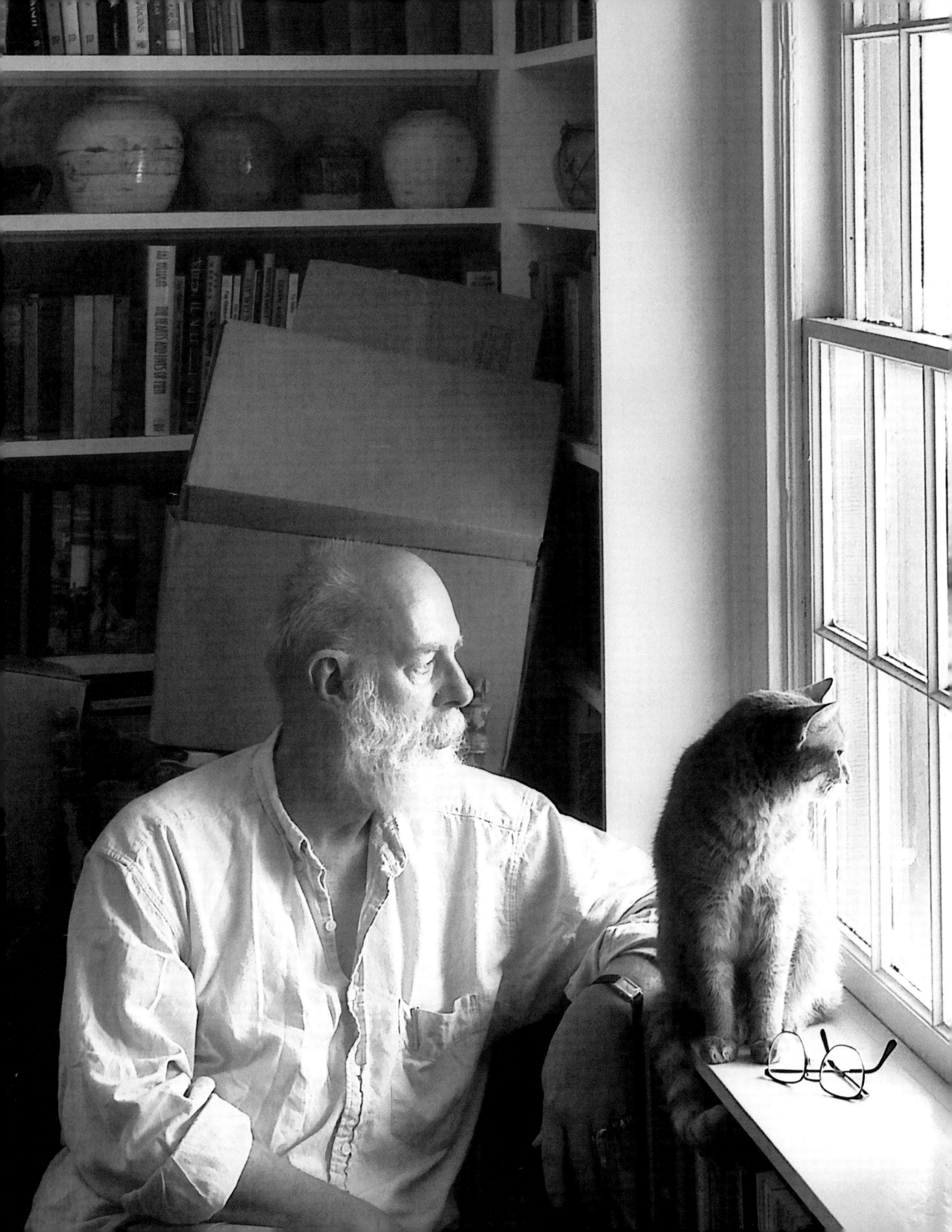

ELEGANT ENIGMAS
the art of EDWARD GOREY

Karen Wilkin

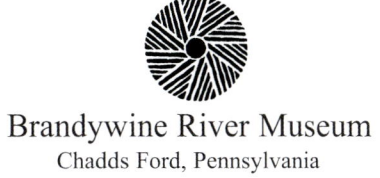

Brandywine River Museum
Chadds Ford, Pennsylvania

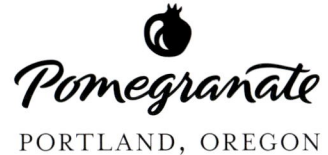

Pomegranate
PORTLAND, OREGON

Pomegranate Communications, Inc.
105 SE 18th Ave., Portland, OR 97214
800-227-1428   pomegranate.com
sales@pomegranate.com

Library of Congress Cataloging-in-Publication Data

Wilkin, Karen
  Elegant Enigmas : the Art of Edward Gorey / Karen Wilkin.
    p. cm.
  Catalog of an exhibition at the Brandywine River Museum, Chadds Ford,
Penn., Spring 2009.
  Includes bibliographical references.
  ISBN 978-0-7649-4804-6 (hardcover)
  1. Gorey, Edward, 1925–2000—Exhibitions. I. Brandywine River Museum.
II. Title.
  NC139.G63A4 2009
  741.973--dc22

                                                                2008029800

ISBN 978-0-7649-4804-6

Item No. A160
Designed by Harrah Lord, www.yellowhousestudio.info

Printed in China
33 32 31 30 29 28 27 26 25 24   18 17 16 15 14 13 12 11 10 9

Half title page: 128. *Verse Advice*
Frontispiece page 2: Photograph © Steve Marsel, Somerville, MA
Page 37: 183. *Self-Portrait with Floating Cats*

Note: Dimensions of works of art listed in this catalogue refer
to borders of the images, not including text.

CONTENTS

FOREWORD

IN every sense of the word, Edward Gorey's lines are sublime. As partners to his distinctively drawn lines, his written lines are also wonderfully crafted and inspire admiration and conjecture. In a few works, his art even reminds us of the qualification Edmund Burke established in the eighteenth century: "Terror is, in all cases whatsoever, either more openly or latently, the ruling principle of the sublime." Like so many readers of recent decades, Burke might have enjoyed Gorey's work, and we may suspect that Gorey would admire Burke's premise in turn.

Burke reminds us that great effect lies in subtlety. Gorey is a master of the sublimated and rarefied. Each image and phrase crafted by his unique, mysterious mind qualifies him as an artist whose very restraint speaks insightfully of human nature.

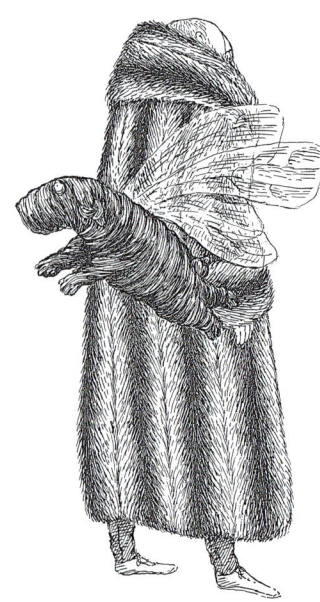

Elegant Enigmas: The Art of Edward Gorey offers a rare opportunity to view a large number of original drawings for Edward Gorey's many pursuits and publications. This current publication devoted to the exhibition may provide for each visitor a record of intimate experiences with the drawings. Such experiences have been made possible by the generosity of the Edward Gorey Charitable Trust in lending for the first time to an extensive traveling exhibition. Everyone who views these works should be grateful to the trustees.

We are also grateful to Karen Wilkin, a widely recognized art historian whose very articulate essay for this is a penetrating introduction to the artist. Lee Wierenga, Assistant Curator at the Brandywine River Museum, has worked diligently and enthusiastically on all aspects of the exhibition. Pomegranate Communications, Inc., having a special relationship with the Edward Gorey Charitable Trust, has been the eager publisher with whose staff it has been a pleasure to work.

The Brandywine River Museum is honored to have the commitment of all these people and to circulate the wonderful work of a singular, unforgettable talent.

James H. Duff
Director, Brandywine River Museum
Chadds Ford, Pennsylvania

166. SELF-PORTRAIT WITH FLYING DOG

ACKNOWLEDGMENTS

DEVELOPMENT of the exhibition *Elegant Enigmas: The Art of Edward Gorey* and this accompanying publication required the assistance and support of many people. Without their cooperation, this endeavor would have been exceedingly difficult.

R. Andrew Boose and Andreas Brown, co-trustees of the Edward Gorey Charitable Trust, are thanked for enthusiastically welcoming the idea of this exhibition. They lent many works from the Gorey archives and permitted them to travel for an extended period of time. Andreas Brown participated throughout all phases of the project. A close friend of Edward Gorey, he provided valuable insight regarding both the man and his work. He willingly answered numerous inquiries and was constantly available during the development of the exhibition. Frances M. Dulaney and Valerie and Matthew Young also graciously lent works from their collections.

It was a pleasure working with Karen Wilkin, author and Edward Gorey scholar. Her keen perception and knowledge regarding Gorey and his work are evident in the fine essay that fills the following pages. Her contribution to this publication is greatly appreciated.

Katie Burke and her staff at Pomegranate Communications, Inc., designed and published this catalogue. They produced a publication that meets the needs and expectations of both the Edward Gorey Charitable Trust and the Brandywine River Museum. Their diligence, expertise, and attention to detail are evident throughout.

Lee Wierenga
Assistant Curator
Brandywine River Museum

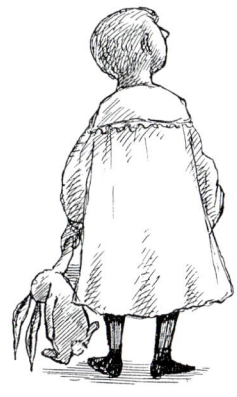

Detail from 12. THE OBJECT LESSON, unpublished cover

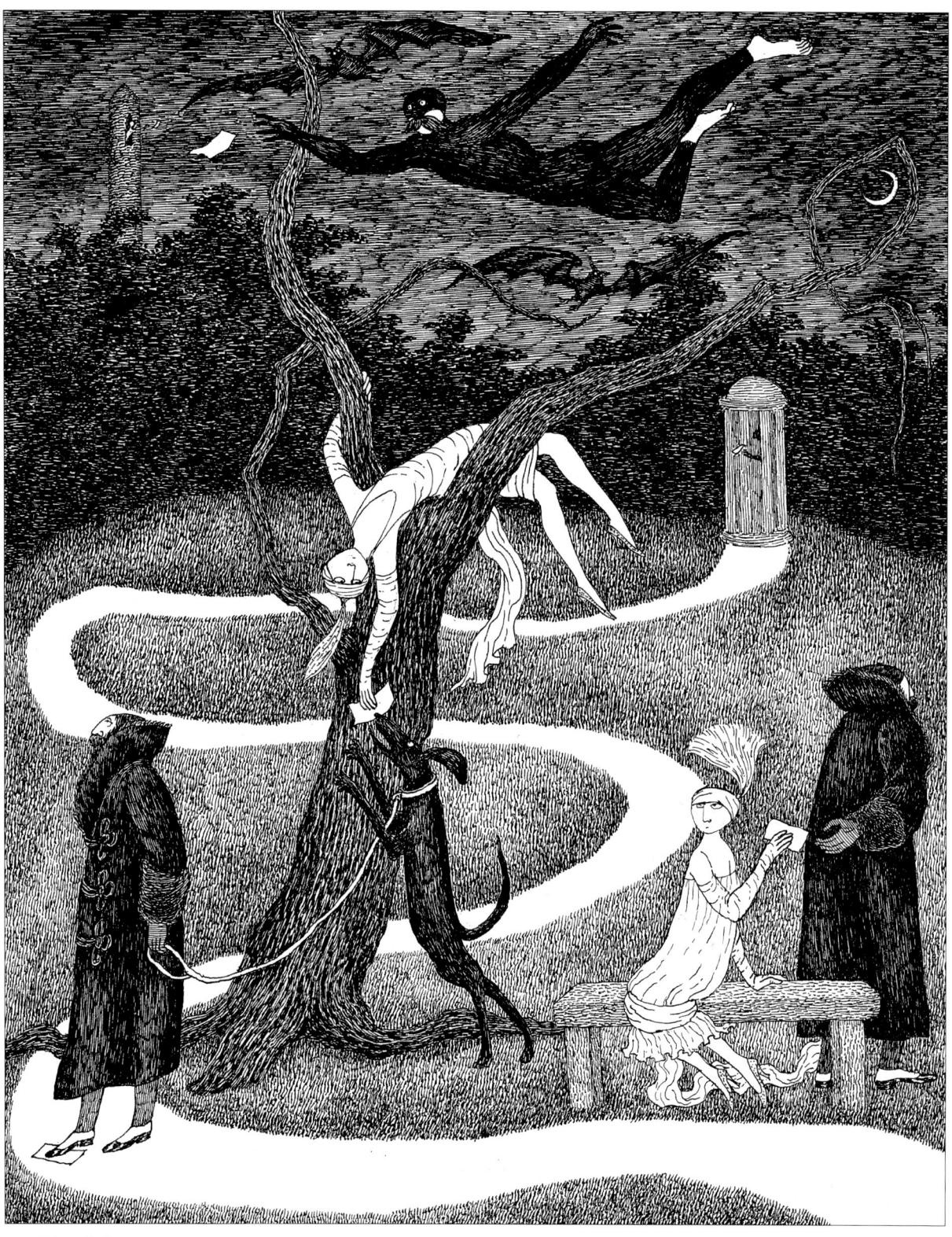

182. Untitled.

EDWARD GOREY
MILDLY UNSETTLING

— KAREN WILKIN —

For some reason, my mission in life is to make everybody as uneasy as possible.
I think we should all be as uneasy as possible, because that's what the world is like.

EDWARD GOREY

SAY "Edward Gorey" and you are most likely to get one of two reactions: a blank "Who?" or an excited outpouring of enthusiasm. With very little encouragement, Gorey's admirers, who often think of him, possessively, as a personal discovery, are inclined to offer detailed catalogues of their favorites among his unnerving little illustrated books, along with nuanced analyses of his drawing style and descriptions of the weirdly threatening, mustachioed men and willowy dowagers, the children in sailor suits and maids in ruffled aprons, the dressing gown—clad patriarchs and hearties in turtlenecks who inhabit his obsessively hatched and patterned *fin de siècle* world. Yet Gorey is far from being an arcane cult figure. Although his laconic fusion of the menacing and the commonplace is a specialized taste, he has entered the public consciousness in surprising ways. Theater-lovers of a certain vintage know him from his

award-winning sets and costumes for a 1977 Broadway production of *Dracula*. Balletomanes, if they were regular patrons of the New York City Ballet before George Balanchine's death in 1983, remember him as the tall, bearded man in the sneakers, fur coat, and long scarf who rarely missed a performance and chatted knowledgeably with a circle of other insiders during the intermissions. While all Gorey initiates pride themselves on their intimate knowledge of his books and drawings, and fortunate ones cherish the stuffed creatures he laboriously sewed by hand, some also comb used bookstores for copies of the paperbacks whose covers he designed during his early years in New York. Other fans boast of having seen his theater pieces, performed in Cape Cod playhouses by amateurs, puppets, and, under extraordinary circumstances, Gorey himself. (On a couple of memorable occasions, versions of these productions reached New York.) True aficionados may even lament having missed the handful of ballet and operetta productions for which he provided sets and costumes. A select group of admirers prizes his prints and drawings made independently of book projects. But beyond this circle of informed devotees, a far wider public has demonstrated an appetite for Gorey greeting cards, T-shirts, note cards, calendars, posters, mugs, jewelry, and the like. There's even a website that purports to cater to "all your Gorey needs." And when the apparently unresponsive are reminded that they probably know Gorey's images from the animated title sequence of the television series *Mystery!*, they look much less blank.

The more you know about Gorey, however, the more difficult it is to define his work. It's probably not surprising, since the man himself was an embodiment of contradiction. He struck people as both amiable and guarded, happy to talk about an astounding variety of topics, including himself, but ultimately reluctant to reveal much. It may be significant that he published a number of his books under fictitious names, usually anagrams of his own, including Ogdred Weary, Mrs. Regera Dowdy, Raddory Gewe, Dreary Wodge, Garrod Weedy, Edward Blutig, and Wardore Edgy. Gorey often said that he wished he had used pseudonyms for all his books, yet it's difficult to decide whether these inventions indicate a genuine desire for concealment or are simply manifestations of Gorey's love of wordplay—in several languages.

The contradictions abound. A man of notably wide-ranging curiosity and imagination, he traveled very little; his only overseas sojourn—apart from a visit to Cuba with relatives in his early youth—was to Scotland, including Fair Isle, the Orkneys, the Shetlands, and the Outer Hebrides, an itinerary inspired by the 1945 film *I Know Where I'm Going*, with Wendy Hiller and Roger Livesey. The trip was apparently most memorable for the failure of the Loch Ness monster to appear. ("The great disappointment of my life, probably," Gorey recalled, punctuating the recollection with one of his epic sighs.[1]) Gorey was famously approachable, willing to accede to all manner of requests for his participation in drawing projects, yet he carefully arranged his life so that for all practical purposes, he was able to spend his time precisely as he wished. Everyone who met him commented on his omnivorous erudition and on the agility of his remarkably well-furnished mind. He bore his weight of information lightly, modestly admitting to "knowing a little about a lot of things," but the breadth and depth of his knowledge was, in fact, dazzling. Gorey's taste embraced the highest of high art and the most popular of popular culture. He was passionate and well informed about nineteenth-century literature and television soap operas, the choreography of George Balanchine and mass market movies, cats and silent films, the Japanese novel and arcane illustrators, and much, much more. He seemed to have read and reread the complete

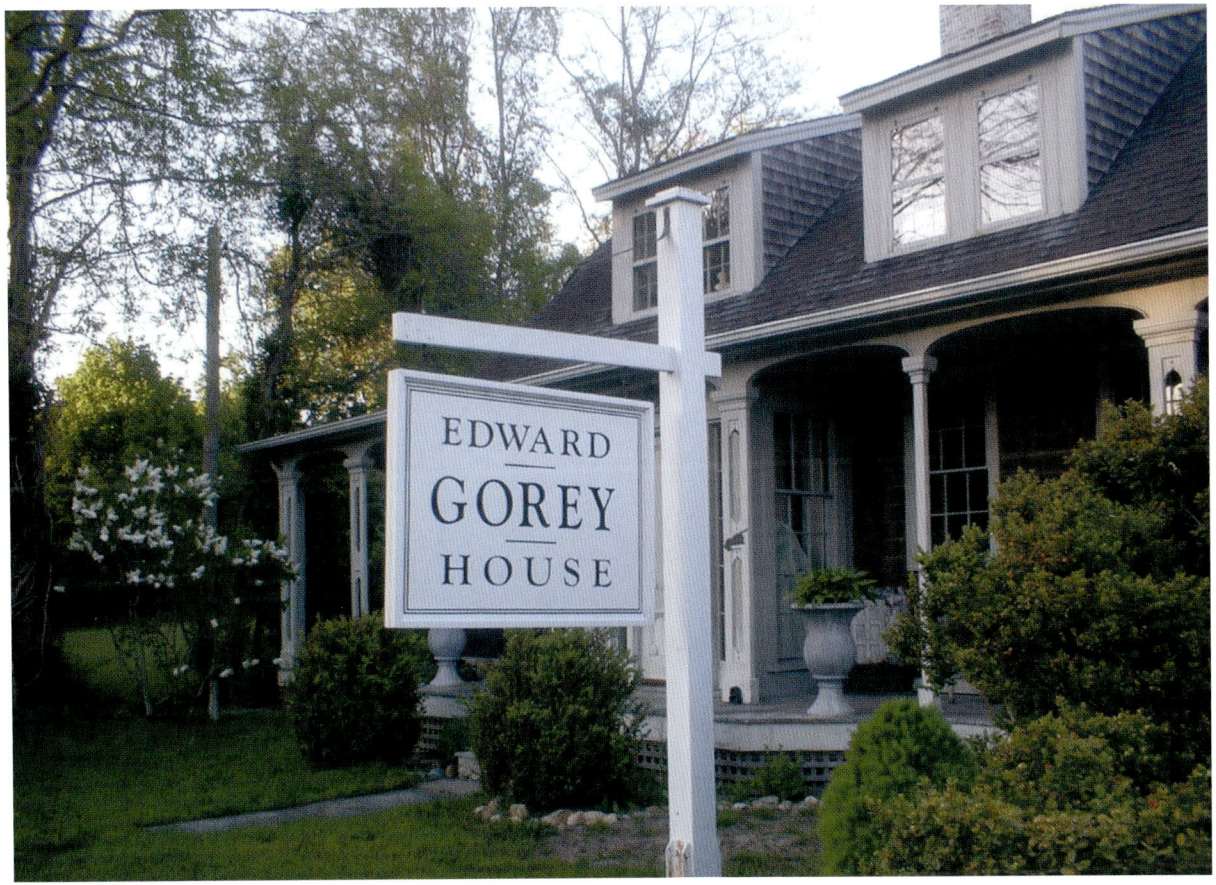

Elephant House, Yarmouth Port, Massachusetts. Photograph © Rick Jones, Director and Curator, Edward Gorey House

works of everyone, to have watched every film ever produced, anywhere, more than once, as well as every episode of every sitcom, and to have remembered all of it in some detail. A connoisseur of yard sales and flea markets, he collected finials, indescribable objects, and African and Tibetan jewelry, which he wore as casually and constantly as he did his habitual sneakers.

Gorey's home was packed with whatever caught his fancy, from rocks to beat-up stuffed toys, but the effect was somehow rather monastic. Despite the accumulation of things, there was a minimum of furniture and a notable absence of elaboration or "décor"—the antithesis of the overwrought interiors he usually drew. Visitors always noted the vast quantities of books, all obviously read and reread, lining the shelves or stacked on the floor. A single wall might contain French symbolist poetry, classic British thrillers, volumes of Jane Austen and the Russians, obscure English novels, complete sets of obsolete children's series, tattered issues of *Punch,* studies of Asian ceramics, compendiums of party games, and a volume on napkin folding. Equally striking were the multiple cats, some omnipresent, others shyly invisible, each with a distinct personality and a distinct relationship to Gorey. If you looked attentively, you also discovered Gorey's art collection, installed with no thought for effect, but rather, placed at the tall, rangy artist's elevated eye level in places that he passed often as he moved through his house. The eclectic assortment ranged from folk art, including nineteenth-century sandpaper pictures, to works on paper by such modern masters as Édouard Vuillard, Pierre Bonnard, Charles Burchfield, and Balthus, photographs by Eugène Atget, paintings by Albert York, and some of the original drawings done by George Herriman, the creator of *Krazy Kat,* for an illustrated version of Don Marquis's *Archie and Mehitabel*—the story of a literary cockroach and his "toujours gai" alley cat friend. In a *New Yorker* magazine profile, Stephen Schiff summed up Gorey's striking catholicity of taste as "cultural voraciousness."[2]

References to all of these sources (and a great deal more) found their way into Gorey's work, usually, he said, without his being fully aware that he was making use of them, so thoroughly had he assimilated particular images from the artists and illustrators who captured his imagination most intensely or passages and turns of phrase from the writers he read most often. The illustrators were mostly British and nineteenth century; the writers ranged from Lady Murasaki, author of the eleventh-century Japanese novel *The Tale of Genji,* to Agatha Christie. Gorey plainly allowed his

voracious reading and viewing habits to inform his work, yet no matter how clear the apparent resemblance, the results always suggest that he arrived at his allusive phrases and images not by conscious appropriation but by a process of free association. A given subject might provoke a host of vague associations—perhaps imperfectly remembered configurations from Gorey's well-stocked mental image bank—that were then given new form by being translated into his unmistakable language. It's undeniable that connections exist between his illustrations for a disparate group of books and such celebrated antecedents as the gnarled figures in Paul Klee's early prints, René Magritte's illogical configurations, Giorgio de Chirico's twilit piazzas, Max Ernst's eerie inventions, Odilon Redon's fantastic *noir* drawings, and Balthus's equivocal images of young girls—to name only a few. It's not, however, necessary to recognize these conscious or unconscious allusions to enjoy the special flavor of Gorey's work. Decoding any of his references can simultaneously confer a sense of having been admitted to an inner sanctum and an awareness of how much else you are undoubtedly missing. Fortunately, these correspondences are always oblique; they are never ends in themselves but create enriching overtones—whether or not they can be specifically deciphered.

Yet there are also moments when Gorey is unequivocal about his inspiration. He said, for example, that he frequently found newspaper photos, particularly from the sports section,

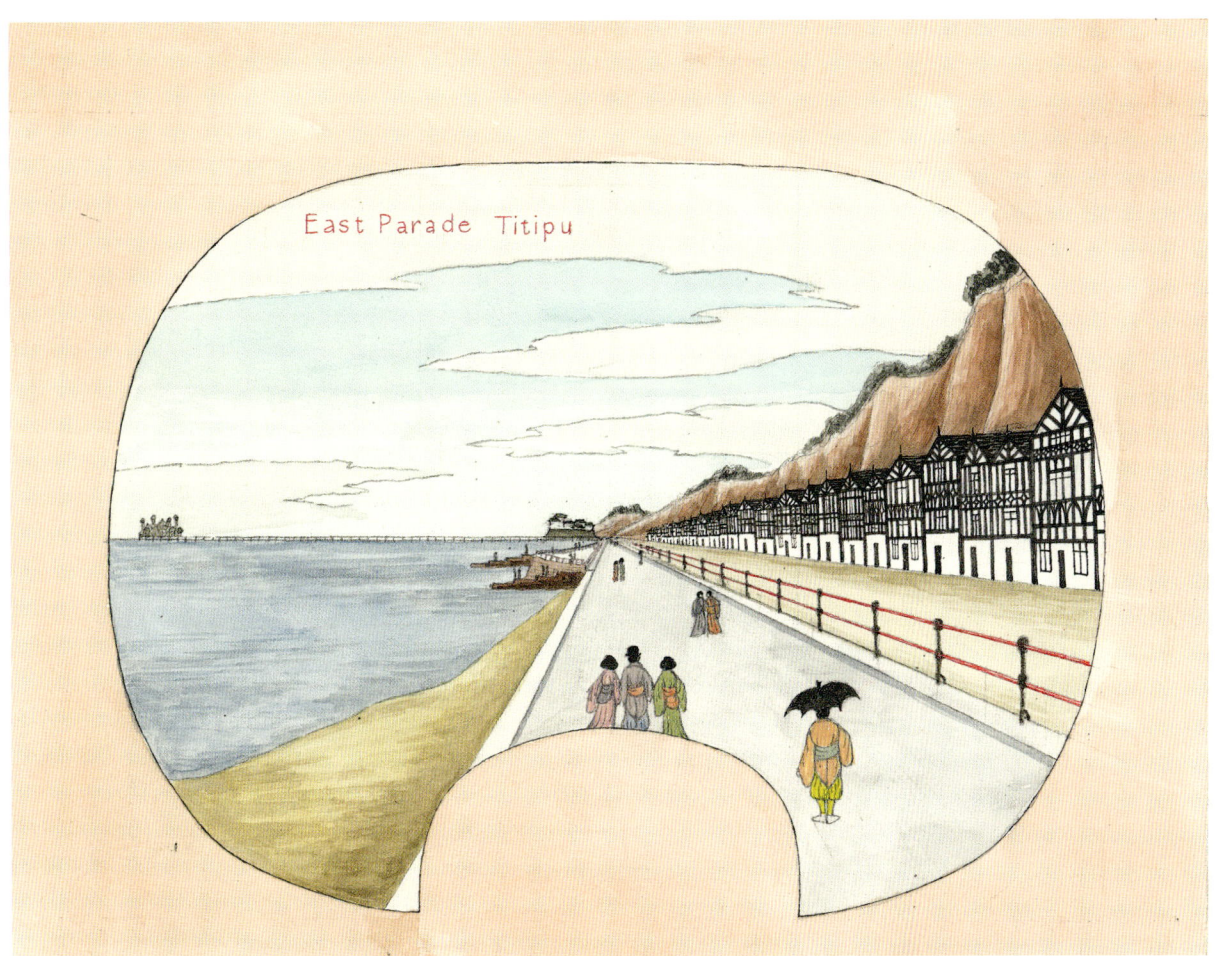

East Parade Titipu

177. Drop curtain design for *The Mikado*

to be useful as starting points for his work, not because of their subject matter but because of their often unexpected combinations of figures in stylized motion. Sometimes the reference is so explicit that it reads as an homage. When Gorey illustrated Edward Lear's marvelous nonsense poems *The Jumblies* (1968) and *The Dong with a Luminous Nose* (1969), he invented a cast of players very different from the Edwardian house-party types with whom he is most closely associated: a sharply characterized group of agile little figures in Regency-derived costumes who

are clearly inspired by the nineteenth-century illustrators Gorey professed to admire most. Similarly, the waves crashing on the rocky coast of the vaguely Scottish settings he devised for the poems evoke the complex scrolls and swirls of the Japanese woodblock master Hokusai's iconic print *The Great Wave off Kanagawa.* In the same way, the sets and costumes Gorey created in 1983 for a Carnegie Mellon University production of Gilbert and Sullivan's *The Mikado* fuse Edwardian postcard views of British seaside towns and Japanese prints, with delicious

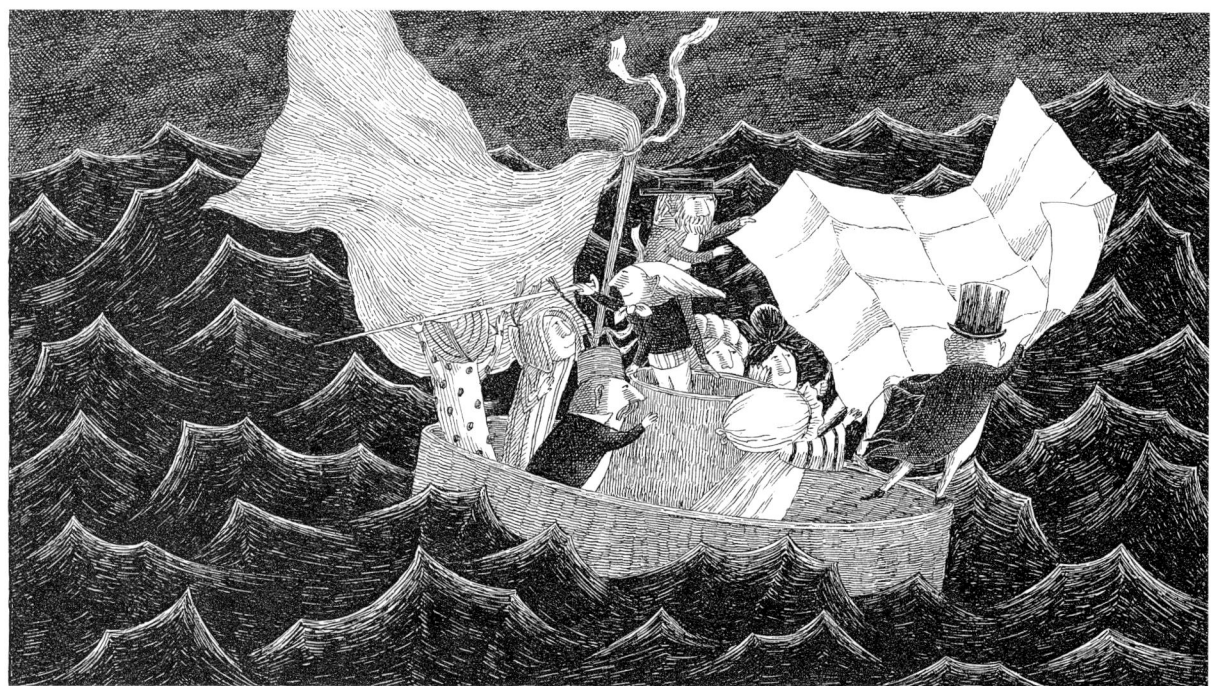

134. THE JUMBLIES, by Edward Lear. *The water it soon came in, it did, / The water it soon came in; / So to keep them dry, they wrapped their feet / In a pinky paper all folded neat / And they fastened it down with a pin.*

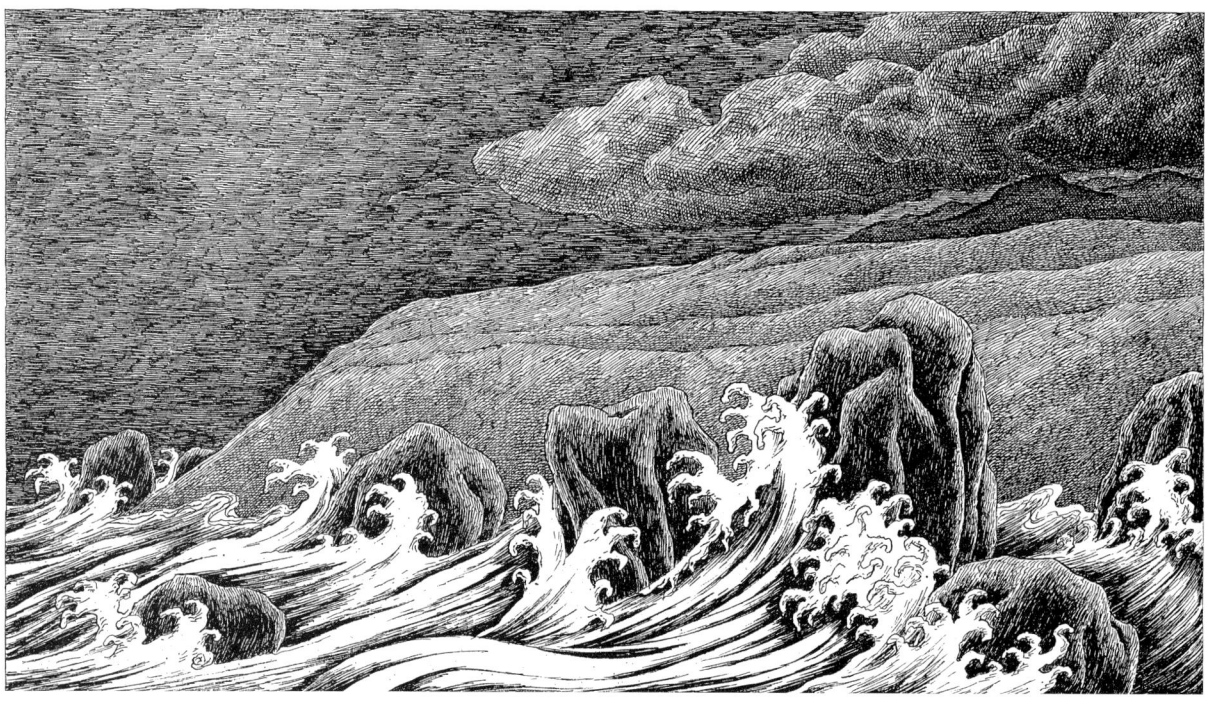

138. THE DONG WITH A LUMINOUS NOSE by Edward Lear. *When awful darkness and silence reign / Over the great Gromboolian plain, / Through the long, long wintry nights;— / When the angry breakers roar / As they beat on the rocky shore;— / When Storm-clouds brood on the towering heights / Of the Hills of the Chankly Bore:—*

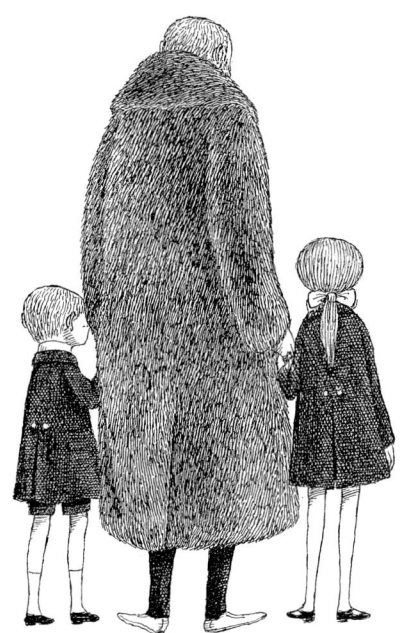

98. The Lavender Leotard; or, Going a Lot to the New York City Ballet. *The author introduces two small, distant, ageless, and wholly imaginary relatives to fifty seasons of the New York City Ballet.*

results—kimono-clad figures promenade past pseudo-Tudor houses beneath a very British seaside cliff—while a poster for the production, showing the Mikado on a bicycle, seems equally informed by French *art nouveau* publicity for that newfangled sport, cycling, and a celebrated photograph of Henri de Toulouse-Lautrec in Japanese costume. There is undoubtedly a great deal more as well, some of it encoded and disguised by this lover of word games, puzzles, and arcana, all of it fueled by a lifetime's avid reading and looking at an amazingly broad range of work in all media.

These allusions, both overt and covert, may help to make Gorey's invented world more plausible, rather in the way that the newspaper and wallpaper pieces in Cubist collages turn the invented context of drawn planes into a new kind of reality, detached from the

actual time and place attested to by the pasted fragments of the everyday world. But the rich underpinnings of Gorey's imagery are always disposed with a light touch, emphasized or downplayed, as required. He himself insisted that the biggest single influence on him was neither literary nor from the world of art but rather the choreography of George Balanchine. Part of it was attitude. Balanchine famously exhorted his dancers to avoid interpretation. "Don't think, dear, just do," he was reported to have said, trusting that meaning would be generated simply by the fact that human beings were articulating his movements in space. "A man dances with a woman," he is supposed to have said. "Isn't that enough?" Gorey's own disjunctive storytelling methods, his reliance on implication rather than explication, may owe something to Balanchine's abstract dances. So, too, may Gorey's economical compositions or his ability to make even minimally rendered gestures eloquent. There are more obvious connections as well, such as Gorey's "ballet books," *The Lavender Leotard* (1973), a direct homage to the New York City Ballet, and *The Gilded Bat* (1966), the story of the rather depressing life of the ballerina Mirella Splatova, née Maud Splaytoes, as well as with a miscellany of acutely observed images of dancers, usually in practice clothes.

Although Gorey rarely spoke of the connection, it's clear that silent films were among the most powerful influences on his imagery and, to an extent, his writing style.

He had an encyclopedic knowledge of the work of such pioneers as Louis Feuillade, who essentially invented the serial thriller between 1913 and 1920 with films whose plots hinge on disguises, doubled identities, and protosurrealist distortions of reality. Feuillade's combination of naturalism and fantasy resonates deeply within Gorey's work. To spend time with Feuillade's films is to become acquainted with women in long dresses and enormous hats with plumes, and men with magnificent moustaches wearing top hats and frock coats, all playing out mysterious dramas in pompously furnished interiors, long corridors with multiple doors, and outdoor settings with rows of iron railings. Once the connection between Gorey and the world of silent movies has been made, the concise bits of text that accompany his drawings begin to read as exceptionally well-written intertitles that help to advance the action. It comes as no surprise to learn that Gorey described the master of deadpan silent comedy, Buster Keaton, as his "idol," or that he wrote a screenplay for a (never-produced) parodic silent thriller titled "The Black Doll."[3]

Just about everyone, whether a devotee of Gorey's work or a casual admirer, will say something about his macabre humor. He is so closely associated with the sinister that puns on his name are all but inevitable; an off-Broadway production inspired by his books was titled *Gorey Stories,* and a website devoted to him is known as "goreydetails.com." Gorey himself acknowledged the association with his pseudonym "Edward Blutig"—German for "bloody" or "cruel"—yet he disliked his books being thought of as "macabre." "In a way I hope it's mildly unsettling," he replied when asked if he ever thought about the effect of his work on readers.[4] His texts deal with minor annoyances: the eponymous protagonist of *The Doubtful Guest* (1957) "has shown no intention of going away" after seventeen years. They involve missed opportunities: Drusilla, in *The Remembered Visit* (1965), finally acts on a promise to send something to an elderly acquaintance and discovers that he died shortly before it was mailed. Gorey's books also itemize murder, misadventure, and the abuse and death of children—a deranged opera fan slays his idol in *The Blue Aspic* (1968); the ballerina heroine of *The Gilded Bat* perishes in a plane crash; the orphaned Charlotte Sophia in *The Hapless Child* (1961) is run over as she escapes from her cruel employers. Yet these unpleasant occurrences are presented with such detachment, both in terms of texts and images, that it's almost impossible to be disturbed by any of it. Gorey's tone is dispassionate; his protagonists remain expressionless. In *The Gashlycrumb Tinies* (1963), an alphabet book that dispatches one tiny tot per letter, from "Amy, who fell down the stairs" to "Zillah, who drank too much gin," you tend to be more engaged by the ingenuity of the paired rhymes than distressed by the sad fates of the twenty-six kiddies: "M is for Maud who was swept out to sea, N is for Neville who died of ennui."

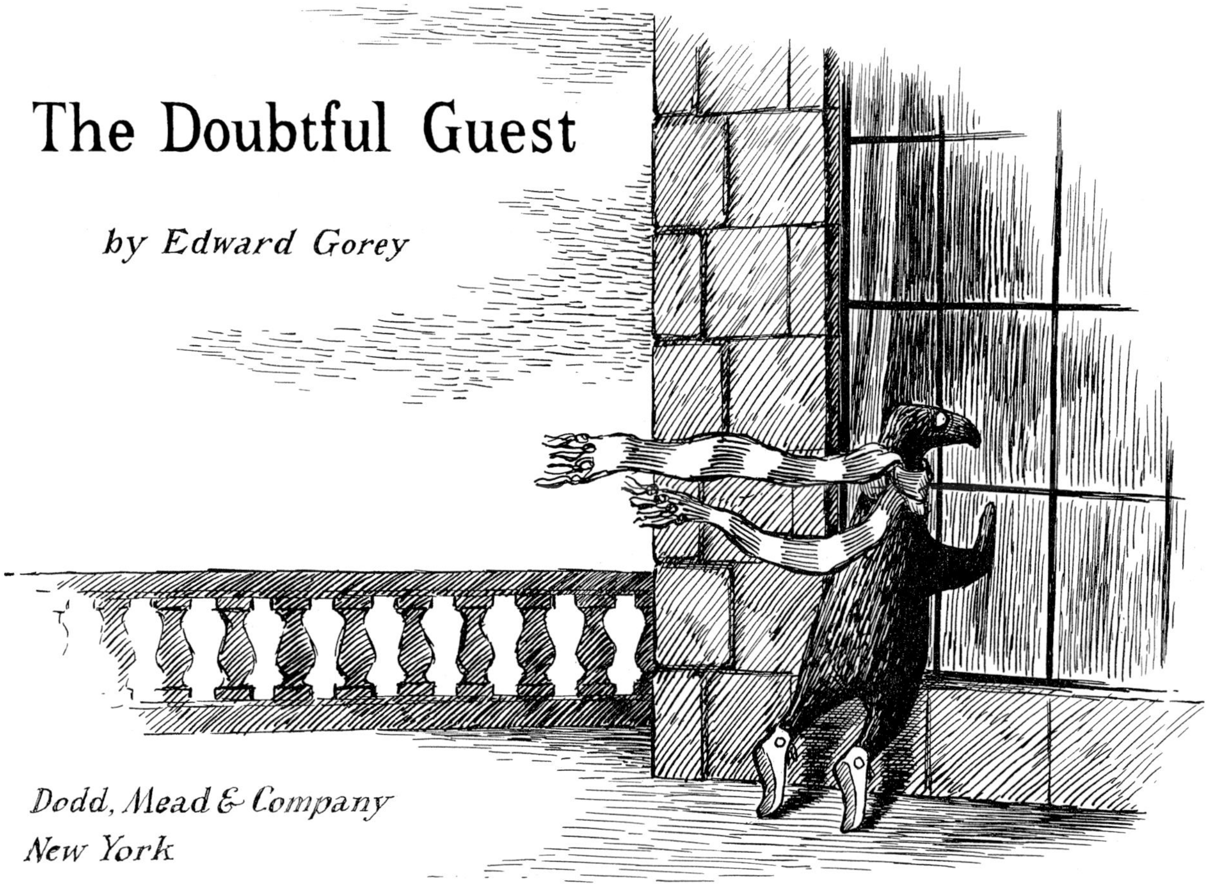

The Doubtful Guest

by Edward Gorey

Dodd, Mead & Company
New York

8. Title page for *The Doubtful Guest*

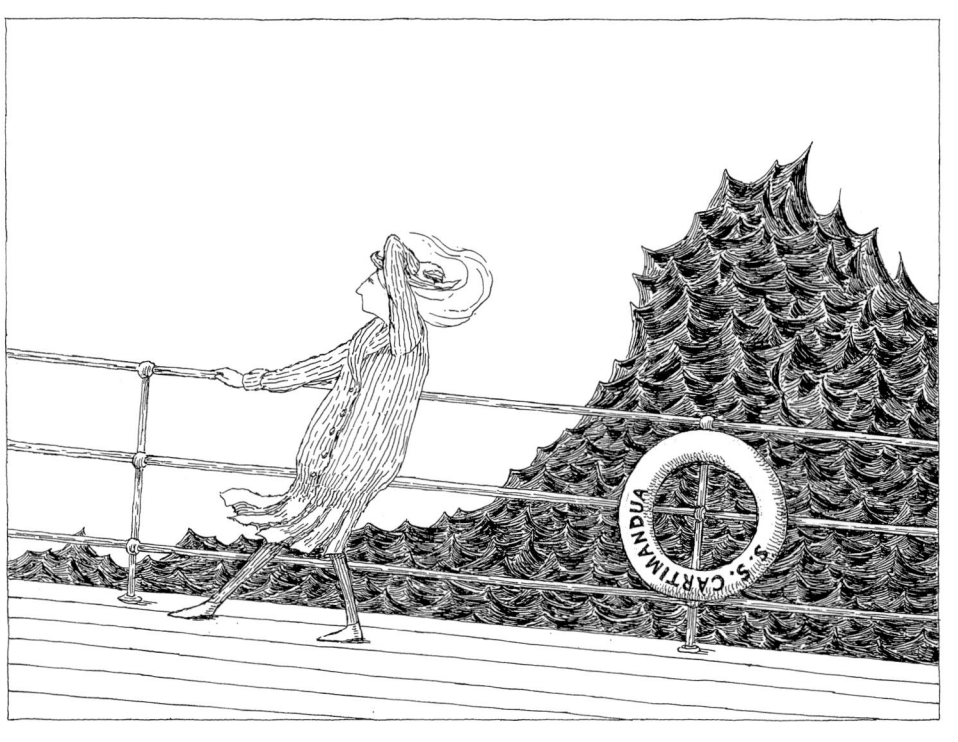

56. THE REMEMBERED VISIT.
Months went by.

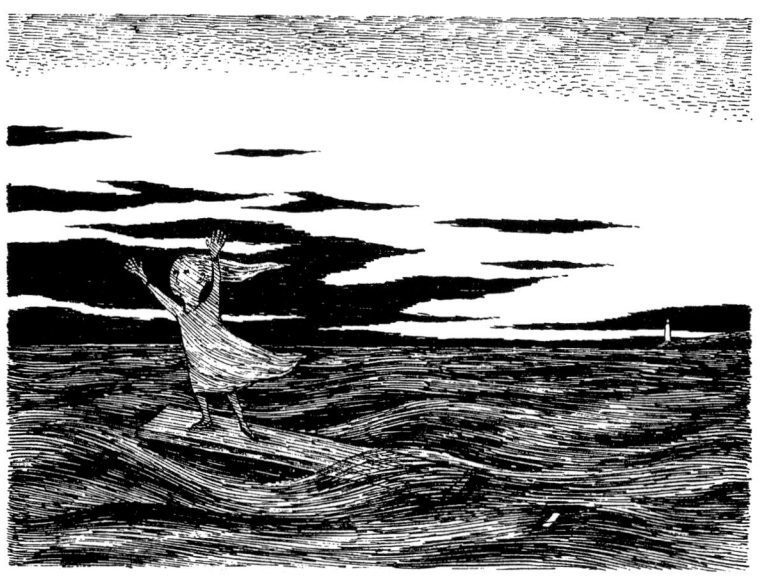

33. THE GASHLYCRUMB TINIES. *M is for Maud who was swept out to sea*

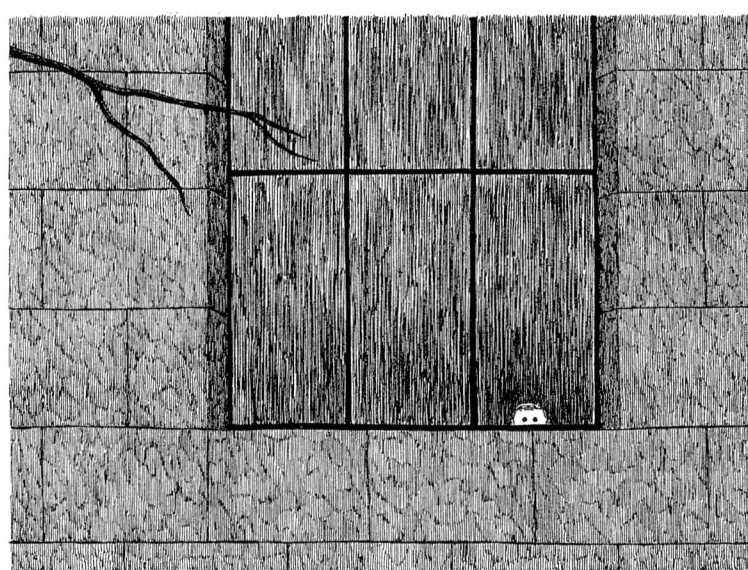

34. THE GASHLYCRUMB TINIES. *N is for Neville who died of ennui*

In *The Deranged Cousins* (1971) and *The Loathsome Couple* (1977), truly grisly things take place—the cousins do each other in or die by misadventure, while the unlovely Mona Gritch and Harold Snedleigh are not merely social misfits but also serial killers. Yet Gorey recounts the dreadful events chronicled by these books so coolly and matter-of-factly that you are simultaneously horrified and kept at a distance. In *The Loathsome Couple*, he tells us that after embarking on their string of lurid crimes—Mona and Harold "spent the better part of the night murdering the child in various ways"—the couple sat down to a meal of "cornflakes and treacle, turnip sandwiches and artificial grape soda." Gorey later said that devising a sufficiently disgusting menu took considerable effort. The images that accompany these flat statements are equally forthright and disengaged; far from depicting anything repugnant, they show only neutral moments. They are also among Gorey's most beautiful, most graphically inventive, and most subtle in tonality, as if he felt that ravishing drawings were required to offset the chilling story. (It has also been pointed out that *The Loathsome Couple* is one of the few books in which Gorey punishes his malefactors; Harold and Mona are tried, jailed, and die in prison.) The reticence of *The Loathsome Couple* is not unique; Gorey never makes images of anything untoward. He was fond of reminding interviewers fascinated by his pseudopornographic tour de force, *The Curious Sofa* (1961), that "the men are totally indistinguishable from the women; everybody

is seen from behind;" there, as in so many of his books, everything is supplied by the reader's imagination.[5]

In Gorey's world, as in classical Greek drama, the most horrific events happen offstage. The audience sees only what leads up to the irrevocable act and its aftermath, never the deed itself. When one cousin brains another with "a brown china doorknob," the actual assault is not depicted; the victim collapses backwards, legs folded under her, arms out-thrust, head outside of the frame of the drawing, while her assailant brandishes the improbable but effective instrument. The melodramatic rendering of another cousin's death after drinking the contaminated "dregs of a bottle of vanilla extract he discovered in the mud" is exceptional. All-over hatching veils the scene, reminding us that the unhappy event takes place at night, but it is still possible to make out plainly the agonized man lying arched and rigid on the floor, with one sneaker-shod foot planted on a chair, his arms raised, and his fingers curled in anguish. Yet, as with all of Gorey's figures, the expression of both the dying man and the surviving cousin witnessing the effects of the poison are preternaturally calm.

"I think of my books as Victorian novels all scrunched up," Gorey told one interviewer.[6] He assured another that he was "a firm believer in the plot as the underpinning of everything else."[7] "Scrunched up" and "plot" are the key words here. Gorey's "novels" unfold as a series of laconic declarations, sometimes in rhyme, so

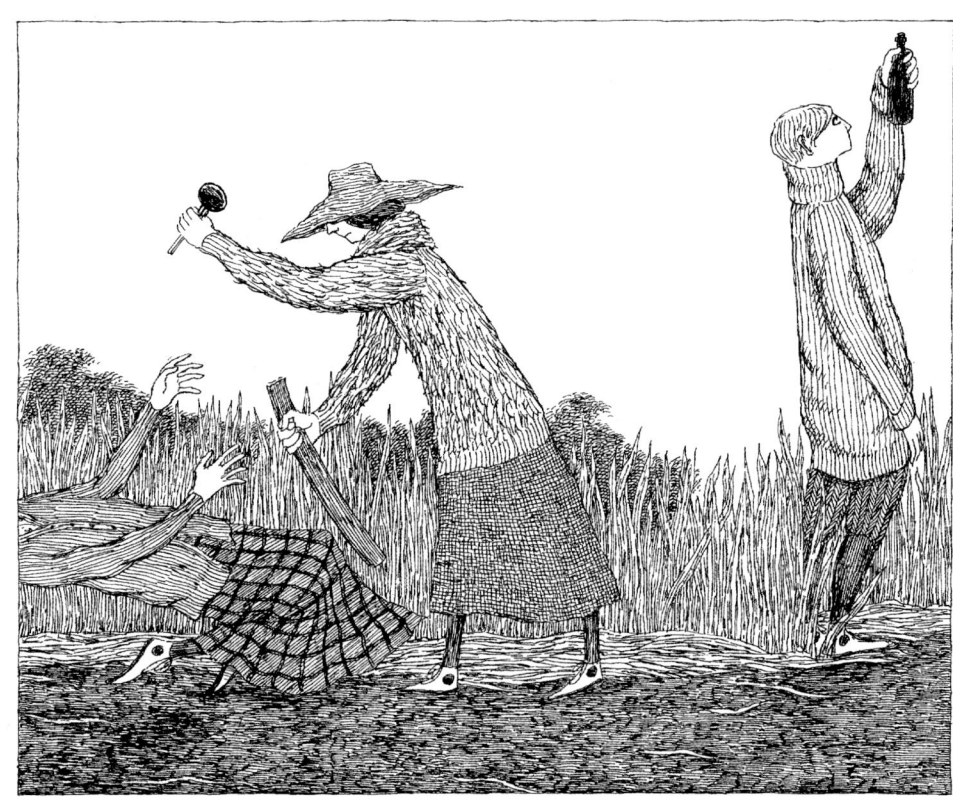

90. The Deranged
Cousins; or, Whatever.
Mary struck Rose with a
brown china doorknob she
had already found and
killed her.

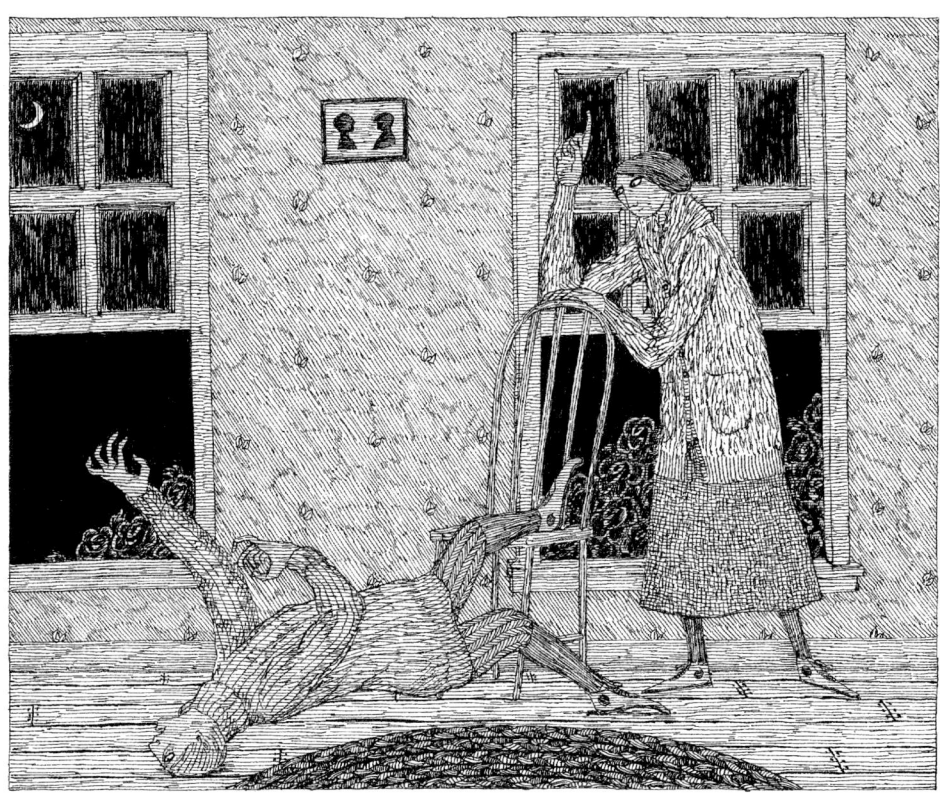

92. The Deranged
Cousins; or, Whatever.
They must have been
contaminated, for he died in
agony during the night.

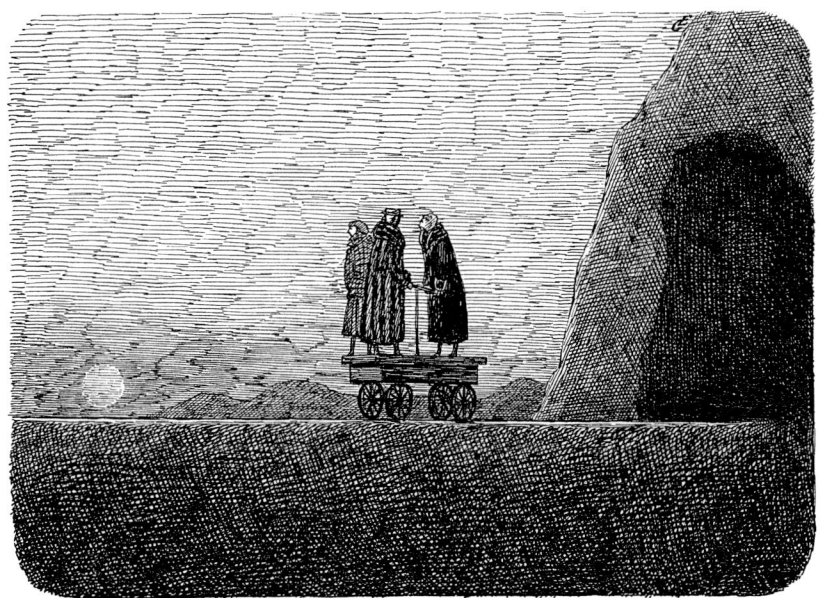

29. THE WILLOWDALE HANDCAR; OR,
THE RETURN OF THE BLACK DOLL.
*At sunset they entered a tunnel
in the Iron Hills and did not
come out the other end.*

pared down that the narrative is carried as much by omission as by description. In *The Willowdale Handcar; or, The Return of the Black Doll* (1962), the protagonists, a woman and two men, begin a journey across America on a summer day, pumping a handcar along a railroad line. They see disasters and also notice things that, individually, seem to be pure happenstance, without apparently attaching much importance to either; cumulatively, they suggest an ominous subtext involving an abandoned, presumably illegitimate child and a distraught mother—a kind of counterpoint to the aimless tranquility of the passengers on the handcar. On the last two pages, the trio, now dressed for winter, the men in long fur coats, are first shown as tourists engaged by the inconsequential: "At Hiccupboro they counted the cannon balls in the pyramids on the courthouse lawn."

Then they are back on the handcar, against a cloudy sky; the viewpoint is strikingly low, so the black mouth of a tunnel on the right side of the page seems overwhelmingly large. "At sunset, they entered a tunnel in the Iron Hills and did not come out the other end." The book has been described as "a subtle yet magisterial view of the human condition."[8] It also includes some of Gorey's most evocative drawings, including prairie landscapes and big skies conjured up with staccato hatching, and an eloquent image of an enormous trestle spanning "Peevish Gorge."

Gorey's deployment of ellipsis and non sequitur can create dreamlike sequences in which logic seems elastic. He can force you to create your own connections, even to complete the narrative for yourself. The most extreme example of this is probably *The Raging*

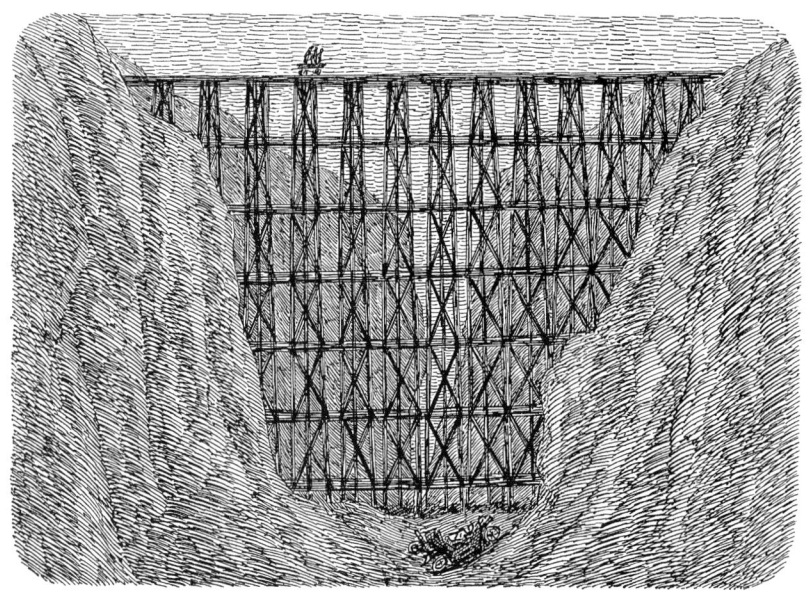

26. The Willowdale Handcar; or,
The Return of the Black Doll.
*From the trestle over Peevish Gorge they
spied the wreck of a touring car at the
bottom. 'I don't see Dick's friend anywhere,'
said Harry.*

Tide; or, The Black Doll's Imbroglio (1987), Gorey's response either to the infinite possibilities of the *I Ching* or to postmodernism's insistence on the instability of the text—or both. The characters in *The Raging Tide* are battered stuffed toys, rather like the ones Gorey collected and made: a faceless rag doll, a wounded teddy bear, something shaggy and unidentifiable, and a long-armed, acrobatic Figbash, one of Gorey's signature creatures. They ambush and assault one another, "erupting through the carpet" or "popping out of a valise," wielding feather dusters, cookie cutters, bootlaces, wet tea leaves, and buttonhooks as weapons. The ambiguous settings, simultaneously indoors and out, include giant thumbs that rise from the patterned carpets like fragments of monumental sculpture. Each caption includes a set of alternatives: "[page] 18. There's no going to town in a bathtub. If you want to get back to the story, turn to [page] 16. If you want to tour the Villa Amnesia, turn to [page] 23." Another caption offers a choice of pages to be selected depending on "If you find this not unamusing" or "If you want to benefit spiritually." Needless to say, in keeping with the stunning illogic of the entire narrative, the images and texts on the specified pages have no obvious relation to the conditions determining the choices.

Alert readers will find innumerable overtones of the nineteenth- and early-twentieth-century novels that Gorey devoured. *The Hapless Child* at once obeys and parodies the conventions of a well-known type of moralizing tale for girls in which a young heroine, accustomed to privilege and comfort, loses everything through the death of a parent, to be plunged into deprivation

22

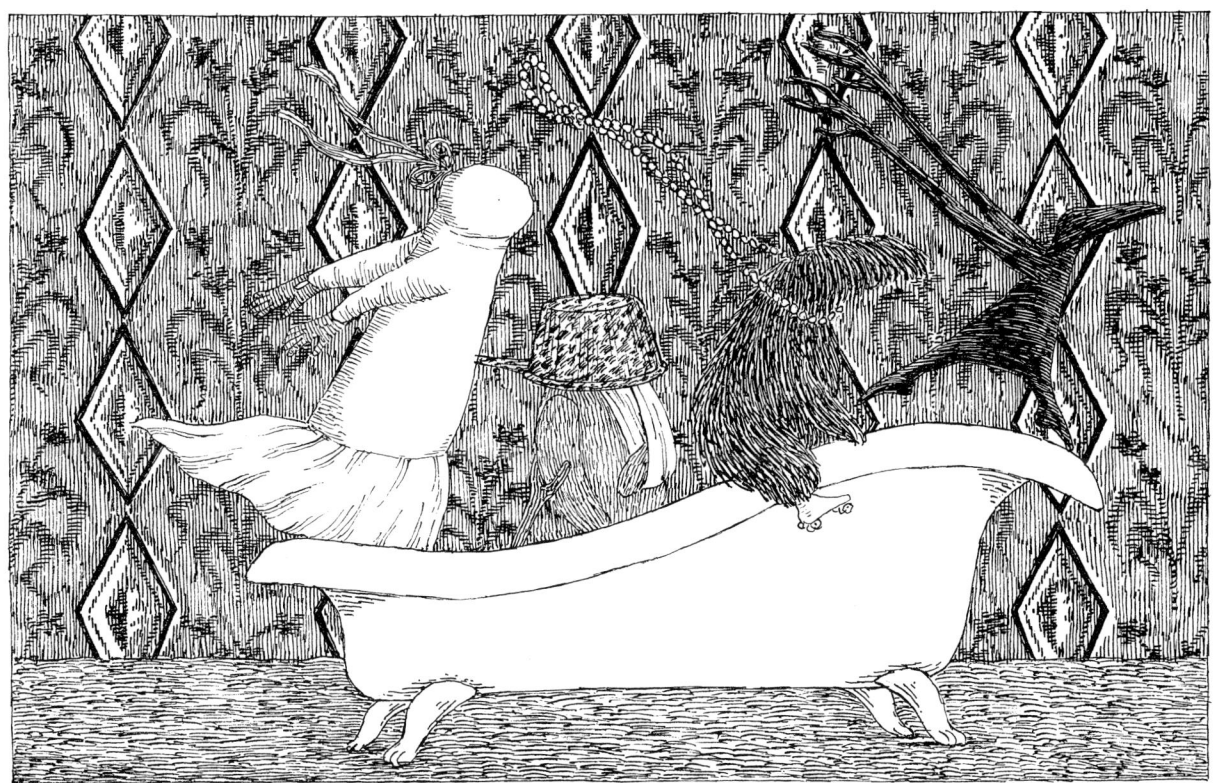

119. The Raging Tide; or, The Black Doll's Imbroglio. *No. 18—There's no going to town in a bathtub. If you want to get back to the story, turn to 16. If you would like to tour the Villa Amnesia, turn to 23.*

and misery. Frances Hodgson Burnett's *Sara Crewe* seems remarkably close to *The Hapless Child,* although Gorey usually traced the spark of the "novel" to *L'enfant de Paris,* a 1913 French silent film, directed by Léonce Perret, in which the cosseted little heroine, like Gorey's Charlotte Sophia, loses her officer father, her widowed mother, and her only relative, in rapid succession, and is sent off to a horrifying boarding school. Both Sara Crewe and the little French girl are eventually rescued, unlike Charlotte Sophia, who is run over, unrecognized, by her own father—who turned out not to have been "killed in a native

uprising" as reported—as he drives through the streets, searching for her. The sad tale provoked memorable images from Gorey. In one, Charlotte Sophia's uncle, seen from the back, in a long coat and top hat, sways and drops his walking stick as he is "brained by a piece of masonry." The drawing is a marvel of economy, with a precise sense of place and space indicated by shifts in scale between the large rusticated blocks of a building, a band of cobblestones, and a fence with bare branches behind it; the contrast between the ample, slightly curved, clothed figure of the uncle and a small, armless nude statue, similarly

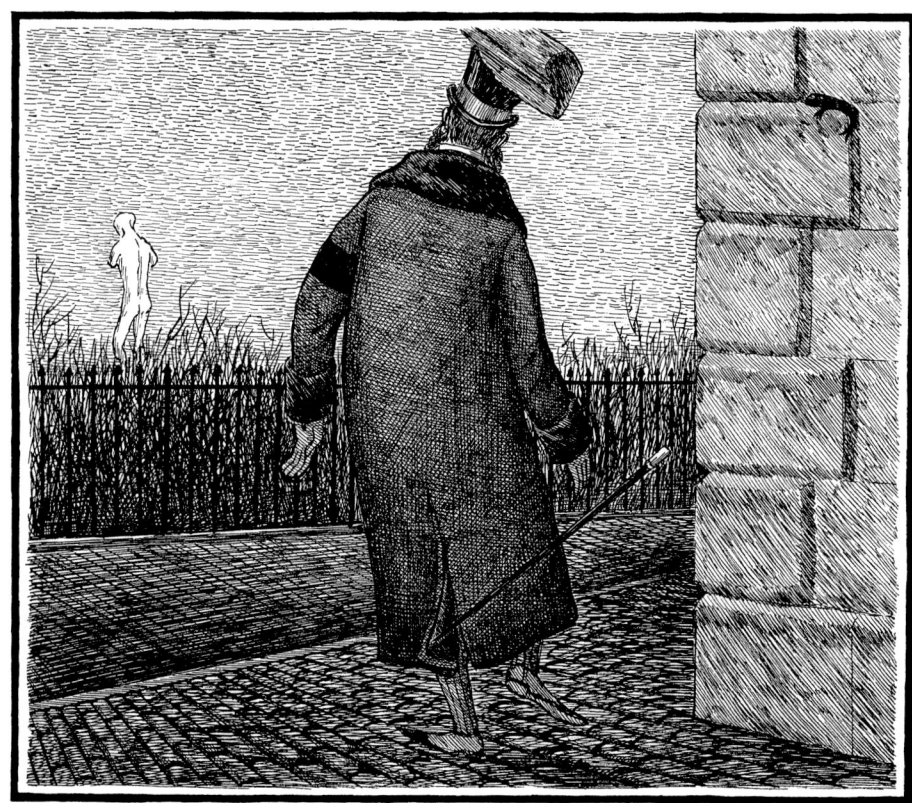

21. THE HAPLESS CHILD.
Her only other relative, an uncle, was brained by a piece of masonry.

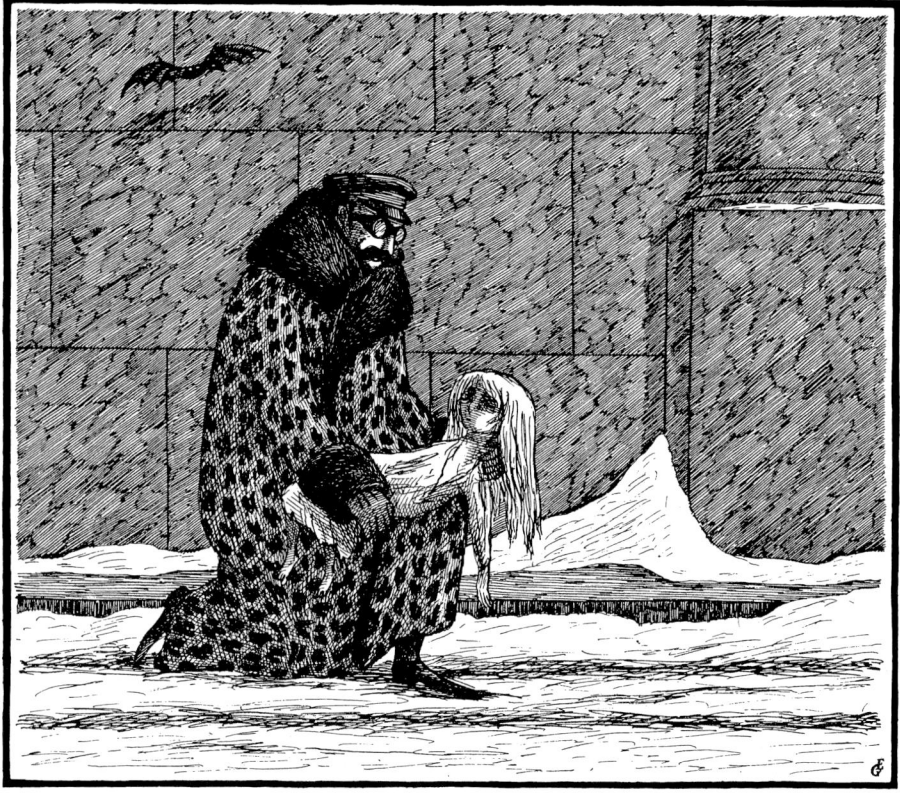

24. THE HAPLESS CHILD.
She was so changed, he did not recognize her.

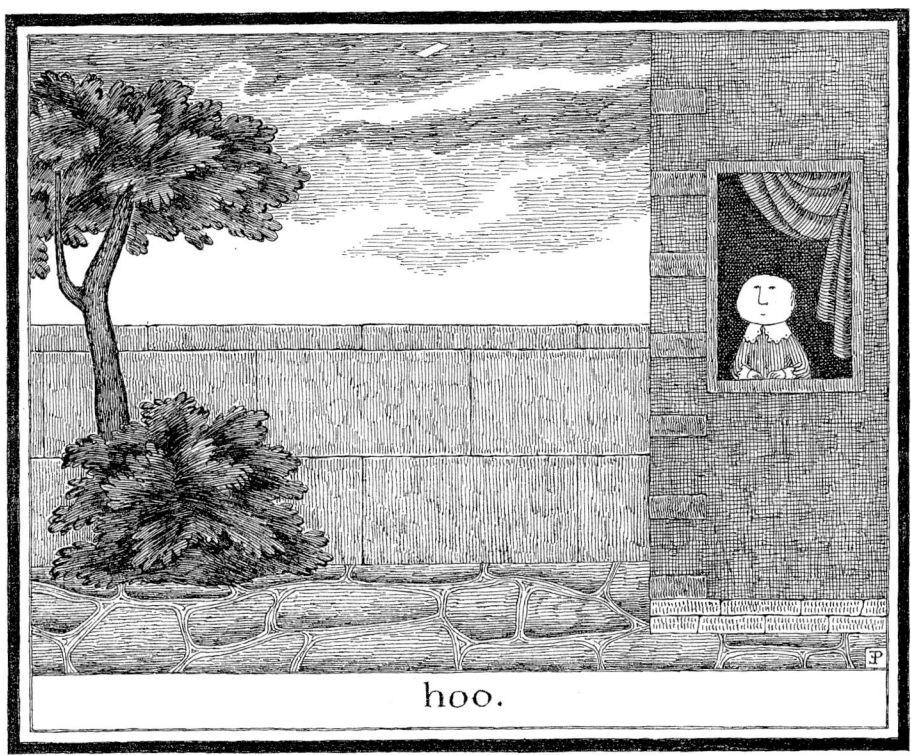

hoo.

97. [The Untitled Book]. *hoo.*

seen from the back, beyond the fence, further opens up the bands of tightly hatched patterns.

By contrast to this masterpiece of eloquent essentials, the final drawing of *The Hapless Child* moves us once again into the realm of parody. Charlotte Sophia's father, in motoring goggles and a nifty leopard-skin coat, kneels in the snow, unaware that the rag doll–like creature he holds is his own child; Gorey's rendering of the tragic moment recalls Oscar Wilde's celebrated quip that "one must have a heart of stone to read the death of Little Nell without laughing."

Occasionally, Gorey's books allude to more current events and even, according to their author, to real experience, of a kind. *The*

Loathsome Couple was based on the serial killers who perpetrated the so-called Moor Murders in England—Gorey said the story particularly upset him—while *The Deranged Cousins,* he claimed, had its origins (absent the murders and deaths) in a routine beach walk and yard sale excursion he made with his own cousins, sisters with whom he spent many summers in Cape Cod before moving there permanently. Other works, perhaps most notably *[The Untitled Book]* (1971), in which a fierce battle between real and invented creatures is elucidated by such captions as "Ipsifendus" and "Quoggenzocker," ending with an enigmatic "Hip, hop, hoo," seem to belong to the tradition of highly serious

Victorian nonsense established by Lewis Carroll and Edward Lear, both of whom ranked high in Gorey's pantheon.

Fascinating as Gorey's elliptical texts are, it is his images that really distinguish his work. His best-known drawings include a highly recognizable group of personages whom he deploys like the stock types in the commedia dell'arte. There are men in smoking jackets, vamps with aigrettes, and innocents with hair bows, along with stiff-backed governesses, callow young men in striped blazers, dignified worthies in top hats, icy butlers, and flappers with long beads, brought to life by the insistent hatchings of his pen. Gorey conjures up opera divas and their besotted fans, sinister impresarios, children both nasty and disturbingly angelic, anthropomorphic cats, and nameless creatures—both benign and threatening—haunting interiors and the occasional eerie landscape. The time seems to be a conflation of the Victorian and Edwardian eras, with occasional notes of the early days of the Roaring Twenties. The place may or may not be England, but wherever it is, these distinctive types inhabit claustrophobic, strangely passé interiors full of riotous wallpapers and relentless paneling—rooms where ferns and aspidistras flourish in elaborate urns, antimacassars protect tufted armchairs, and pelmets are trimmed with opulent tassels. When Gorey's people venture outside, through the wrought-iron gates of their slightly creepy dwellings, they don enormous hats with veils and ankle-length fur coats; they ride on archaic bicycles and drive in open cars that have to be started with cranks. Cats and indescribable creatures behave like humans or lurk in corners.

These "Edwardian"—in both the historical and personal sense of the word—pen-and-ink drawings are not simply illustrations but achieved works of art in their own right, extraordinarily various and unexpected in their imagery, and deeply evocative. Gorey's urgent, meticulous hatchings suggest a wealth of textures from stone to fur, and patterns from flamboyant wallpapers to the brocade of an acclaimed soprano's evening wrap. The spectrum of grays created by the textures in Gorey's finest drawings is as wide as in the most beautifully printed vintage photograph. In *The West Wing* (1963), one of Gorey's most beautiful and poetic achievements, there is no text; the images alone carry the burden of meaning. (*The West Wing* is dedicated to the critic Edmund Wilson, an admirer who wrote the first important, generally enthusiastic critical notice of Gorey's work in *The New Yorker* in 1959. Since Gorey maintained that Wilson "was always castigating me for my prose," he chose to dedicate a book without text to him, to forestall further reprimands.[9]) Confrontational, richly inflected, and uncanny, the drawings for *The West Wing* thrust the viewer into the corners of unfurnished rooms, some wallpapered, some with elaborate paneling, some with elegant carpets. A staircase appears to lead to nowhere; three sneakers have been abandoned beneath

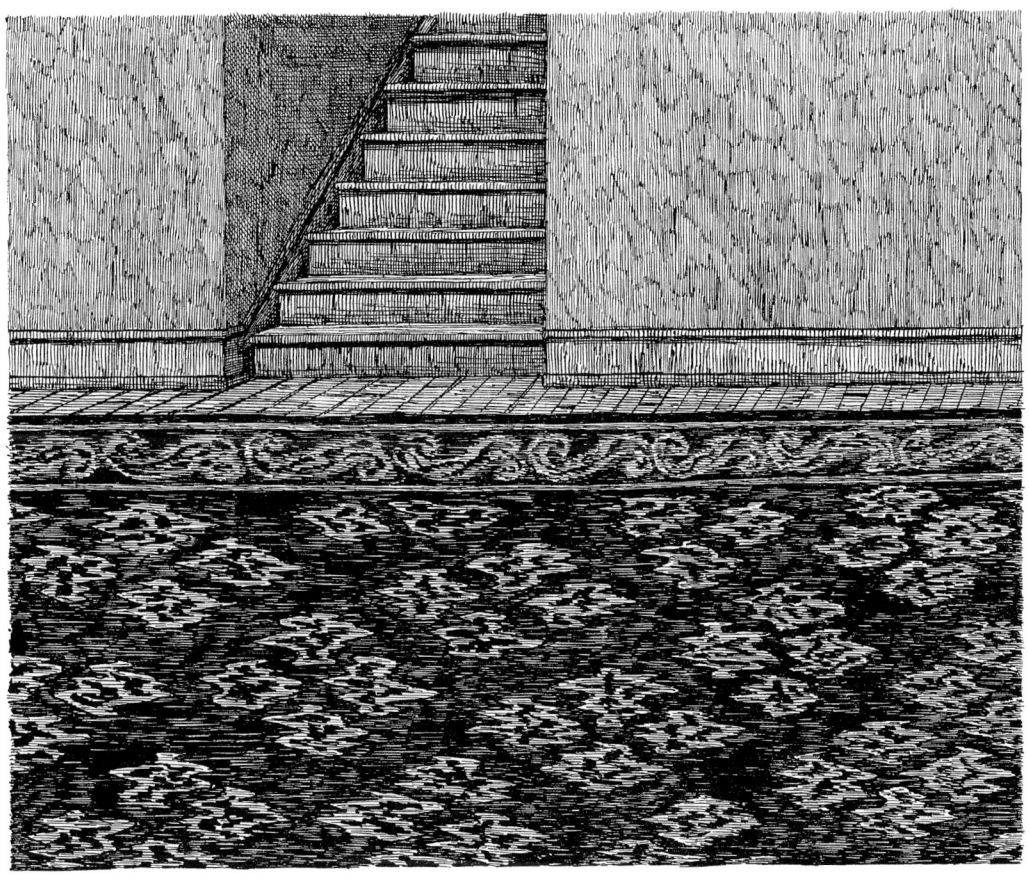

39. THE WEST WING. Panel I

a window; doors open into incomprehensible spaces; an interior sea rises, waist deep, against a paneled door; twisted cloths—or are they papers?—float in the air; a naked man in carpet slippers stares over a balustrade at nothingness. Nothing is specified, but the aura of disquiet and resonant silence evoked by the images, along with the sheer beauty of the orchestration of pen marks, make the book one of Gorey's most compelling.

Despite the potentially unsettling view of the world that pervades Gorey's books, his work often appeals to children. It may be because the elegantly produced volumes in which he presents his idiosyncratic illustrated stories are notably small or because their texts are kept to a minimum—one or two lines to a page, frequently in rhyme. Children are often the protagonists of Gorey's books, almost always—except for some cloyingly well-behaved, sanctimonious types—cast in the role of victims to whom dreadful things happen. The wretched Charlotte Sophia is typical, as are the systematically dispatched kiddies in *The Gashlycrumb Tinies,* or Theoda, the "heroine" of *The Tuning Fork* (1990), labeled by Gorey "a Gothic

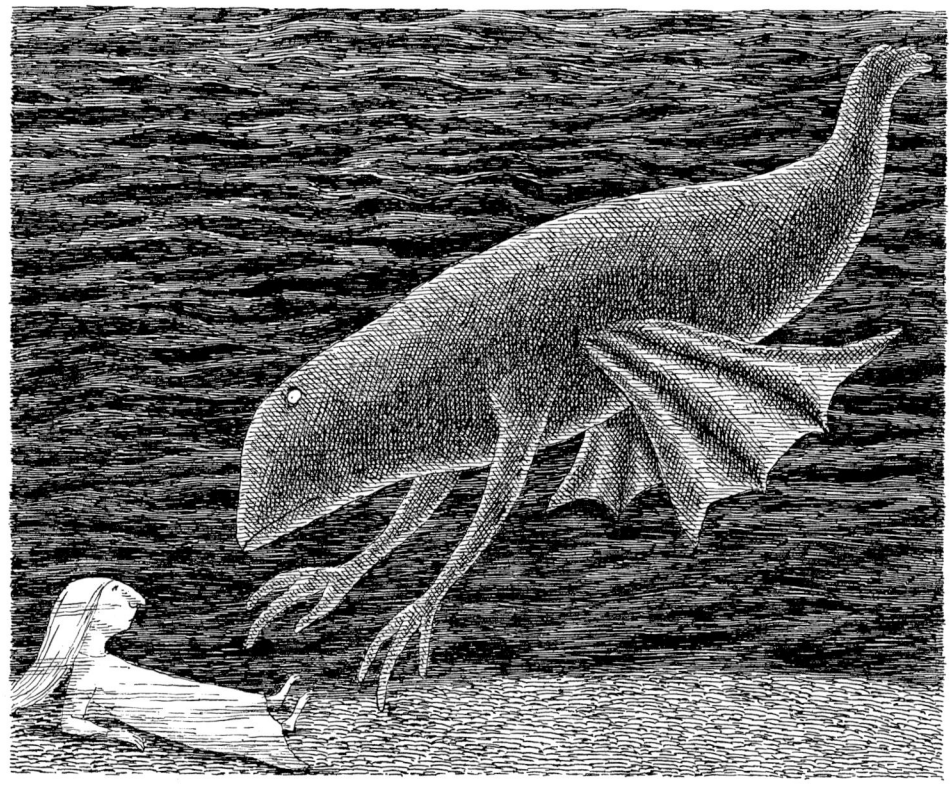

126. THE TUNING FORK. *A monster of alarming size / Was peering at her in surprise*

tale of the Generation Gap, alienation, and despair, driving parents and children into monstrous behavior which solves nothing"— despite the discreet presence in some of the images of a tuning fork, symbol of harmony and accord. Gorey himself was equivocal about his relationship to children. He occasionally said that he intended some of his work for young readers, while at other times he declared that he was perplexed when told that children liked his books, claiming to know few children and insisting that he hadn't thought about anyone but adult readers. The subtle references to literary and visual precedents with which his books are laced bear out the accuracy of this last statement, although while it's obvious that few children are likely to pick up on Gorey's nods at obscure nineteenth-century novels or to little-known images by celebrated artists, even extremely well-read adults can have trouble unraveling the complicated allusions embedded in his work. Gorey recalled urging one of his publishers to market his books to children and being told that they were unsuitable for young audiences. He was, however, frequently commissioned to create covers and interior illustrations for young people's books; his art adorns children's editions by a remarkable list of authors, including, among many others, T. S. Eliot, Muriel Spark, Florence Parry

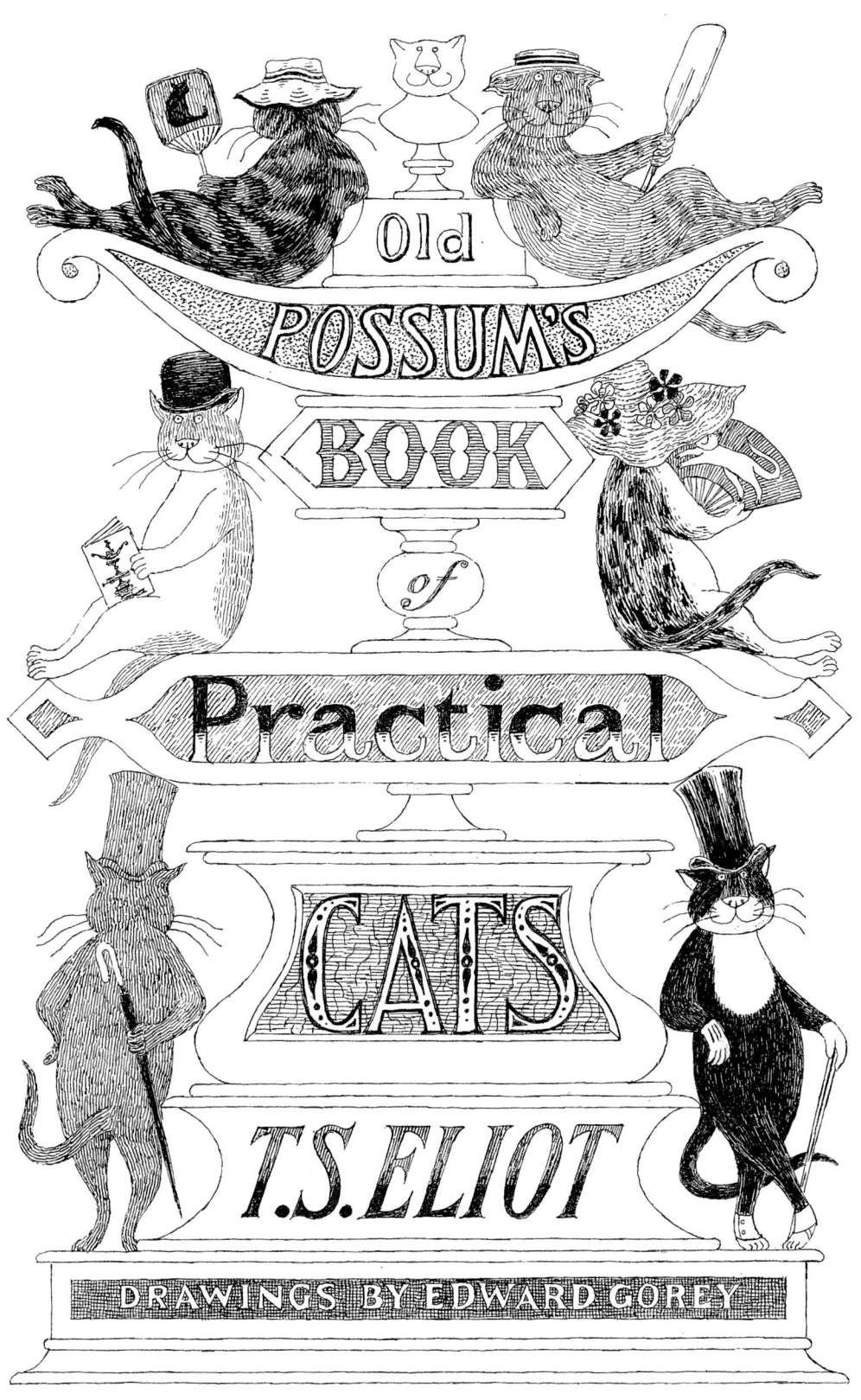

Old POSSUM'S BOOK of Practical CATS

T.S. ELIOT

DRAWINGS BY EDWARD GOREY

145. Front cover for *Old Possum's Book of Practical Cats* by T. S. Eliot

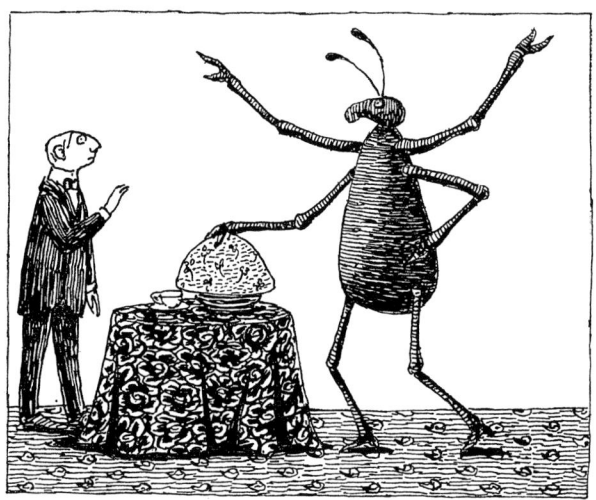

132. The Haunted Tea-Cosy. *'I am the Bahhum Bug,'* it declared; *'I am here to diffuse the interests of didacticism.'*

Heide, Joan Aiken, Peter Neumeyer, John Ciardi, Hilaire Belloc, H. G. Wells, and Edward Lear.

Gorey's parody of Charles Dickens's *A Christmas Carol,* titled *The Haunted Tea-Cosy* (1997), has a special place among his responses to the work of celebrated writers. Originally commissioned as a Christmas project by the *New York Times* (which canceled its commitments to all the other artists involved in favor of Gorey's inventions), *The Haunted Tea-Cosy* is clearly indebted to the hoary classic but moves into a territory that is entirely Gorey's own. Tiny Tim is mercifully absent. Scrooge becomes a generic parsimonious recluse, confronted by a multilimbed insect, the Bahhum Bug, whose role is "to diffuse the interests of didacticism." Various "subfusc but transparent personages,"

identified as the Spectre of Christmas That Never Was, the Spectre of Christmas That Isn't, and the Spectre of Christmas that Never Will Be, show the recluse "affecting," "distressing," and "heart-rending" scenes that include the discovery of missing wallpaper. Deeply moved by what the spectres show him, the recluse gives a party at which "giggling, dancing, and shrieking prevailed and, as the evening wore on, were carried to the very edge of the unseemly."

When questioned about his methods, Gorey's reply was always the same—along the lines of his written response to a questionnaire sent to "writers who draw": "I have to have the finished text of a book before I start on the drawings."[10] A connoisseur of arcane words—a book he claimed as a favorite, *The Nursery Frieze* (1964), consists of a parade of

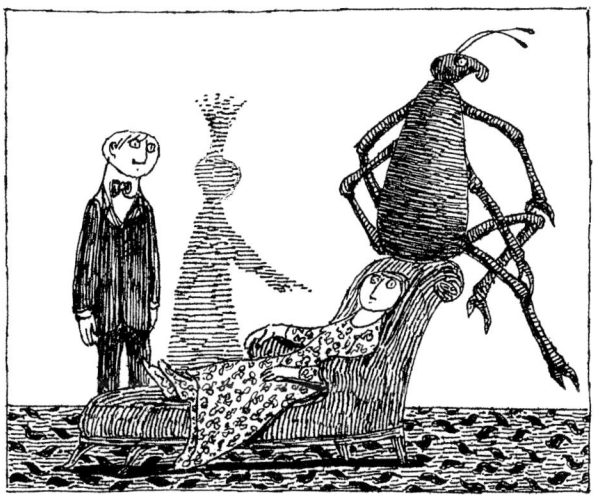

133. THE HAUNTED TEA-COSY. *Albinia Fennel reclined on a chaise longue and waited for a letter from her brother in far-off Hokkaido, Japan.*

blunt-nosed, unidentifiable creatures, uttering words such as "antigropelos," "badigeon," and "febrifuge"—he complained of agonizing over the first sentence of a text until he was satisfied enough to complete the entire, economically told story, long before beginning to draw. "I have to get the first sentence right or I can't do the second, and so forth. I can cover several hundred pages with versions of the first sentence," he told an interviewer, with typical hyperbole, but added later in the same conversation, with typical indifference to consistency, "quite often I throw away the first sentence and start with the second, as it were."[11] (Though fond of describing himself as "a great one for drift," Gorey worked hard and methodically, filling pages—often neatly typed—with possibilities for books and then filing

them for future consideration. Occasionally he developed these ideas as small, extremely schematic images, rather like miniature film storyboards—which he confessed he was not always able to decipher.)

Gorey was famously unwilling to allow himself to be categorized. "I am a person before I am anything else," he insisted in 1980 when a journalist pressed him for details about his life. "I never say I am a writer. I never say I am an artist . . . I am a person who does those things."[12] In the late 1990s, though, he told another interviewer that since he had been doing "mainly theater" for the last decade, "now there are three of me—the writer, the artist, and the theater person."[13] That "the writer" comes first in this trinity is significant. "If push comes to shove I consider myself

The Nursery Frieze

Archipelago, cardamon, obloquy, tacks,

Ignavia, samisen, bandages, wax,

Gavelkind, turmeric, imbat, cedilla,

Cassation, hendiadys, quincunx, vanilla,

Corposant, madrepore, ophicleide, paste,

Jequirity, tombola, sphagnum, distaste,

Aceldema, lunistice, yarborough, cranium,

Febrifuge, ampersand, hubris, geranium,

Opopanax, thunder, dismemberment, baize,

Hellebore, obelus, cartilage, maze,

Antigropelos, piacle, occamy, whistle,

Maremma, accismus, badigeon, epistle,

Quodlibet, catafalque, hiccup, remorse,

Idioticon, gibus, botargo, divorce,

Phylactery, gegenschein, clavicle, sago,

Bellonion, thurible, aphthong, plumbago,

Amaranth, rhoncus, pantechnicon, hymn,

Diaeresis, purlicue, sparadrap, whim,

Cicatrix, salsify, palindrome, Bosphorus,

Narthex, betrayal, chalcedony, phosphorus,

Ligament, exequies, spandrel, chandoo,

Gehenna, etui, anamorphosis, glue,

Wapentake, orrery, aspic, mistrust,

Ichor, ganosis, velleity, dust.

Idea 30/4/63.
30/11/63 - 7/1/64
Drawings 9/1/64 - 1/2/64

47. Final manuscript for *The Nursery Frieze*

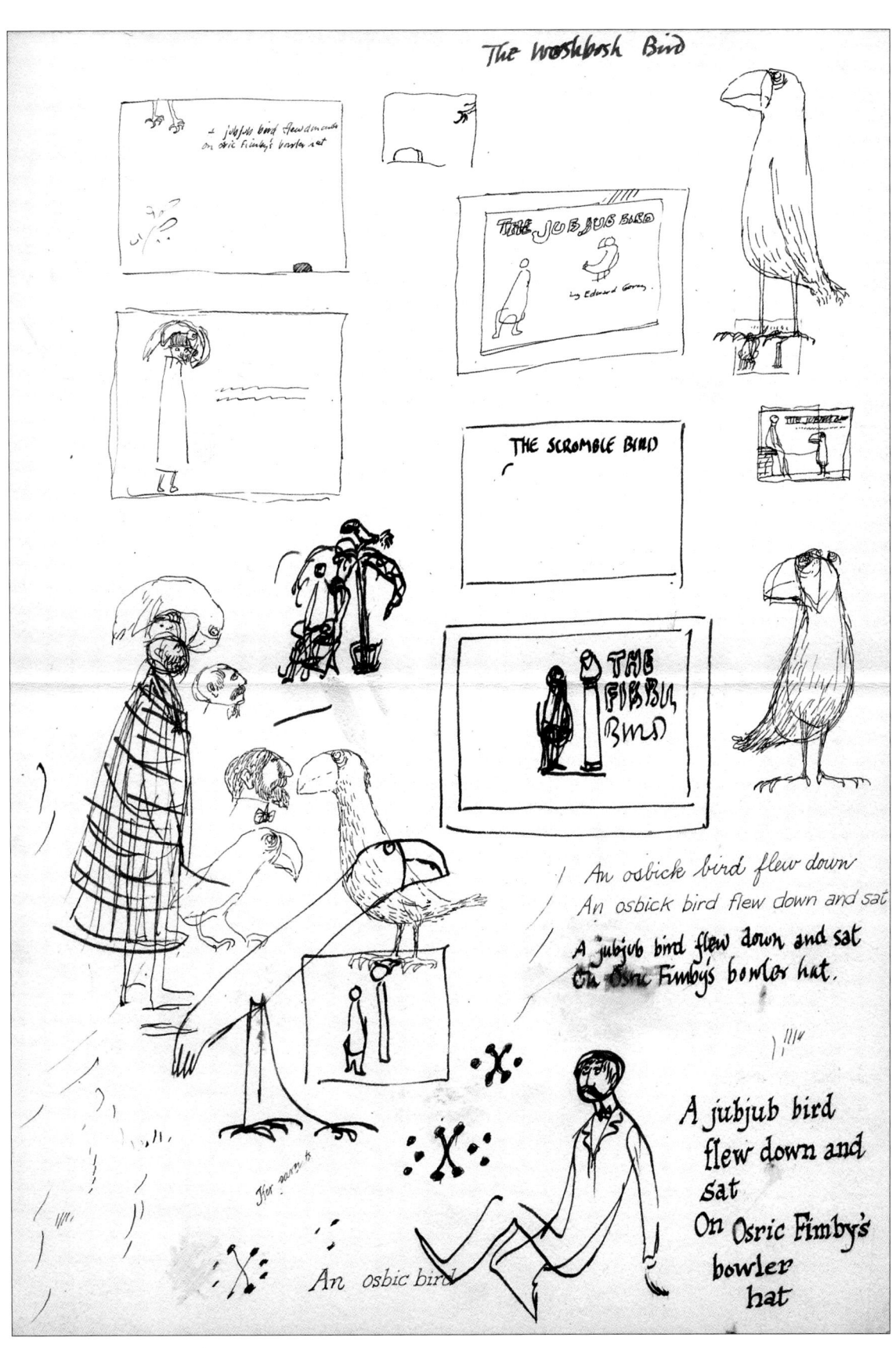

81. Page of studies for *The Osbick Bird*

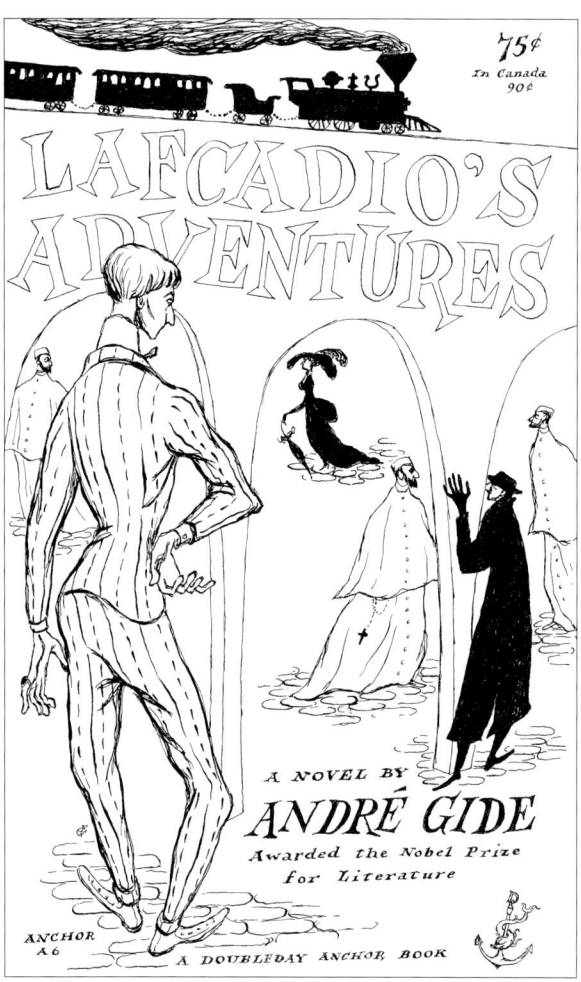

161. Cover for *Lafcadio's Adventures* by André Gide

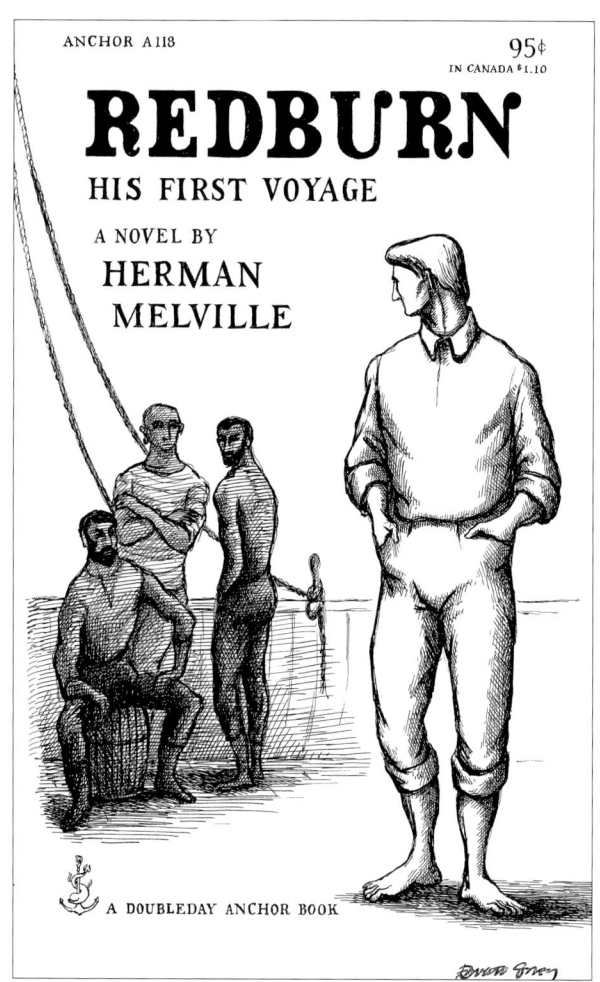

162. Cover for *Redburn: His First Voyage* by Herman Melville

more of a writer," Gorey told more than one interviewer, a conception attested to by his images.[14] That his first book, *The Unstrung Harp*, published in 1953, deals with the tribulations of "Mr C(lavius) F(rederick) Earbrass . . . the well-known novelist" always seemed to surprise Gorey, since, as he said, when he wrote the book, "I wasn't an author and I really knew nothing about it."[15] (He had, however, been working at several different publishing houses, as a designer of book covers.) The slope-browed

Mr. Earbrass bears little overt resemblance to his creator, apart from his thick turtleneck and his air of bemused hysteria. But the many self-portraits, both overt and disguised, in Gorey's books include several that identify their subject specifically as a writer. In the alphabet rhyme *The Chinese Obelisks* (1970), a tall, bearded figure in a fur coat and sneakers witnesses or is the victim of a series of miniature dramas—"I was an Infant who clung to his sleeve, J was the Jam that he gave it to leave," and "Q was the

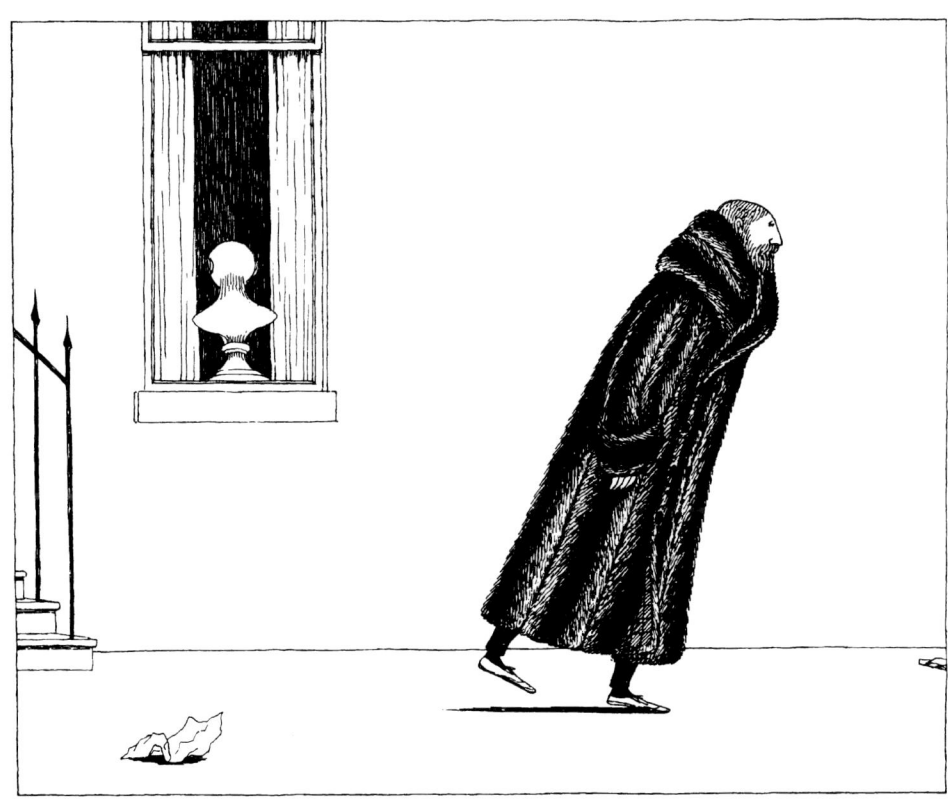

80. THE CHINESE
OBELISKS; FOURTH
ALPHABET. *A was an
Author who went for a walk*

Question he asked of a stranger, R the Reply that his life was in danger." He is identified as "A"—"an Author who went for a walk." He turns up again, looking older, now wearing glasses but still sporting the fur coat and the sneakers, and writing in a notebook, at the end of yet another alphabet book, *The Glorious Nosebleed* (1975); here, we are told, "He wrote it all down Zealously." There is no equivalent image of an artist.

In the end, however, Gorey remains, like the steepest ascents in bicycle races, *hors catégorie*. Describing him as—for example—a maker of, in his phrase, "mildly unsettling" books about an imagined past (possibly intended for children) fails to capture the many facets of this elusive polymath. So does labeling him as writer, artist, poet, or theater person. He is something far more complicated and interesting: a true American original whose work, at once wholly his own and informed by a wealth of often unexpected sources, refuses to be classified. Offered interpretations of his work, Gorey proved characteristically agreeable and evasive. "I always feel 'what you see is what you get,'" he said, "but if you want to read something into it, then you can. Occasionally, someone will come up to me and say 'Oh, I figured out what your book was about.' And I say, 'Oh, what?' And they'll tell me something completely bizarre. And I'll think, 'If that's what you want to see, it's okay by me.'"[16]

Karen Wilkin
New York, April 2008

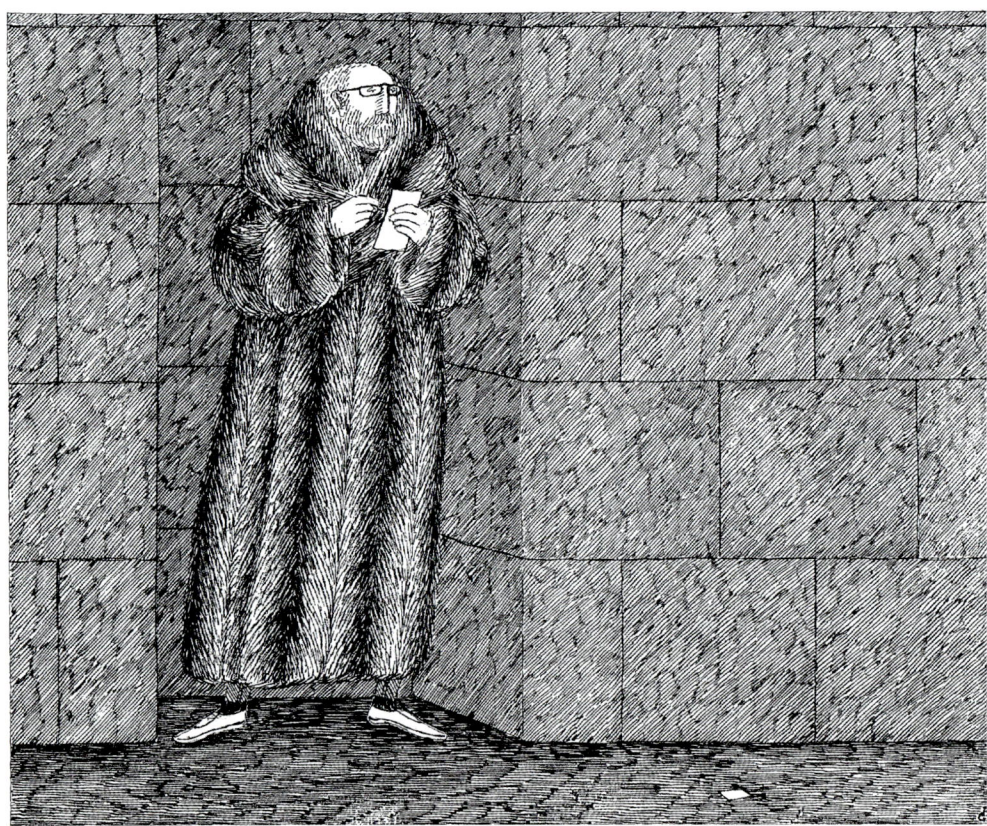

109. THE GLORIOUS
NOSEBLEED: FIFTH
ALPHABET. *He wrote it all
down Zealously.*

NOTES

Epigraph. Edward Gorey, quoted in Richard Dyer, "The Poison Penman," *Boston Globe Magazine,* 1 April 1984.

1. All uncited quotations from Edward Gorey are from conversations with the author on various dates between 1995 and 2000.

2. Stephen Schiff, "Edward Gorey and the Tao of Nonsense," *The New Yorker,* 9 November 1992, reprinted in *Ascending Peculiarity: Edward Gorey on Edward Gorey,* interviews selected and edited by Karen Wilkin (New York: Harcourt, 2001), 139.

3. Annie Nocenti, "Writing 'The Black Doll': A Talk with Edward Gorey," *Scenario,* Spring 1998, reprinted in *Ascending Peculiarity,* 200.

4. Ed Pinsent, "A Gorey Encounter," *Speak,* Fall 1997, reprinted in *Ascending Peculiarity,* 192.

5. Robert Dahlin, "Conversations with Writers: Edward Gorey," in *Conversations with Writers,* ed. Matthew J. Bruccoli et al., vol. 1 (Detroit, Mich.: Gale Research Co., 1977), reprinted in *Ascending Peculiarity,* 40.

6. Mary Rourke, "Strange Things Happen When Gorey Is Afoot," *National Observer,* 11 September 1976, in *Ascending Peculiarity,* 239.

7. Dahlin, "Conversations," *Ascending Peculiarity,* 37.

8. Schiff, "Tao of Nonsense," *Ascending Peculiarity,* 145.

9. Gorey, in Dahlin, "Conversations," *Ascending Peculiarity,* 48.

10. Jean Martin, "The Mind's Eye: Writers Who Draw," *Drawing,* July/August 1980, reprinted in *Ascending Peculiarity,* 86.

11. Dahlin, "Conversations," *Ascending Peculiarity,* 37, 41.

12. Lisa Solod, "Edward Gorey," *Boston Magazine,* September 1980, in *Ascending Peculiarity,* 102.

13. Pinsent, "A Gorey Encounter," *Ascending Peculiarity,* 189.

14. Ibid.

15. Carol Stevens, "An American Original," *Print,* January/February 1988, in *Ascending Peculiarity,* 127.

16. Nocenti, "Writing 'The Black Doll,'" *Ascending Peculiarity,* 202.

ELEGANT ENIGMAS
the art of EDWARD GOREY
PLATES

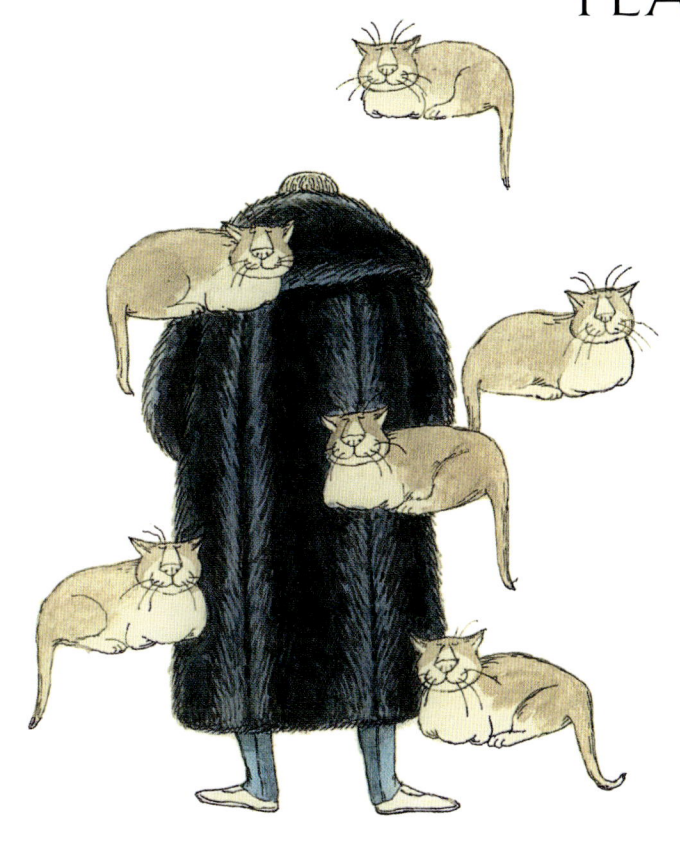

BOOKS BY
EDWARD GOREY

The Unstrung Harp;
or, Mr Earbrass Writes a Novel, 1953

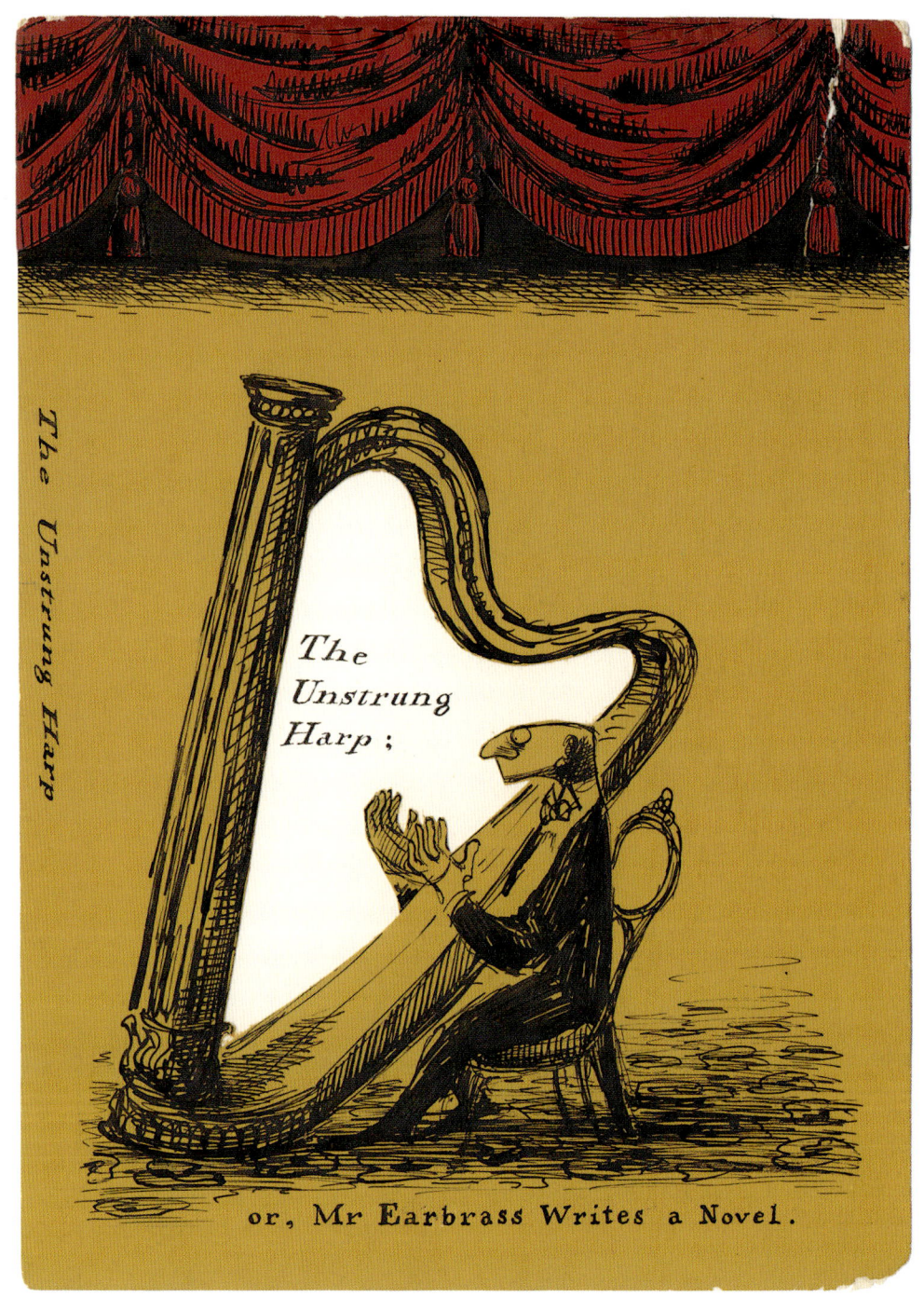

2. Study
for cover

3. *Mr C(lavius) F(rederick) Earbrass is, of course, the well-known novelist. Of his books,* A Moral Dustbin, More Chains Than Clank, Was it Likely?, *and the* Hipdeep *trilogy are, perhaps, the most admired. Mr Earbrass is seen on the croquet lawn of his home, Hobbies Odd, near Collapsed Pudding in Mortshire. He is studying a game left unfinished at the end of summer.*

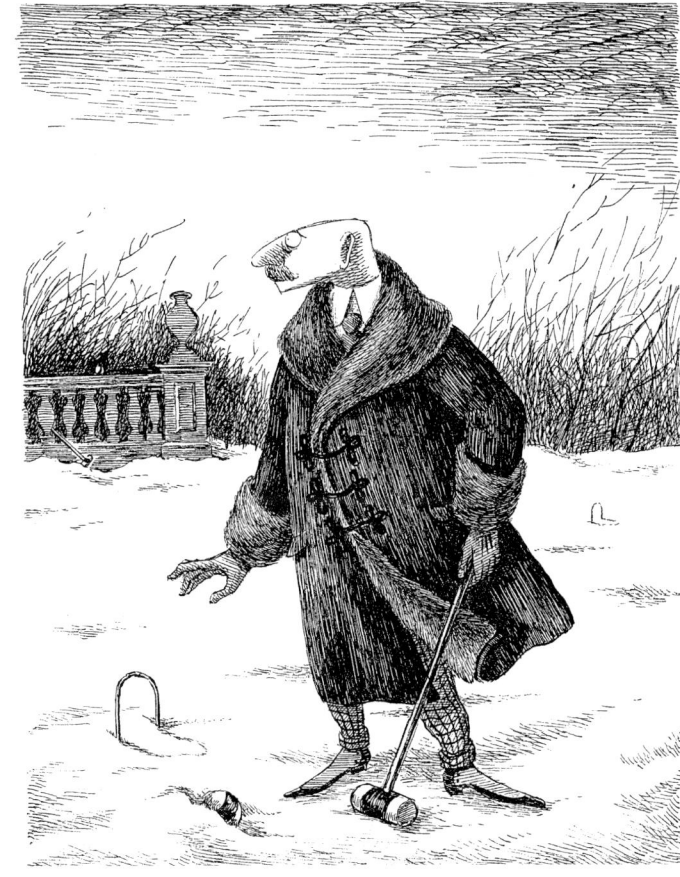

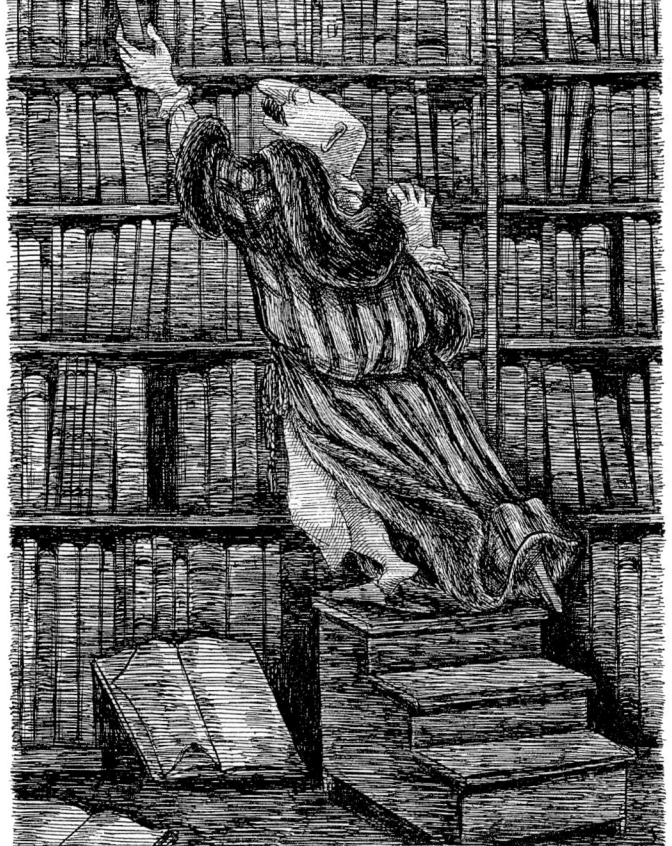

4. *Mr Earbrass was virtually asleep when several lines of verse passed through his mind and left it hopelessly awake. Here was the perfect epigraph for* TUH:

A horrid ?monster has been [something]
  delay'd
By your/their indiff'rence in the dank
  brown shade
Below the garden . . .

His mind's eye sees them quoted on the bottom third of a right-hand page in a (possibly) olive-bound book he read at least five years ago. When he does find them, it will be a great nuisance if no clue is given to their authorship.

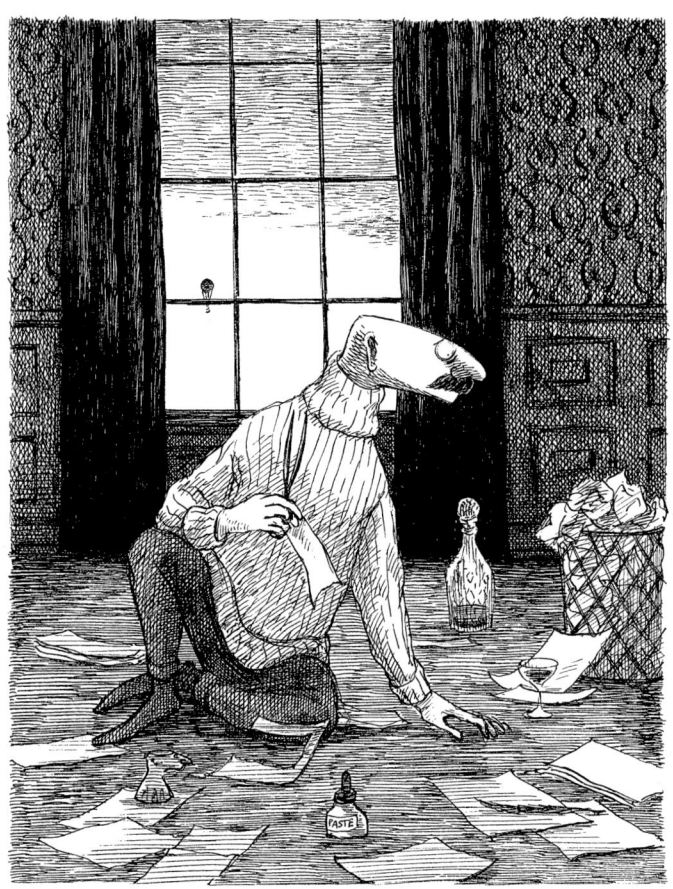

5. *Some weeks later, with pen, ink, scissors, paste, a decanter of sherry, and a vast
reluctance, Mr Earbrass begins to revise* TUH. *This means, first, transposing
passages, or reversing the order of their paragraphs, or crumpling them up
furiously and throwing them in the waste-basket. After that there is rewriting.
This is worse than merely writing, because not only does he have to think up new
things just the same, but at the same time try not to remember the old ones. Before
Mr Earbrass is through, at least one third of* TUH *will bear no resemblance
to its original state.*

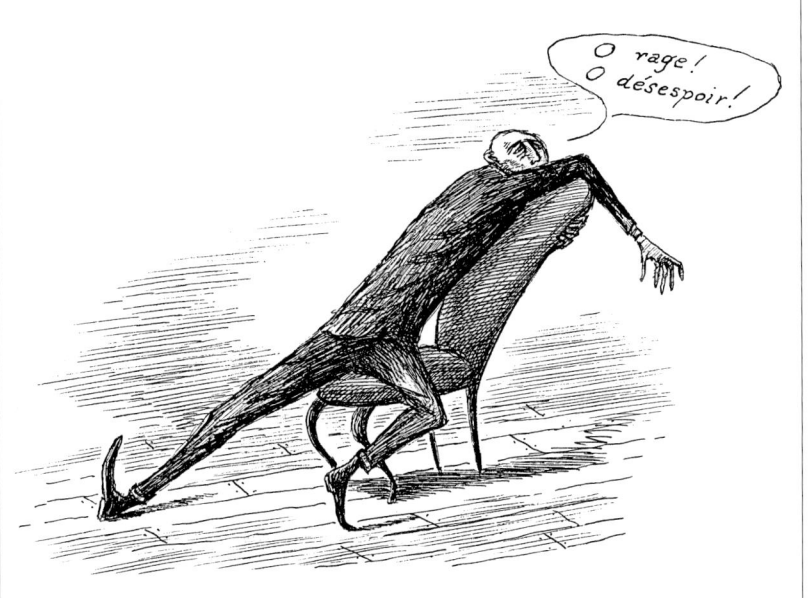

6. Cover

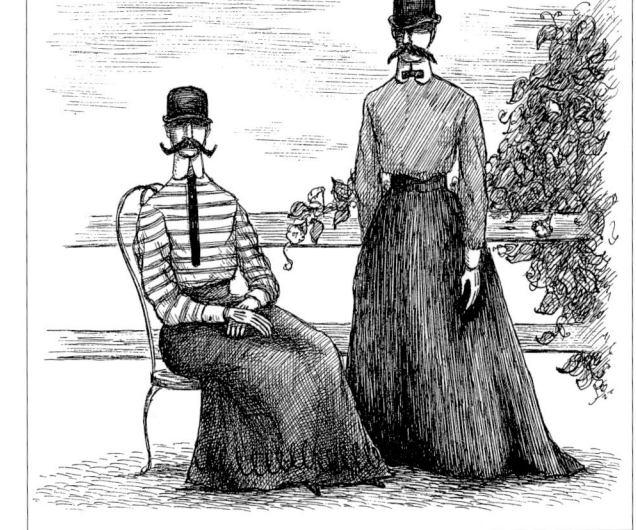

7. There's a rather odd couple in Herts
Who are cousins (or so each asserts);
    Their sex is in doubt
    For they're never without
Their moustaches and long, trailing skirts.

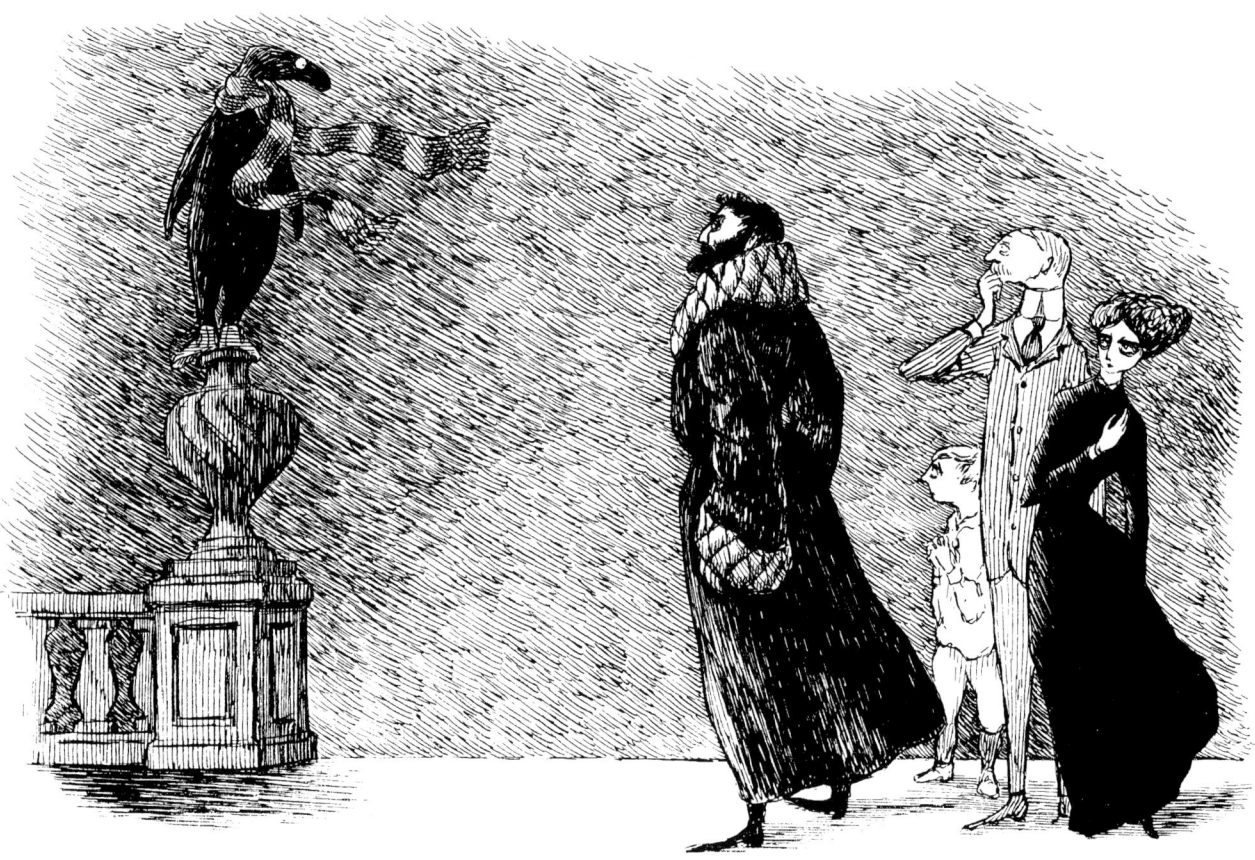

9. *Then they saw something standing on top of an urn,*
Whose peculiar appearance gave them quite a turn.

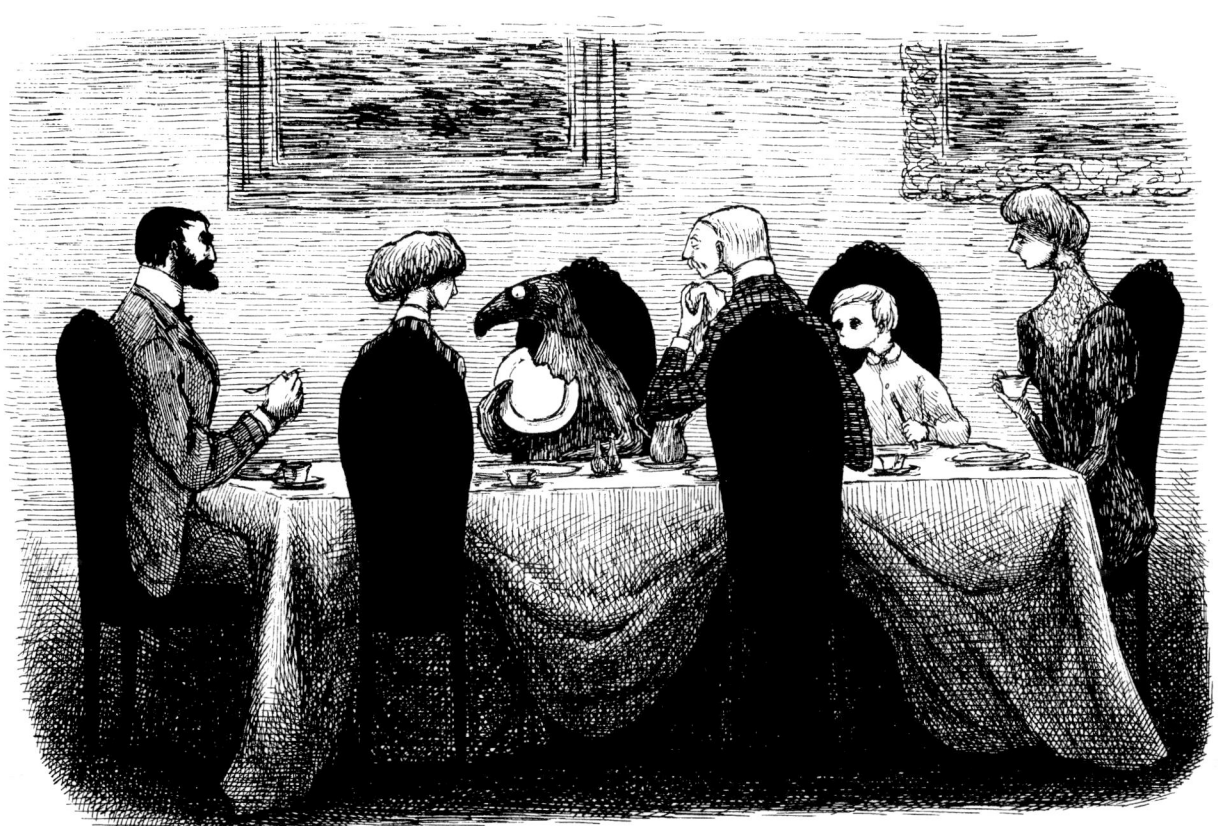

10. *It joined them at breakfast and presently ate*
All the syrup and toast, and a part of a plate.

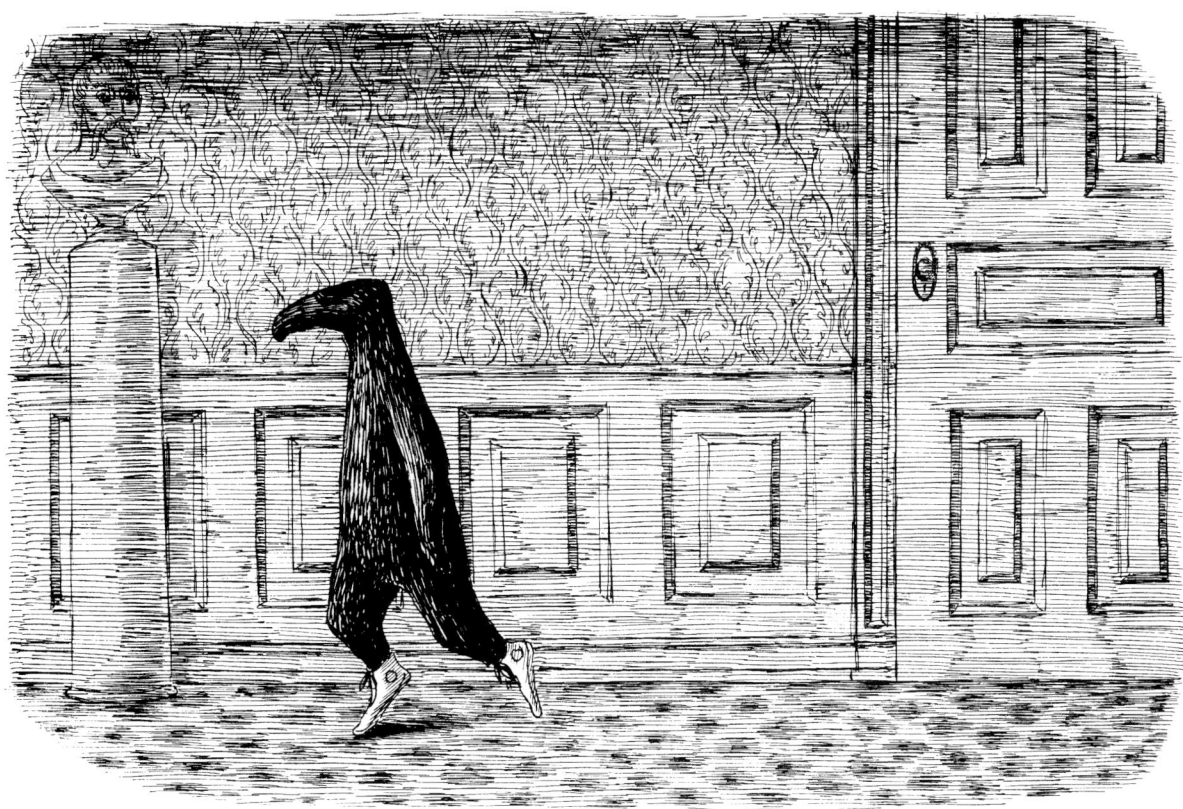

11. *In the night through the house it would aimlessly creep,*
In spite of the fact of its being asleep.

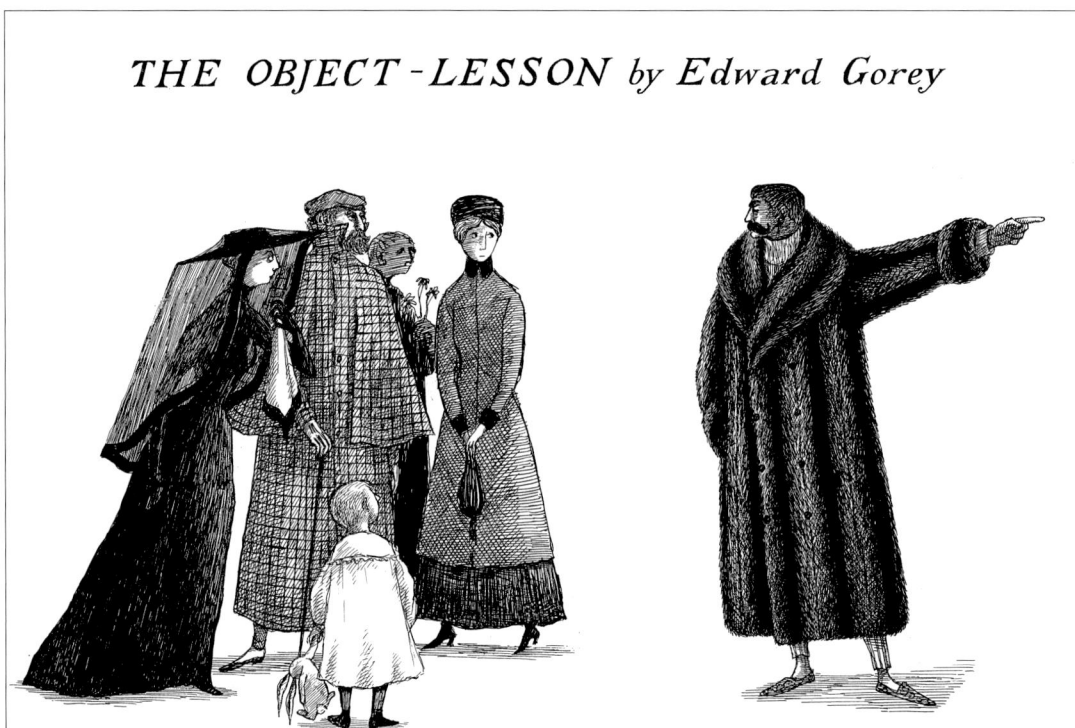

THE OBJECT-LESSON by Edward Gorey

12. Cover (unpublished)

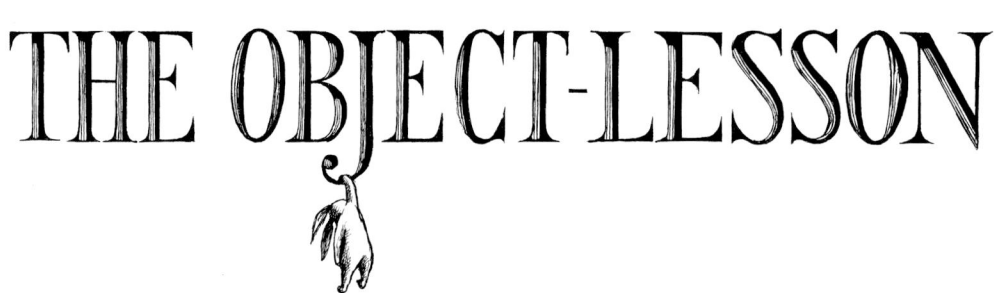

THE OBJECT-LESSON

EDWARD GOREY

13. Cover

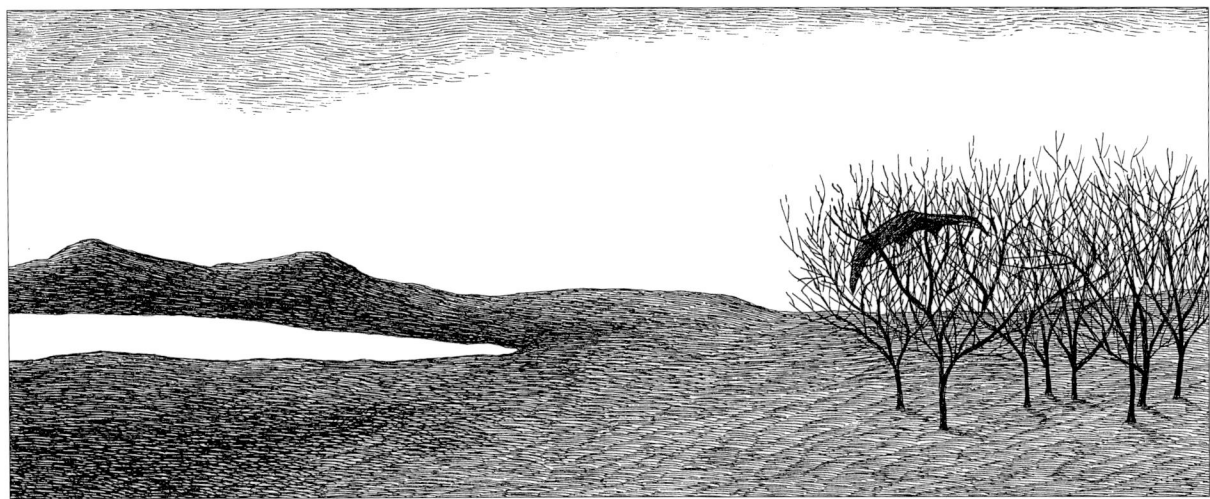

14. *On the shore a bat, or possibly an umbrella,*

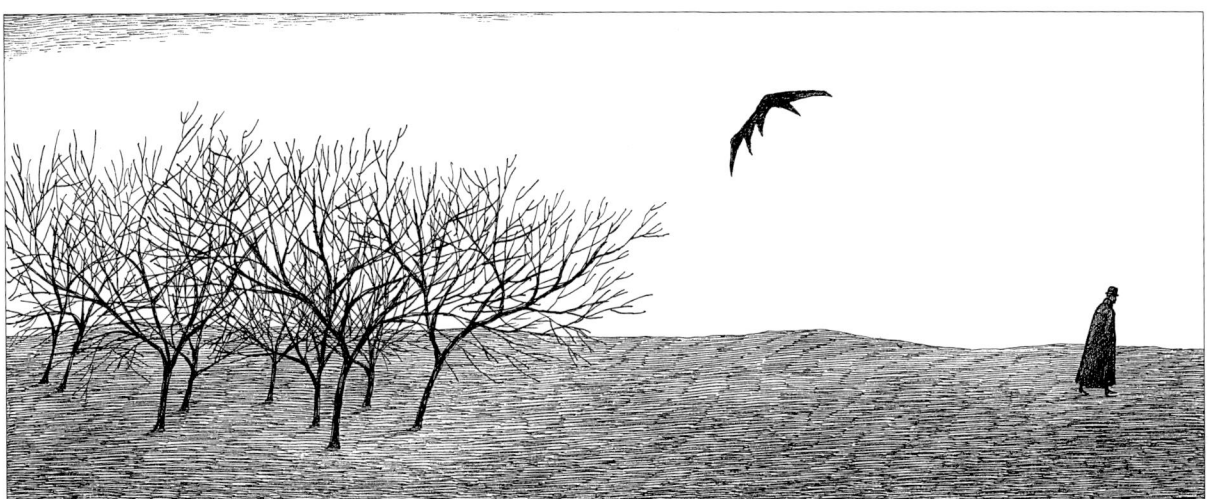

15. *disengaged itself from the shrubbery,*

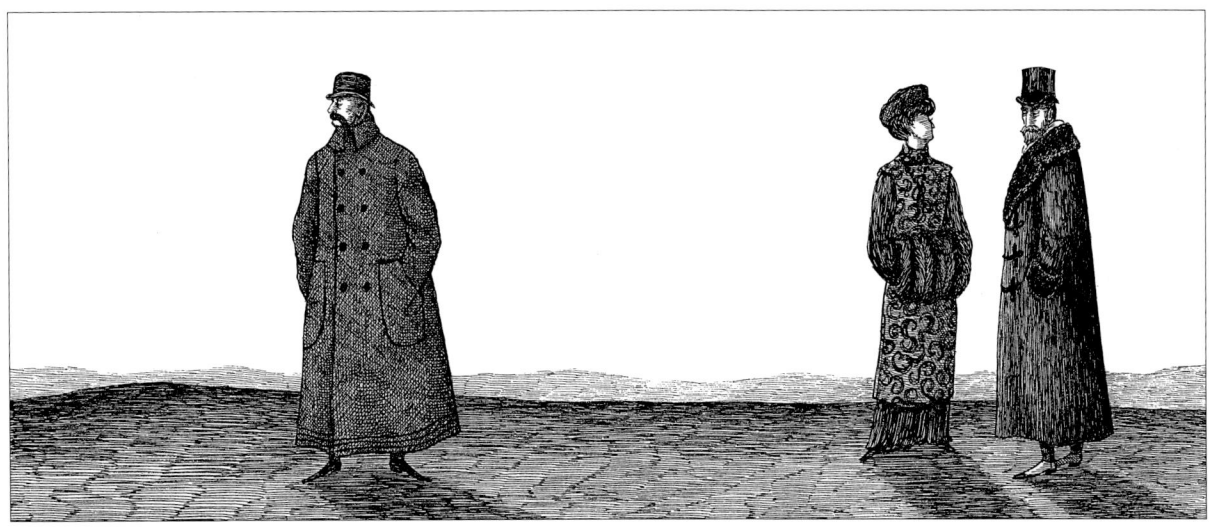

16. *causing those nearby to recollect the miseries of childhood.*

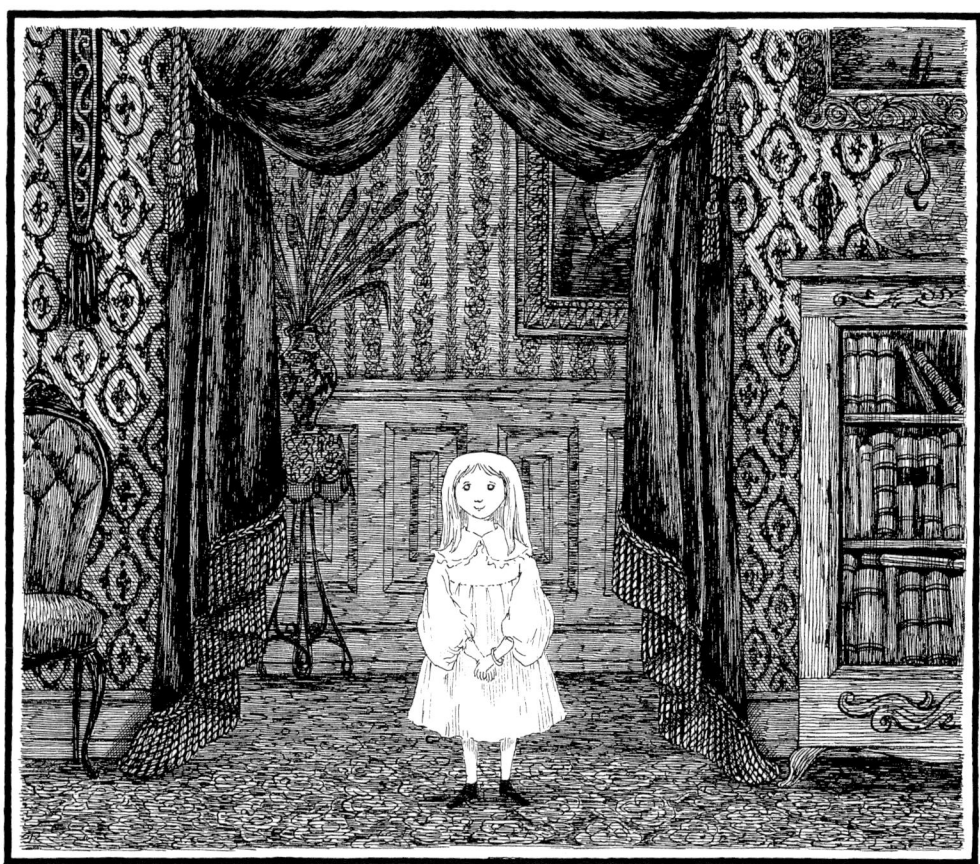

20. *There was once a little girl
named Charlotte Sophia.*

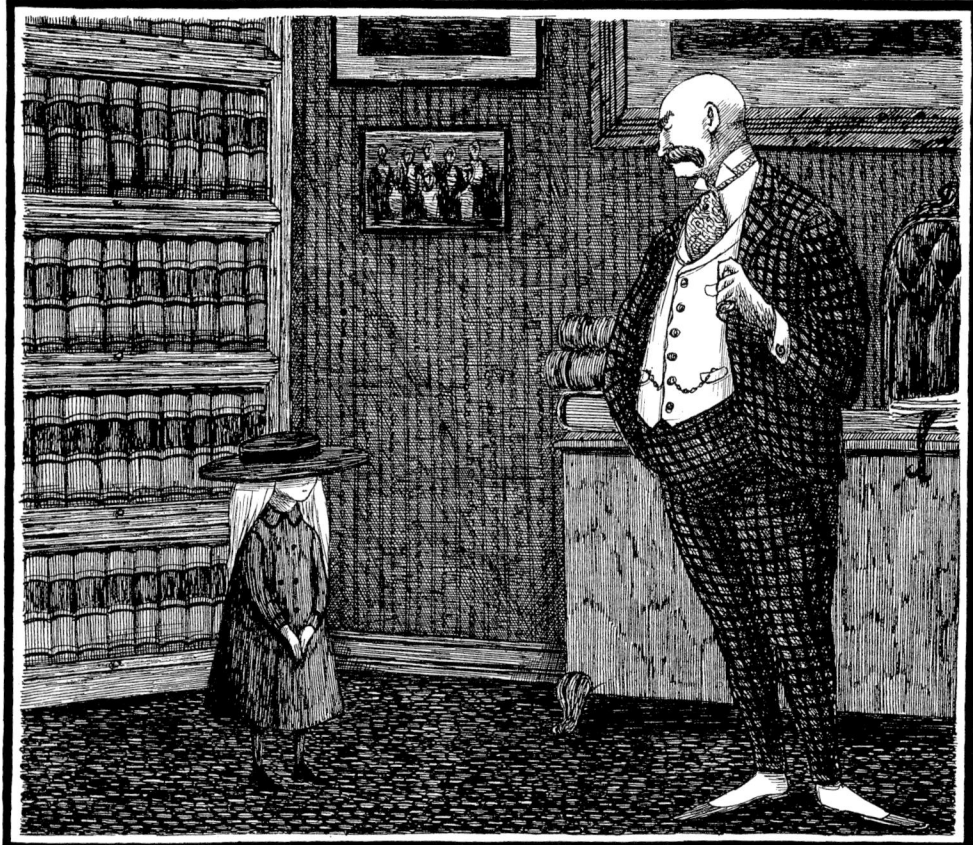

22. *Charlotte Sophia was left in
the hands of the family lawyer.*

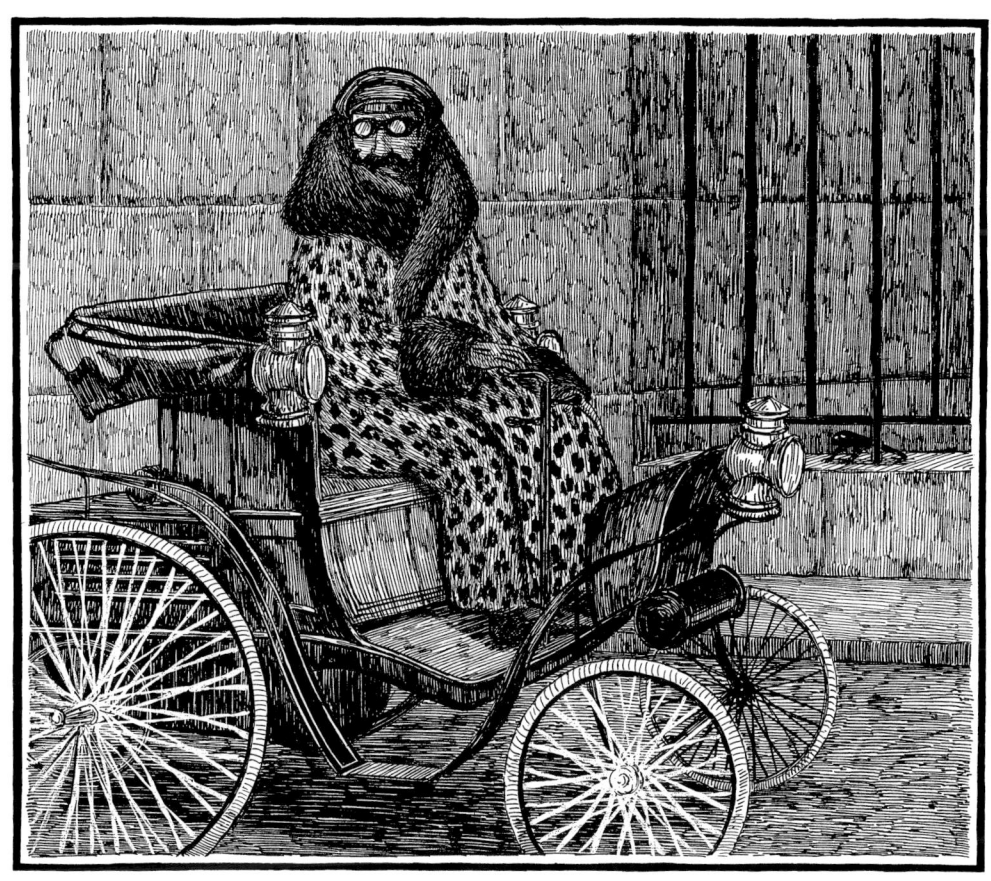

23. *Every day he motored through the streets searching for her.*

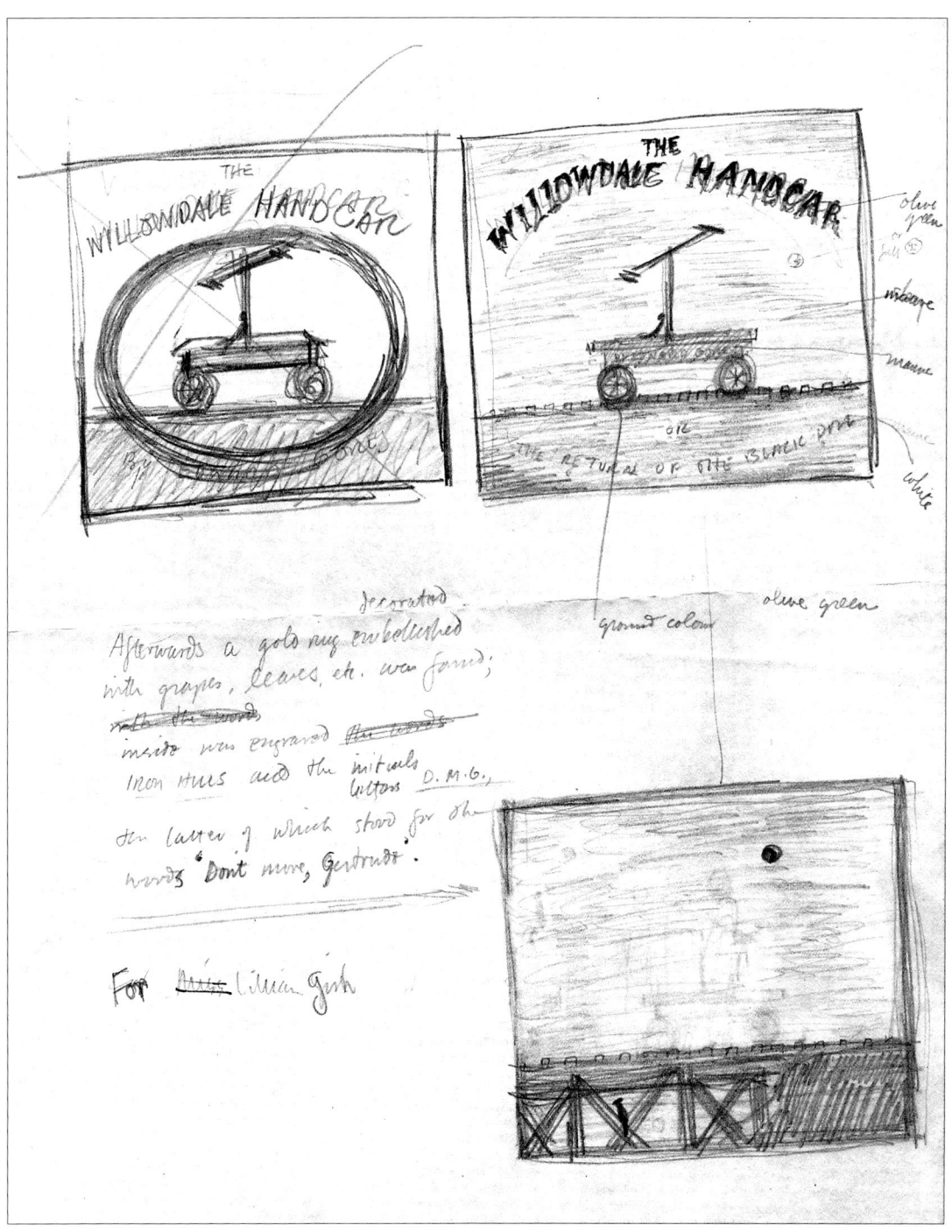

25. Page of studies for cover

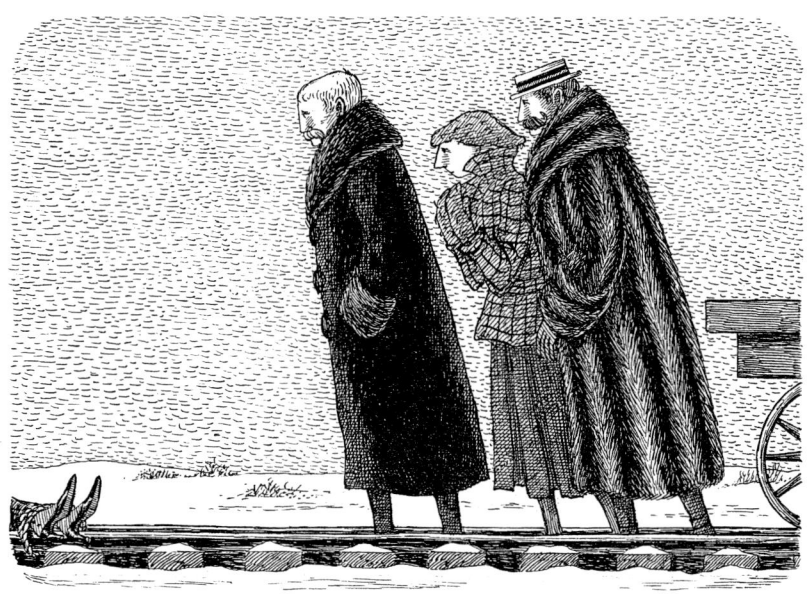

27. *Between West Elbow and Penetralia they almost ran over someone who was tied to the track.*
It proved to be Nellie.

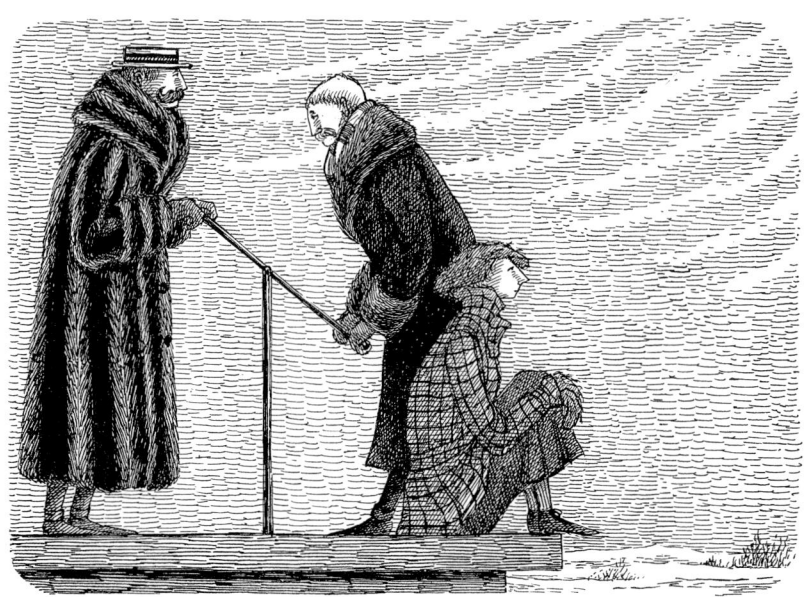

28. *Some months went by, and still they had not returned to Willowdale.*

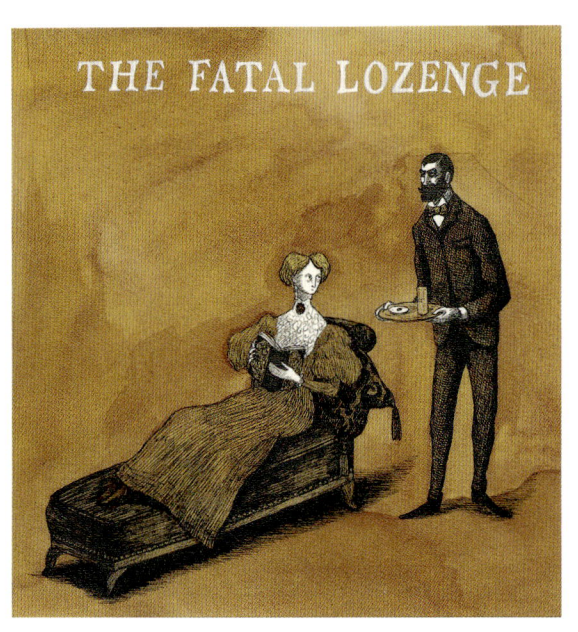

17. Cover (unpublished)

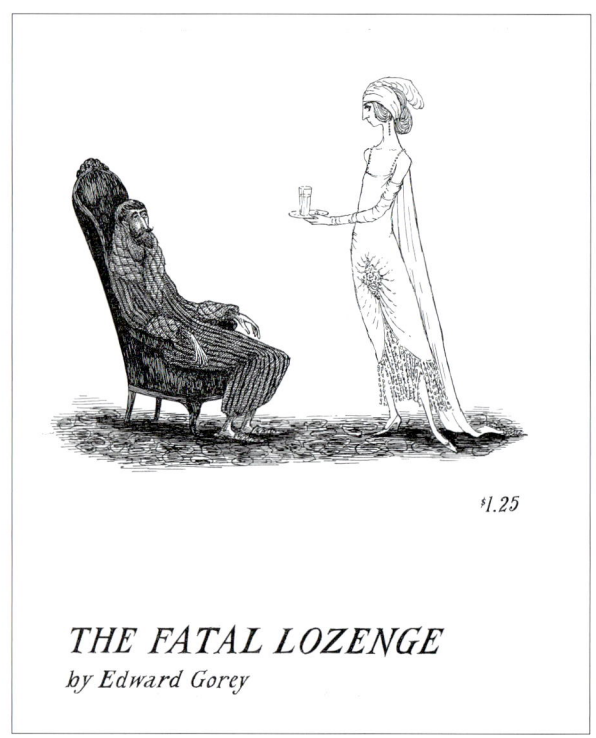

18. Cover

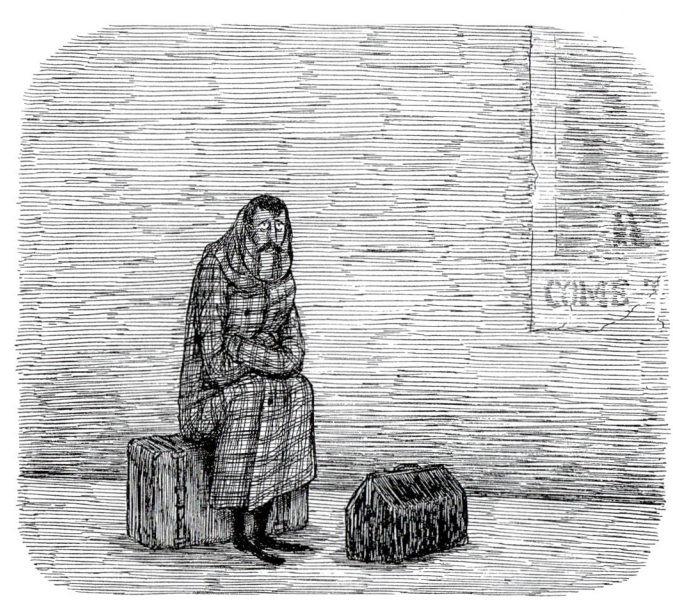

19. *The* Tourist *huddles in the station*
While slowly night gives way to dawn;
He finds a certain fascination
In knowing all the trains are gone.

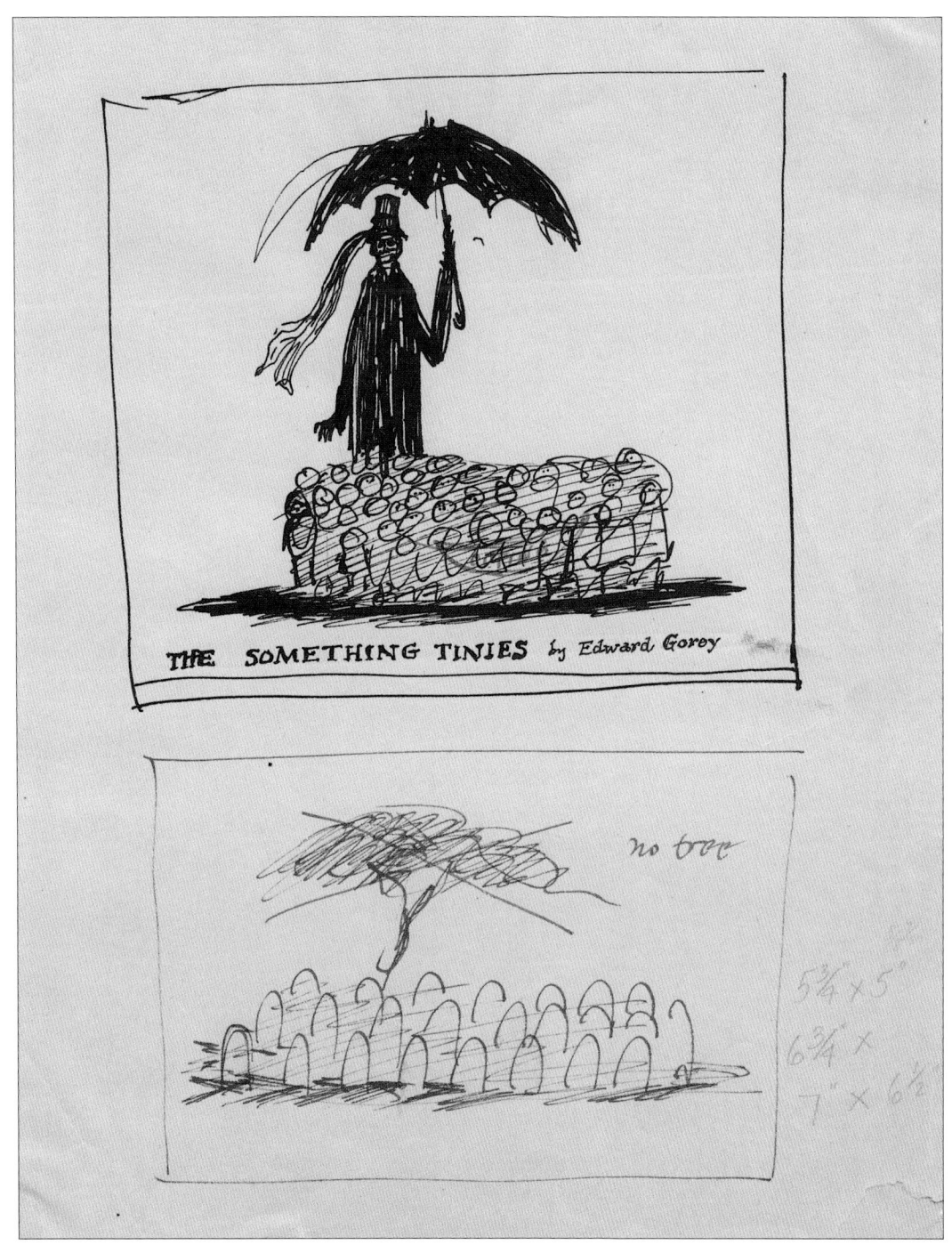

30. Page of studies for front and back covers

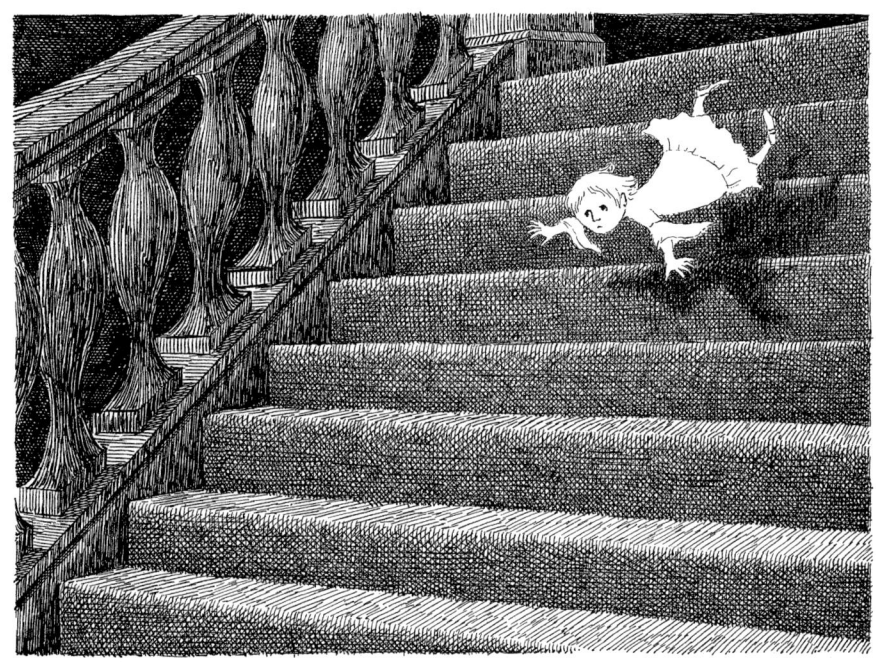

31. *A is for Amy who fell down the stairs*

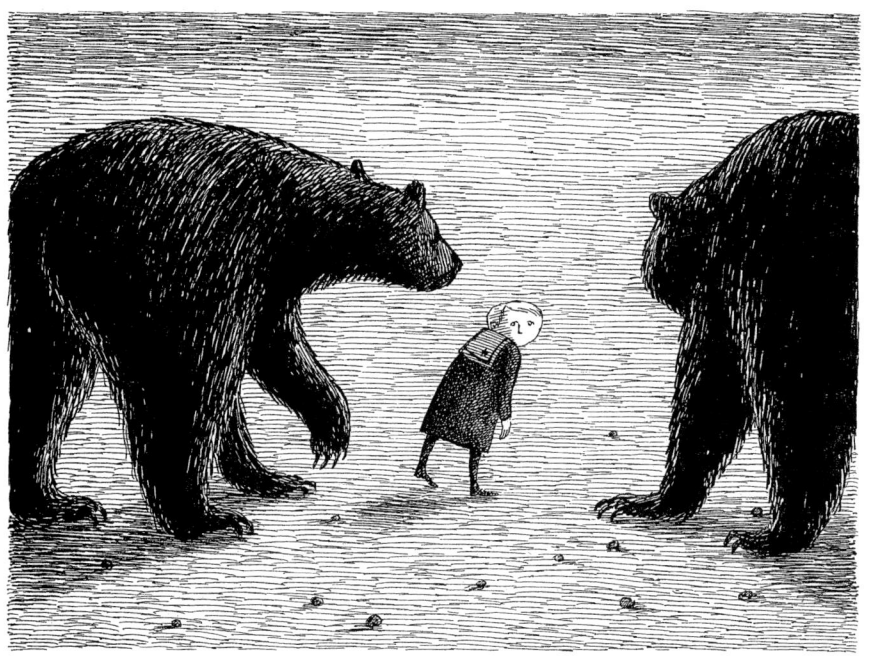

32. *B is for Basil assaulted by bears*

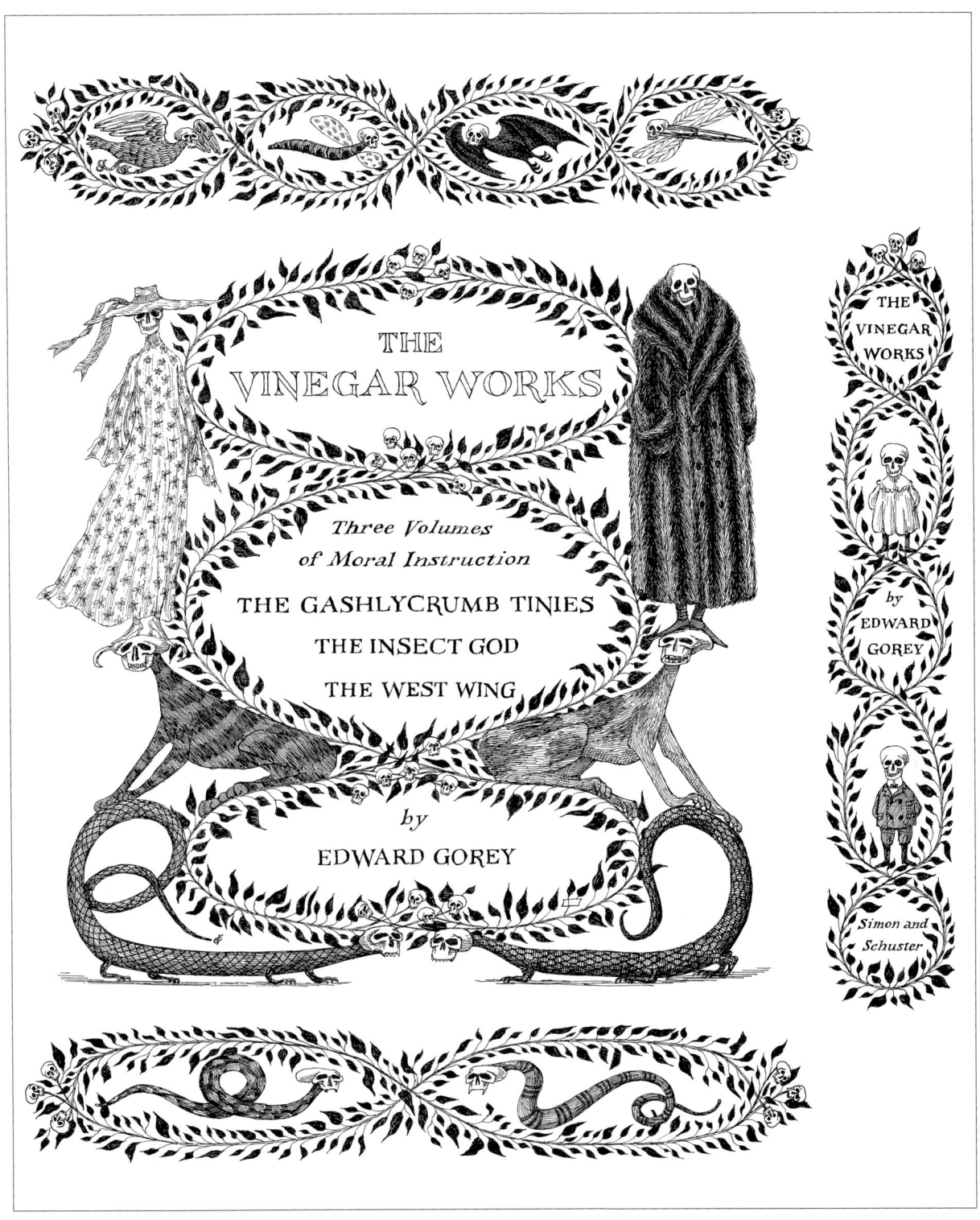

The Vinegar Works
Three Volumes of Moral Instruction
THE GASHLYCRUMB TINIES
THE INSECT GOD
THE WEST WING
by
EDWARD GOREY

THE VINEGAR WORKS
by
EDWARD GOREY
Simon and Schuster

35. Cover for slipcase (front, top, side, and bottom panels) for *The Vinegar Works: Three Volumes of Moral Instruction*

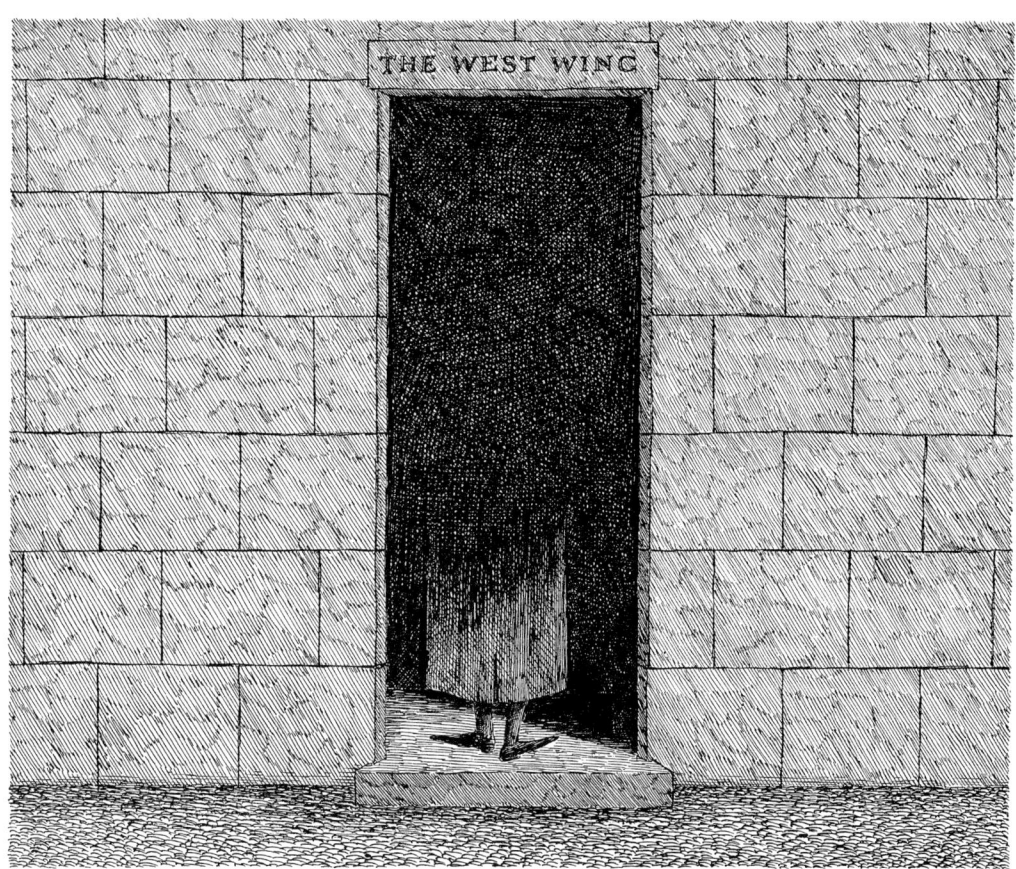

THE
WEST WING
1963

38. Title page

by Edward Gorey   *Simon and Schuster, New York, 1963*

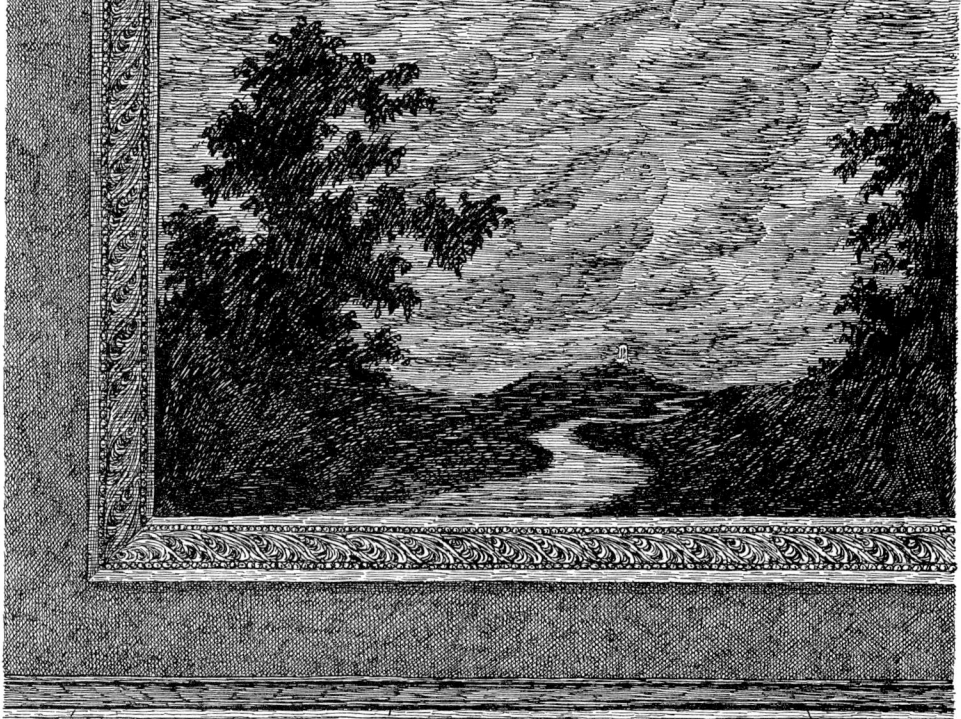

40. Panel 5

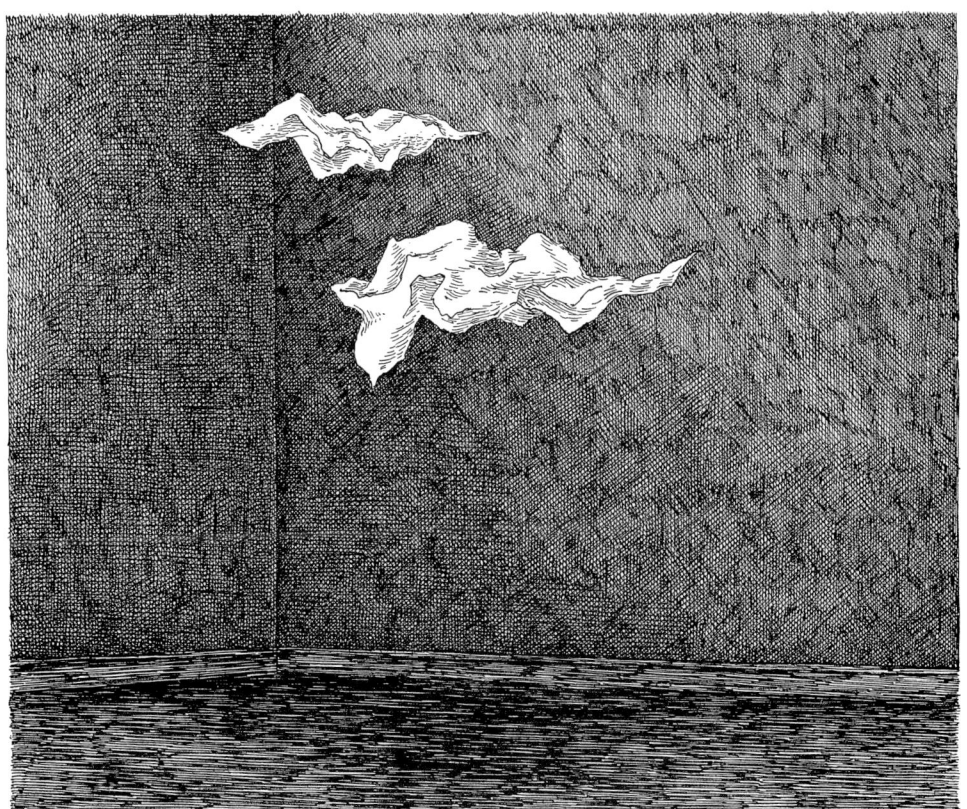

41. Panel 13

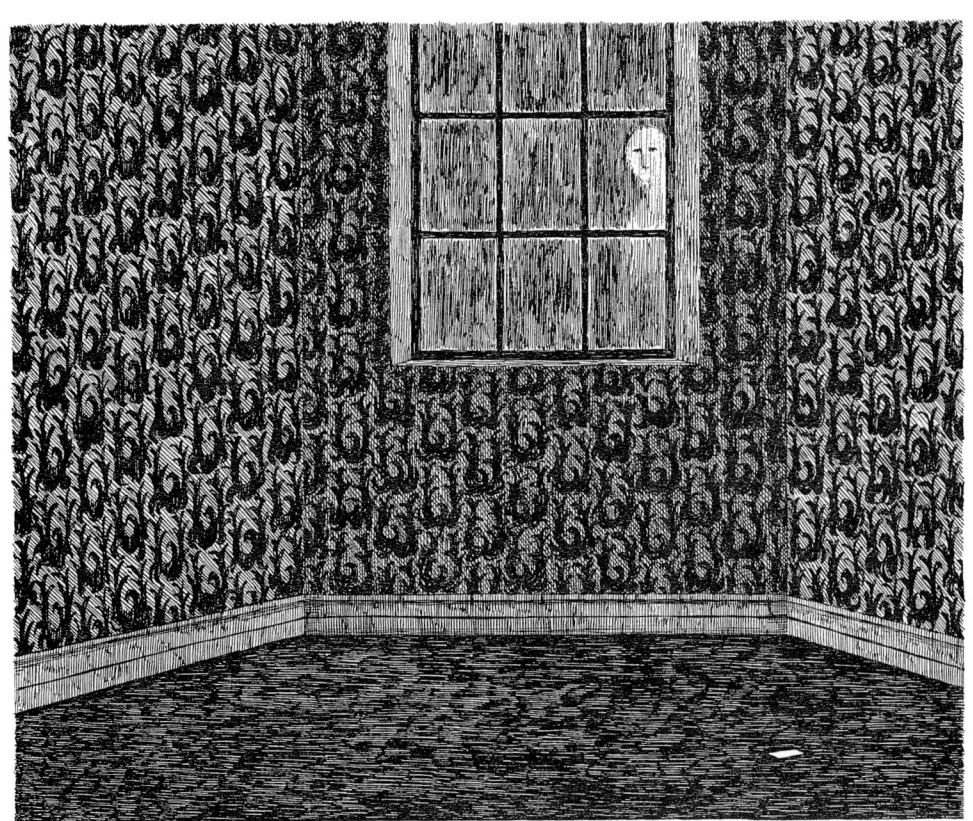

42. Panel 17

55

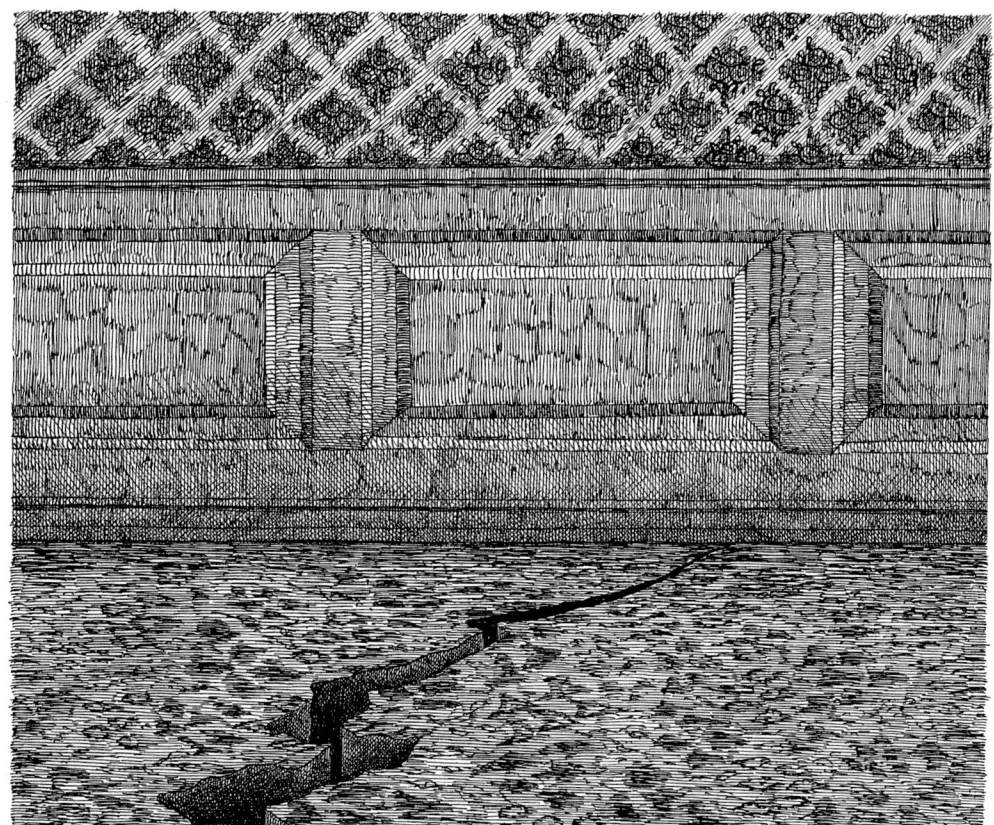

43. Panel 22

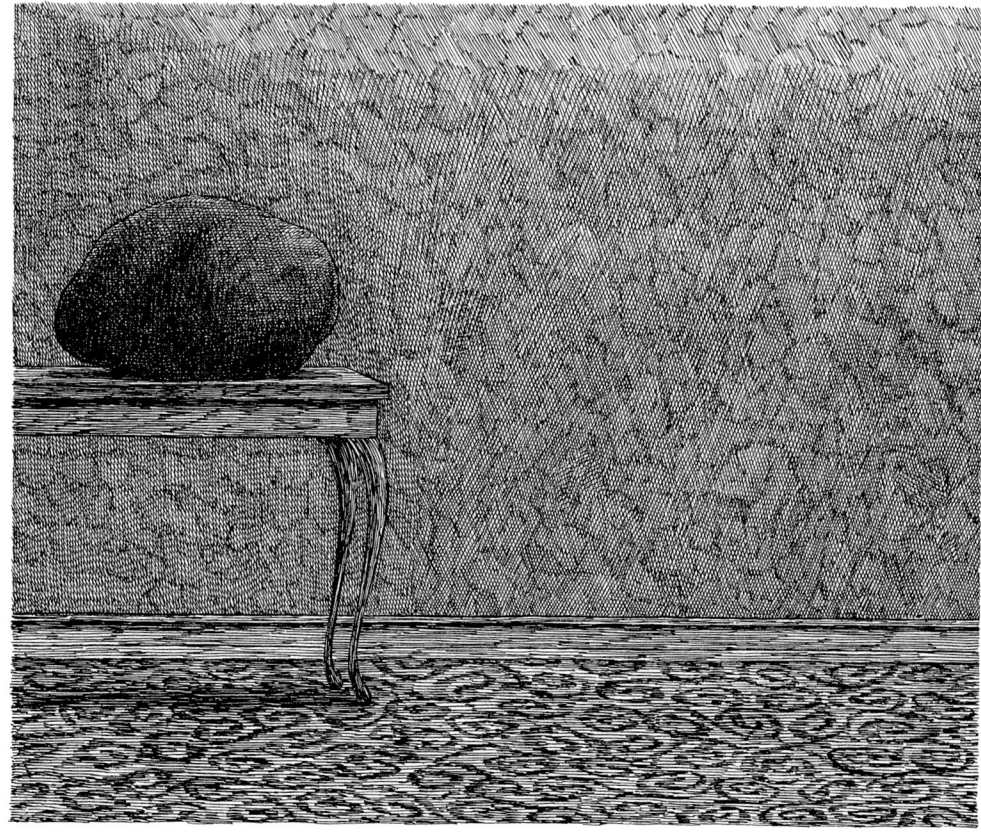

44. Panel 27

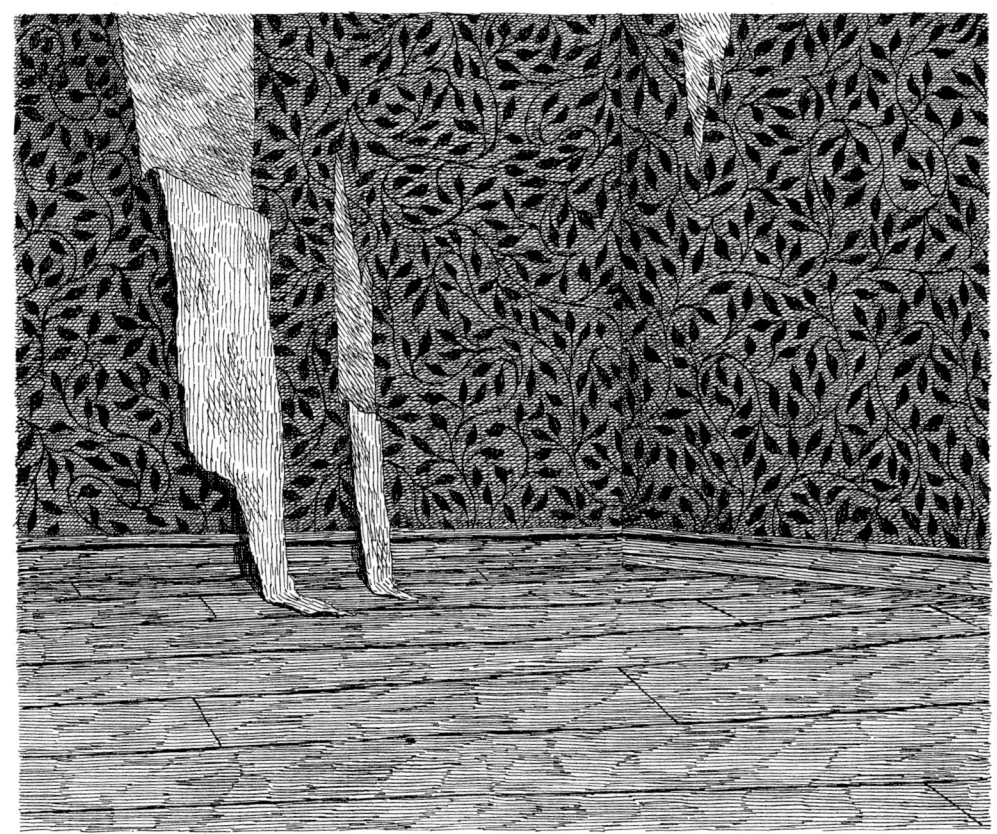

45. Panel 29

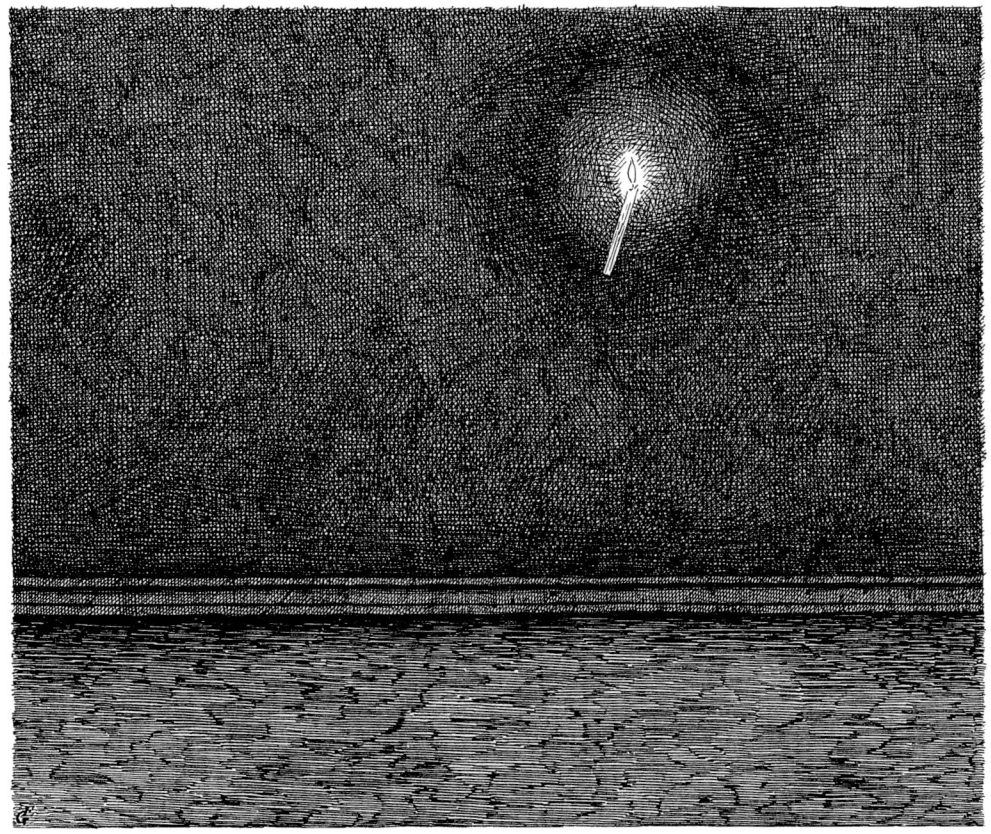

46. Panel U

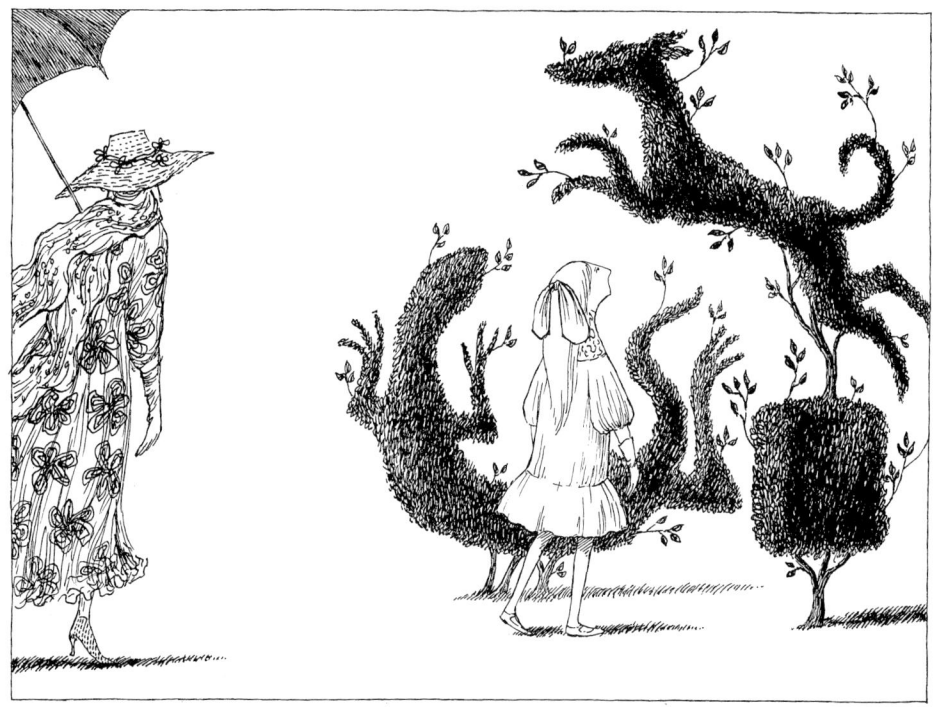

54. *They were shown into a garden where the topiary was being neglected.*

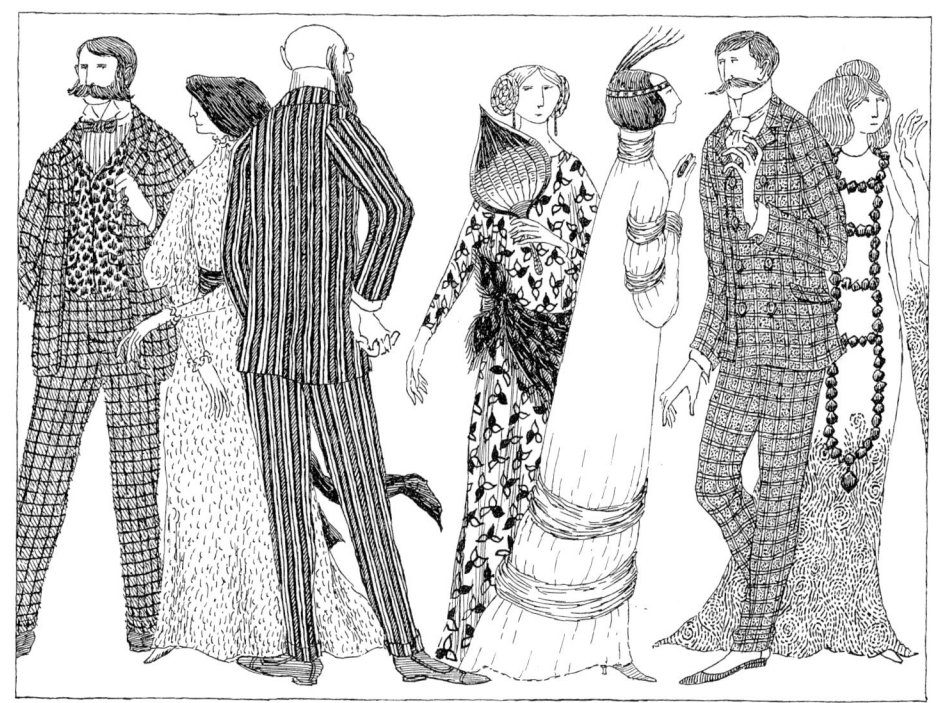

55. *He and Miss Skrim-Pshaw mentioned a great many people who had done things in their conversation.*

THE NURSERY FRIEZE, 1964

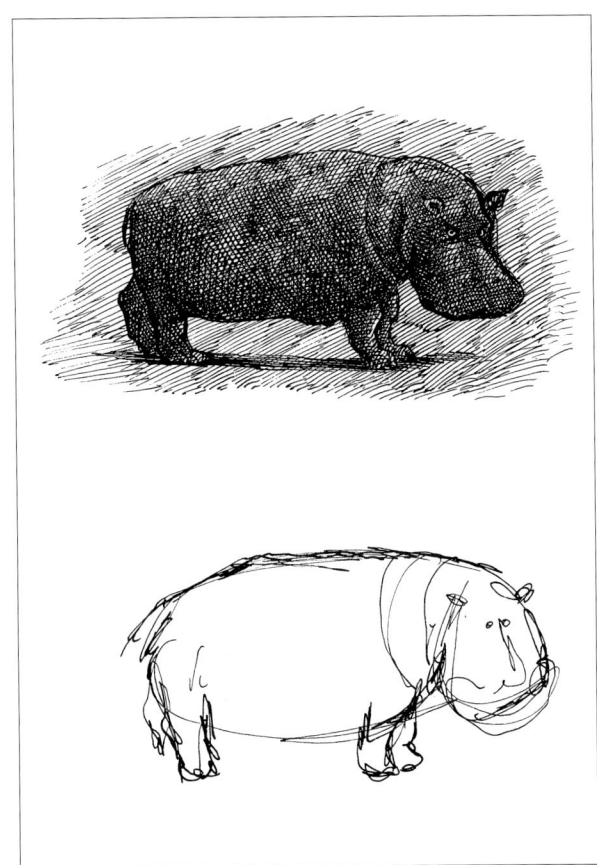

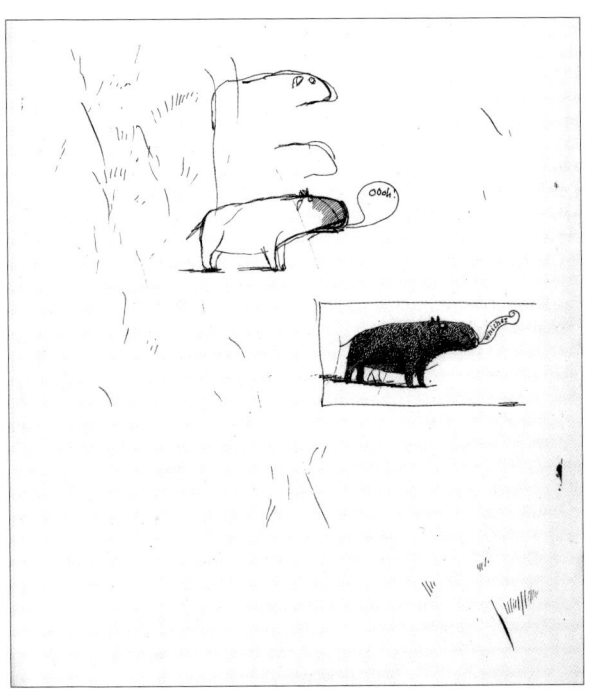

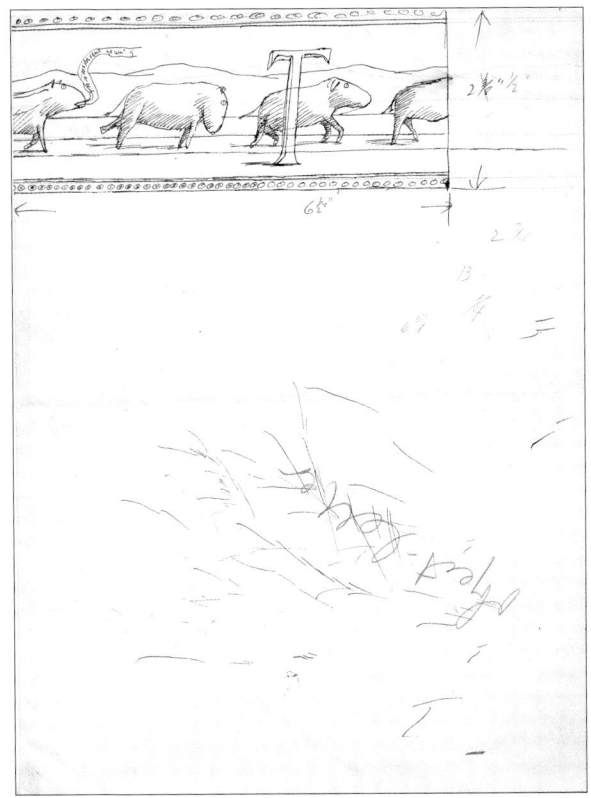

48, 49, AND 50. Three pages of studies

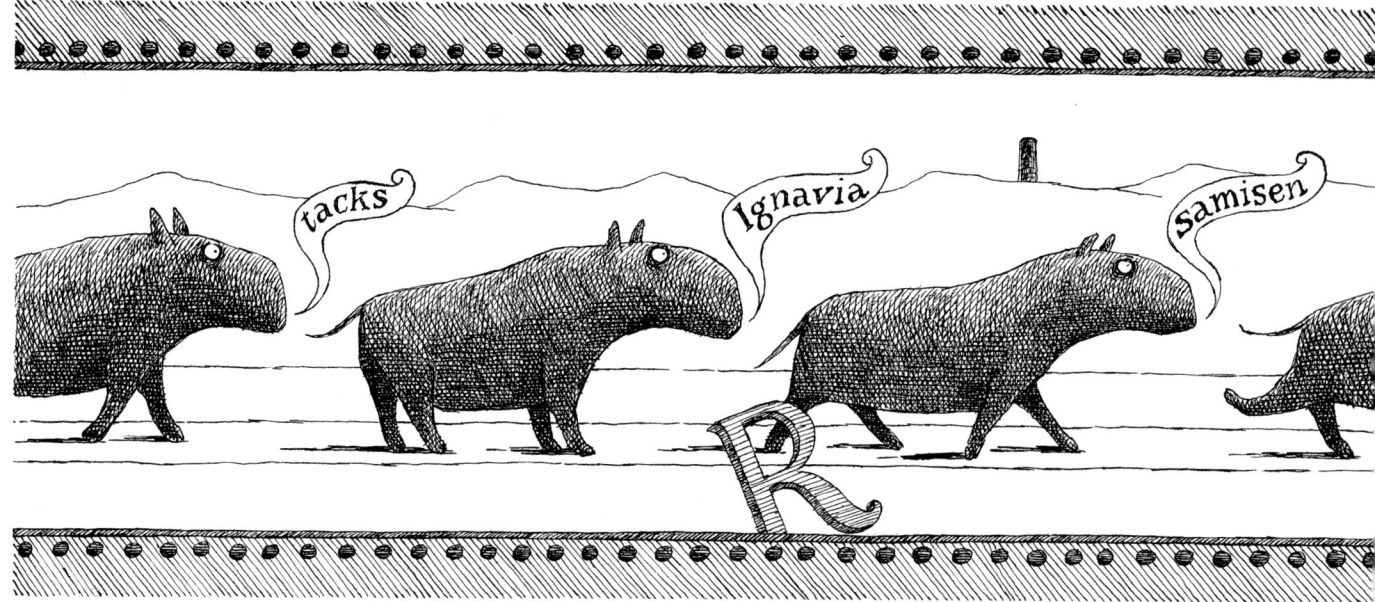

51.

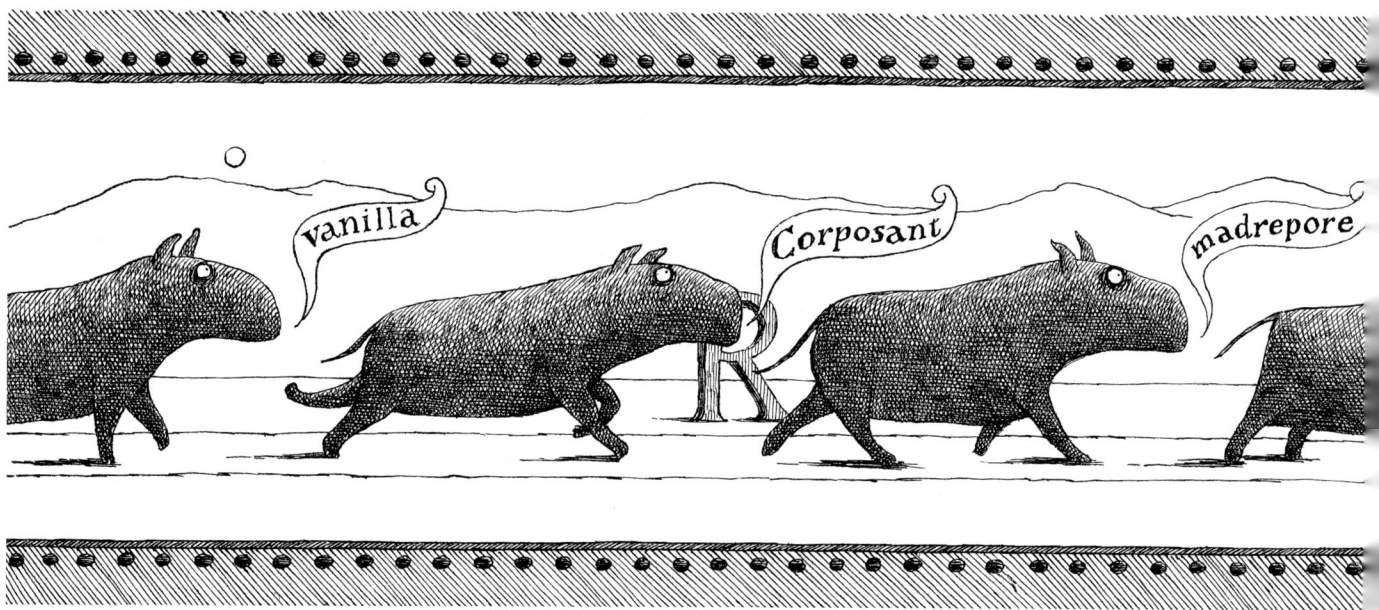

52.

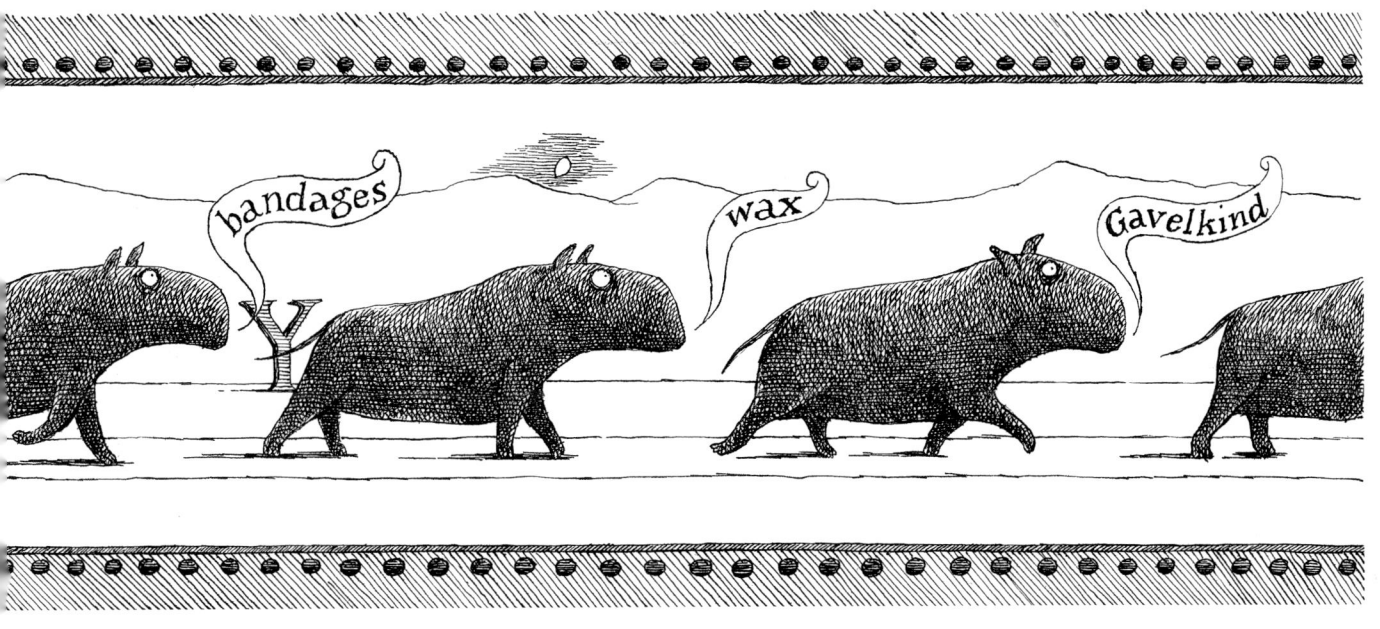

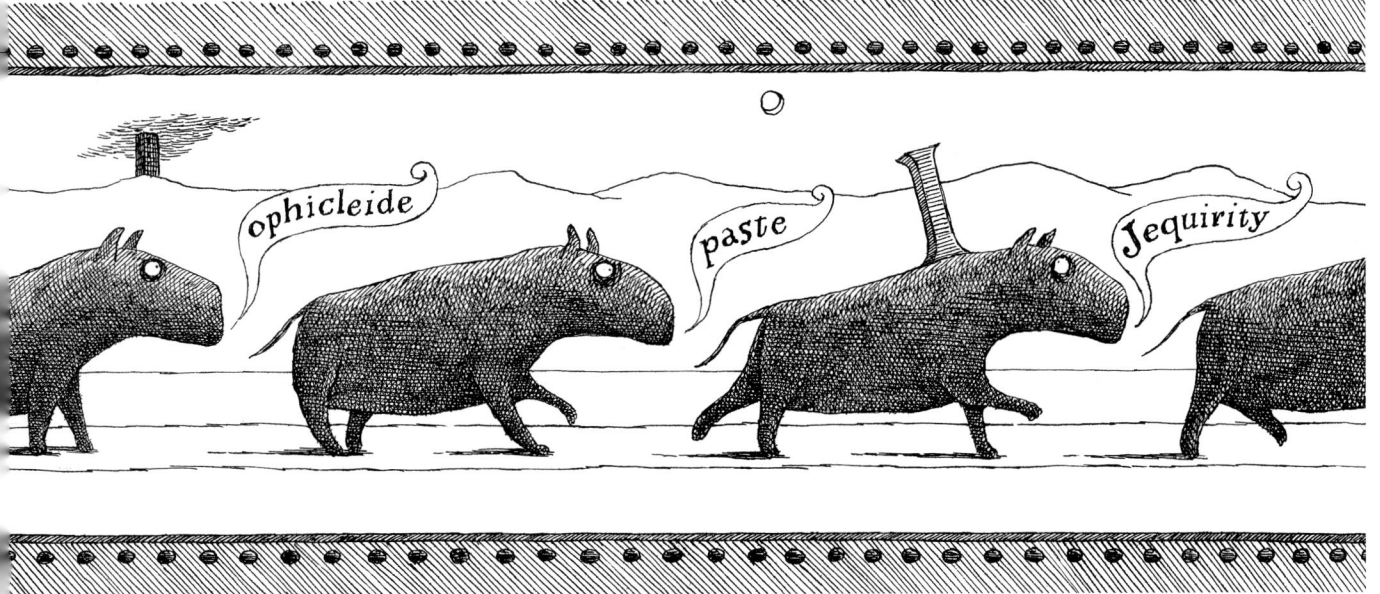

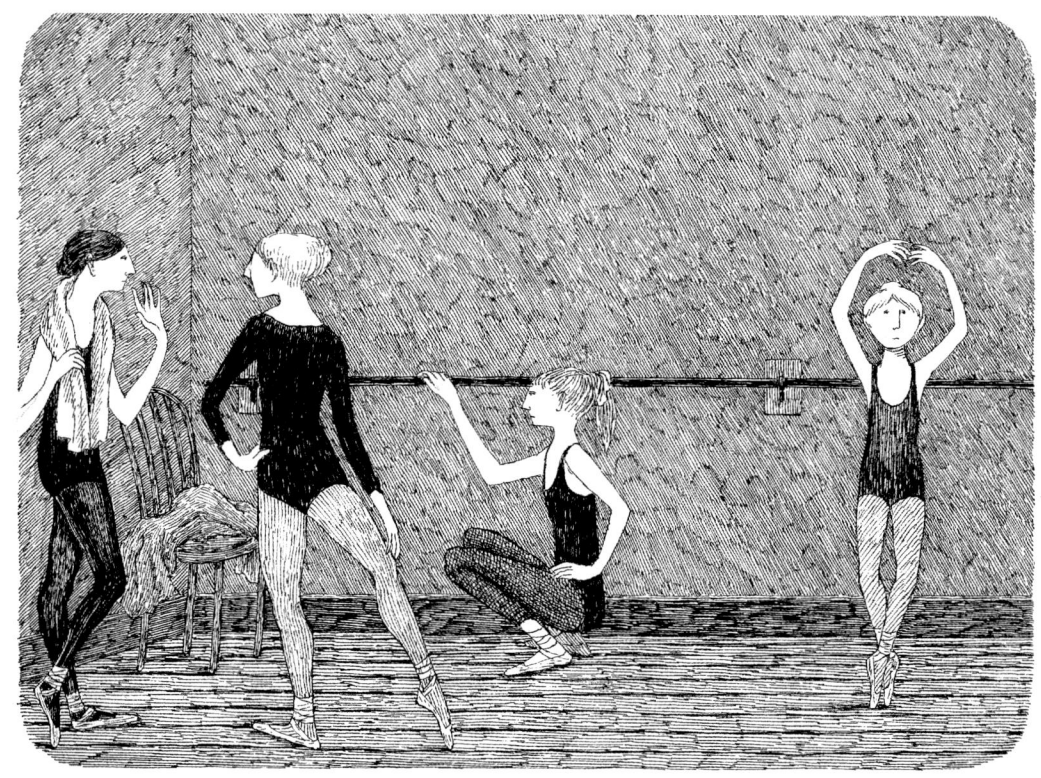

57. *Eventually she was allowed to go up on point.*

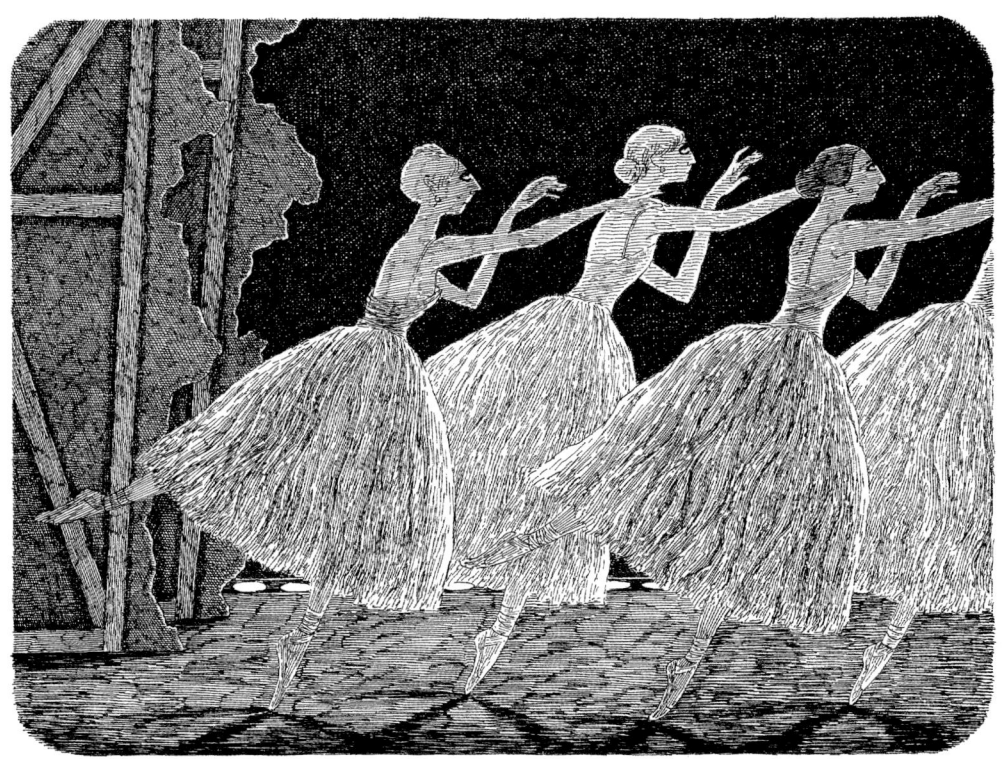

58. *Maud obtained a place in the corps of the Ballet Hochepot.*

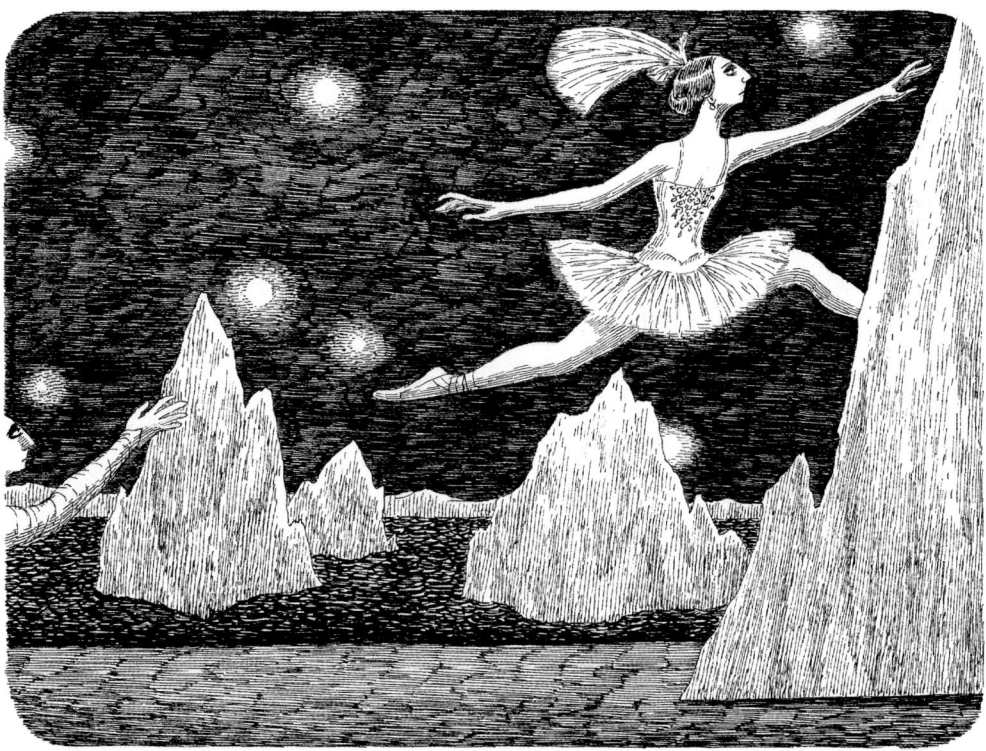

59. *After Federojenska did a grand jeté into the wings one matinee and was never seen again, Maud took over* Oiseau de Glace *to great acclaim.*

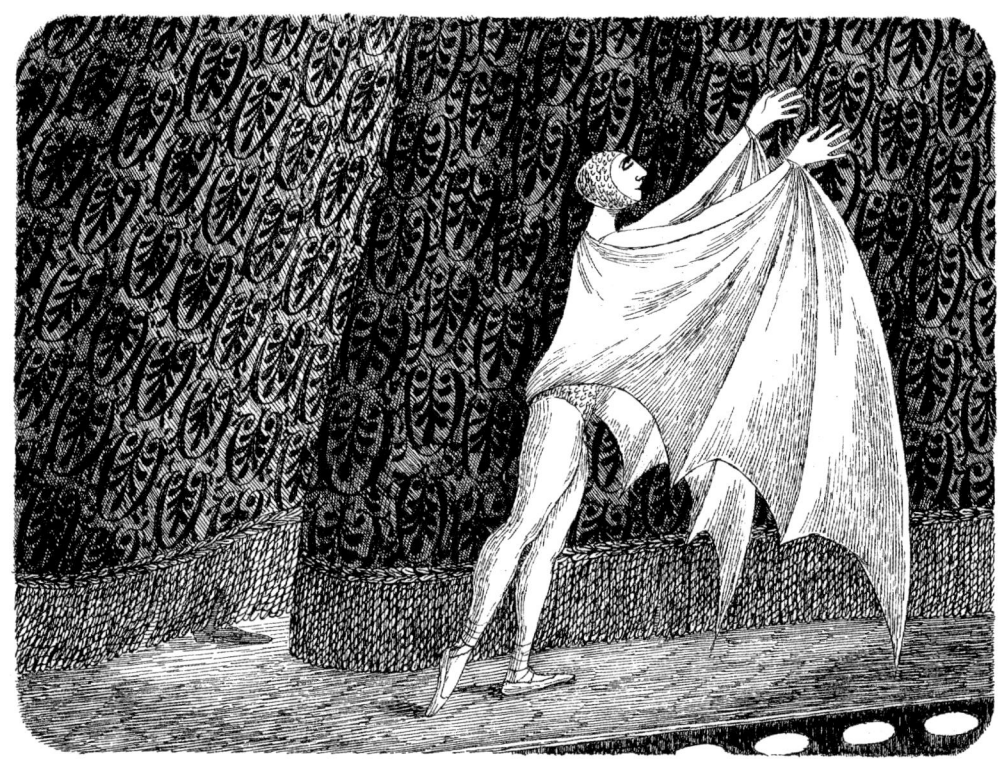

60. *She had become the reigning ballerina of the age, and one of its symbols.*

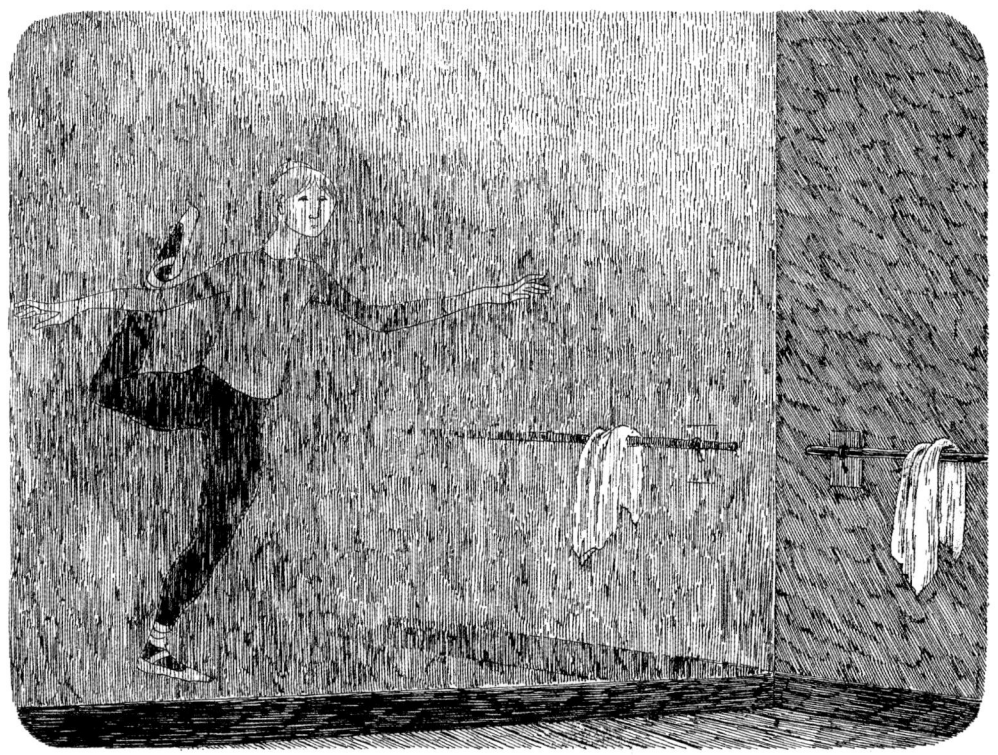

61. *Her life was really no different from what it had ever been.*

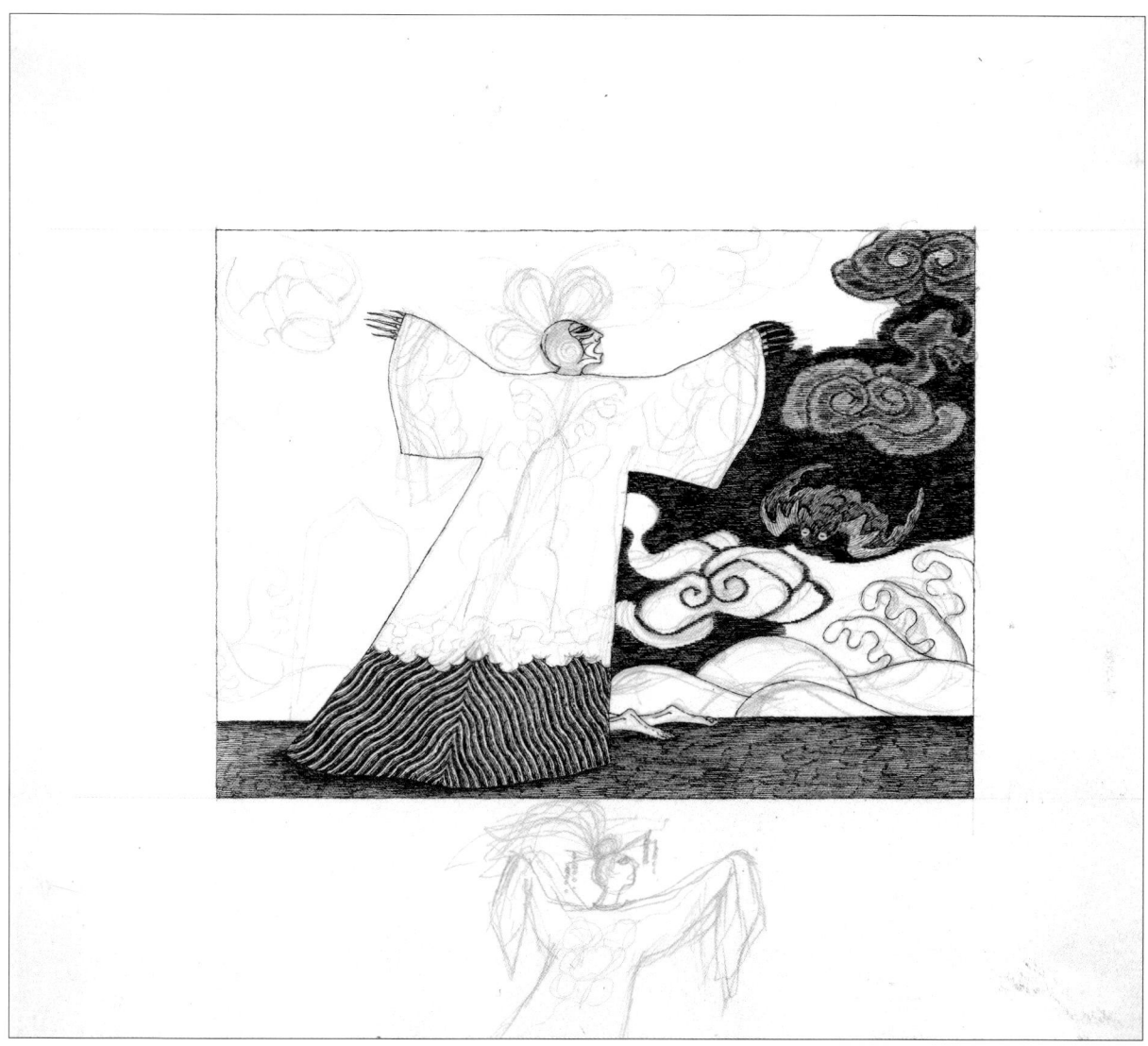

62. *As Tsi-Nan-Fu Caviglia had her greatest triumph to date.* (working draft)

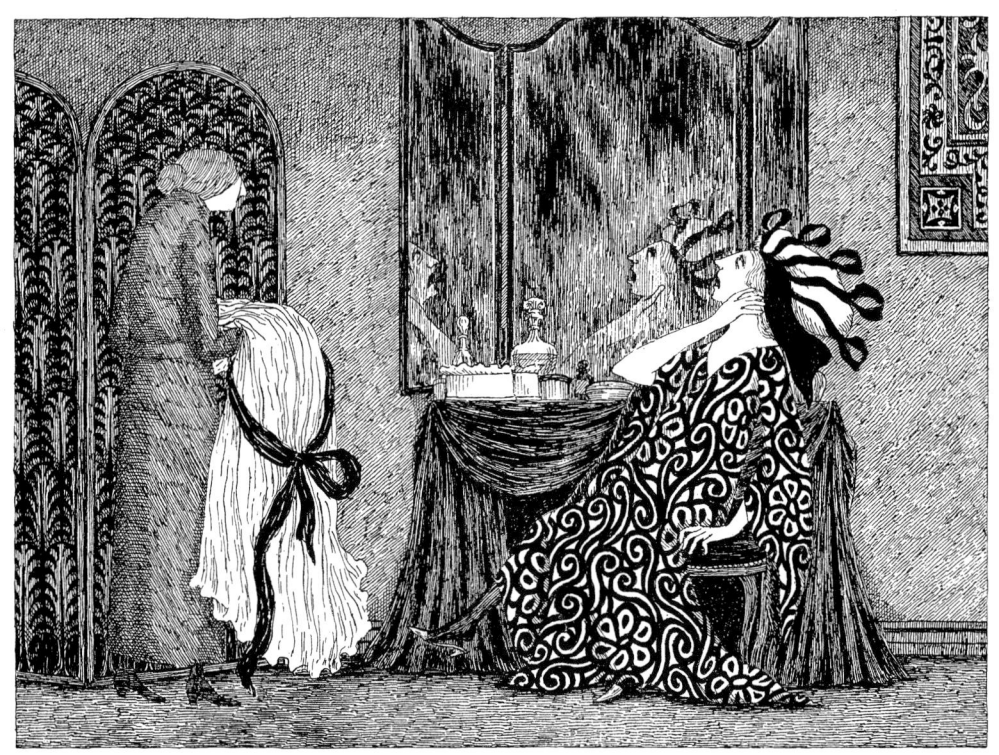

63. *While dressing, Gertrúdis Callosidad dipped into a box of candied violets from an unknown admirer.*

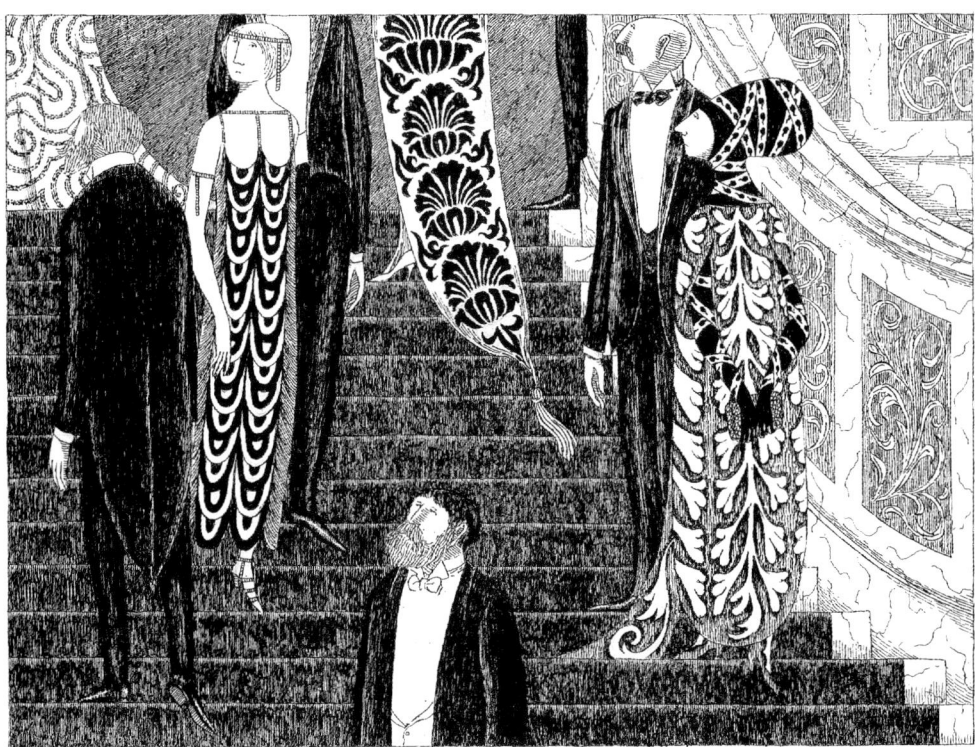

64. *A statue fell on the Duke of Whaup during the second interval of* Amable Tastu.

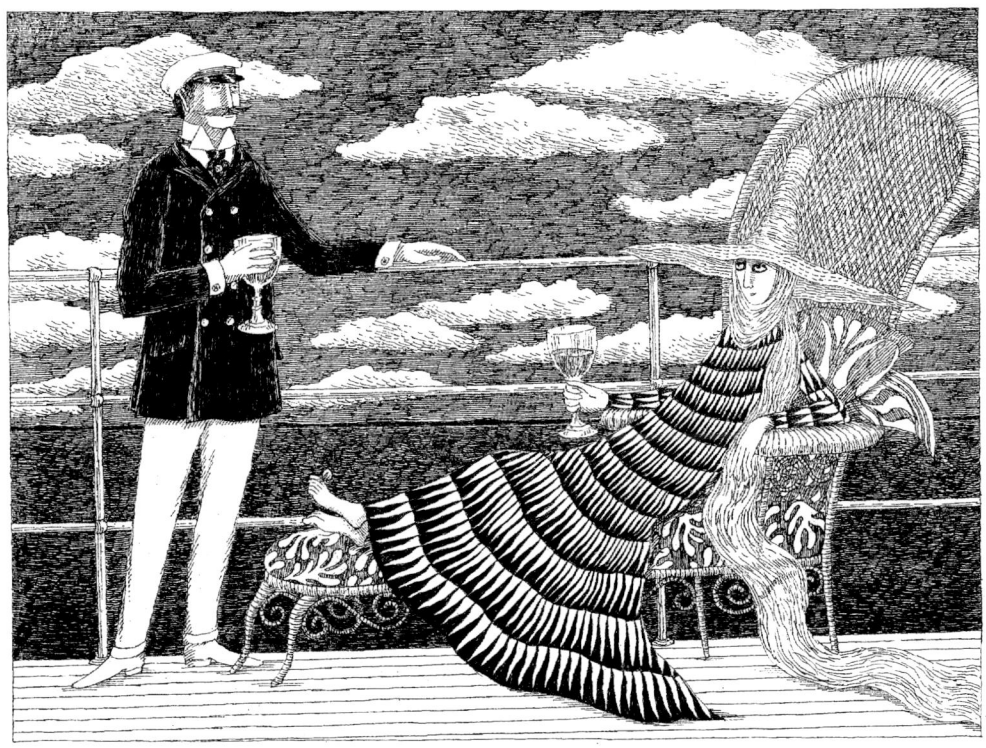

65. *Caviglia cruised the Adriatic with Basil Zaribaydjian, the financier, on his yacht, the* Maud.

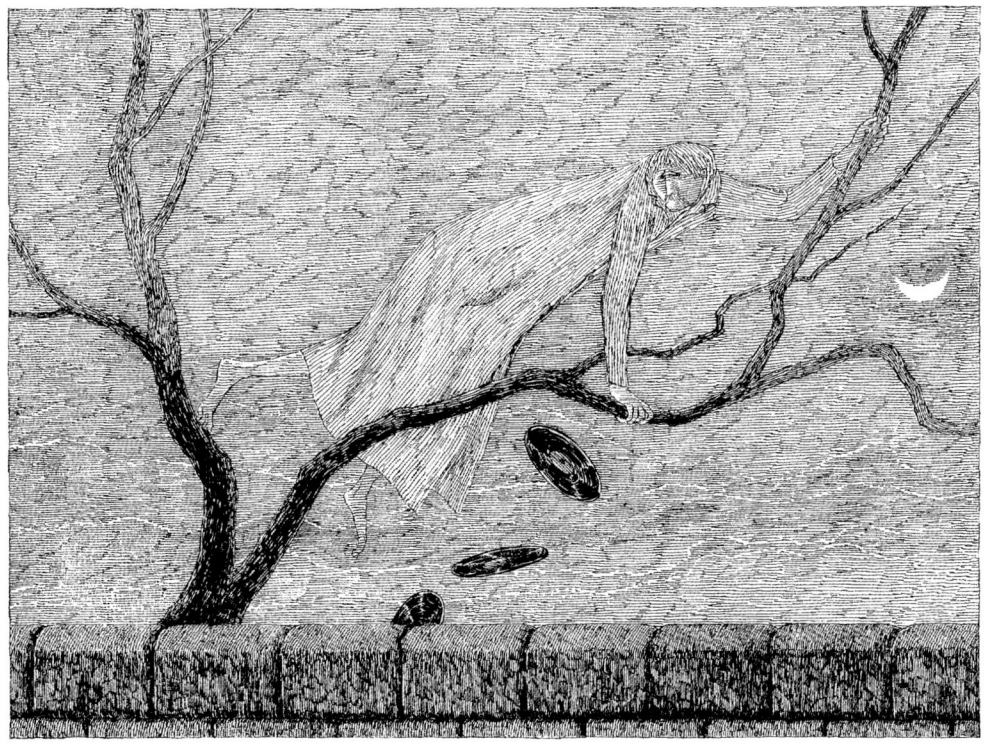

66. *Jasper's records got broken as he was escaping from the asylum.*

THE SECRETS: VOLUME ONE, THE OTHER STATUE, 1968

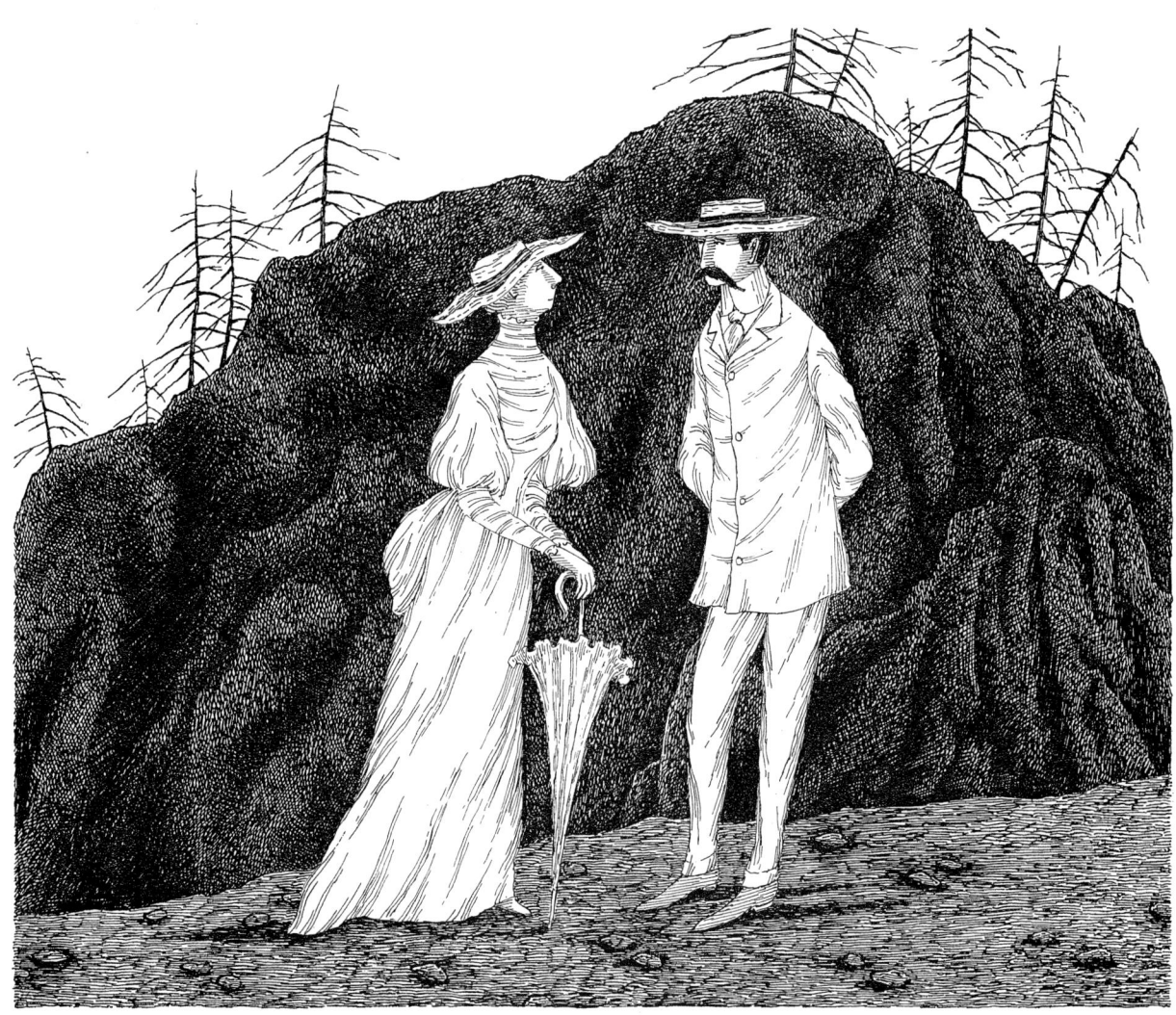

67. *He was recognized at once by Lady Isobel Stringless, Lord Wherewithal's aunt, although they had last met seventeen years before on St Clot in the Maladroit Islands.*

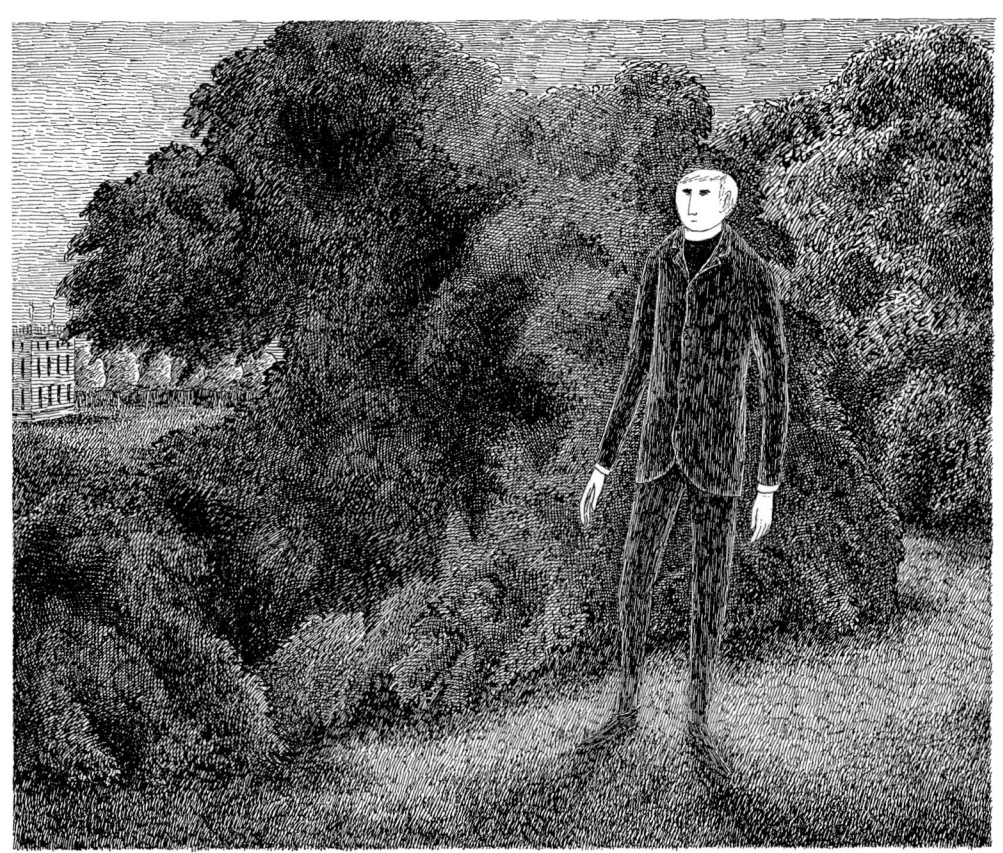

68. *A clergyman staying at the Upturned Pig, the Rev. O. MacAbloo, wandered in a remote corner of the shrubbery.*

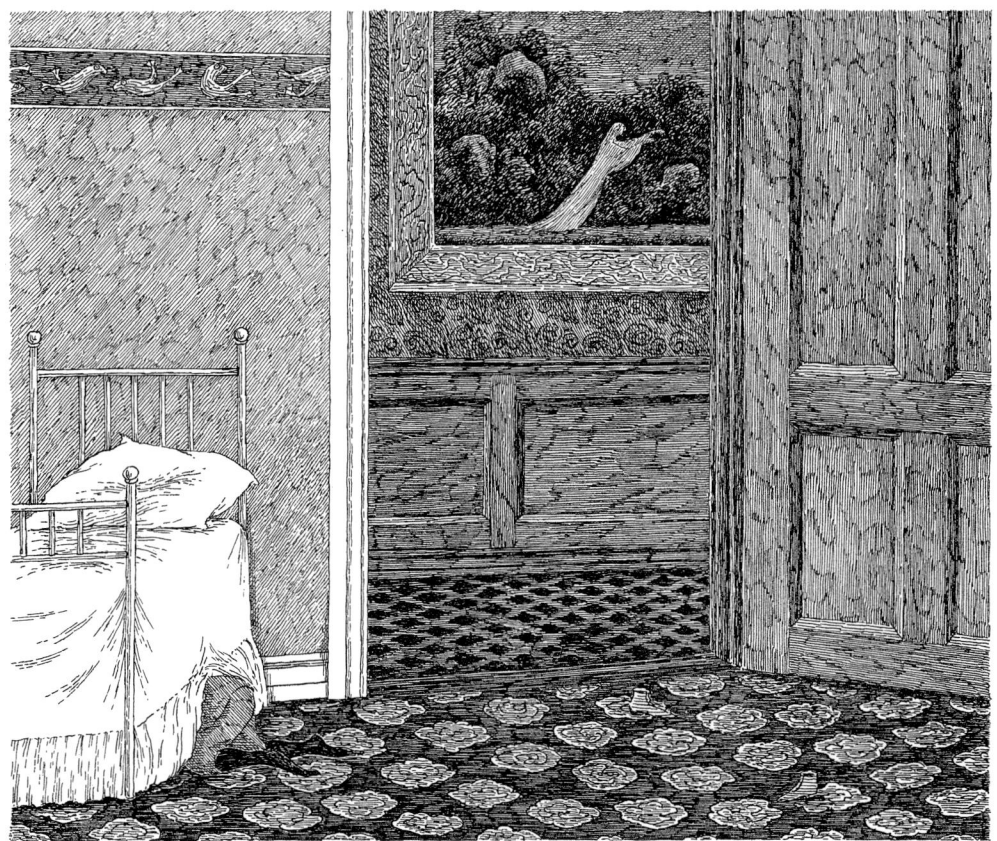

69. *Augustus woke up to find his stuffed twisby was missing.*

69

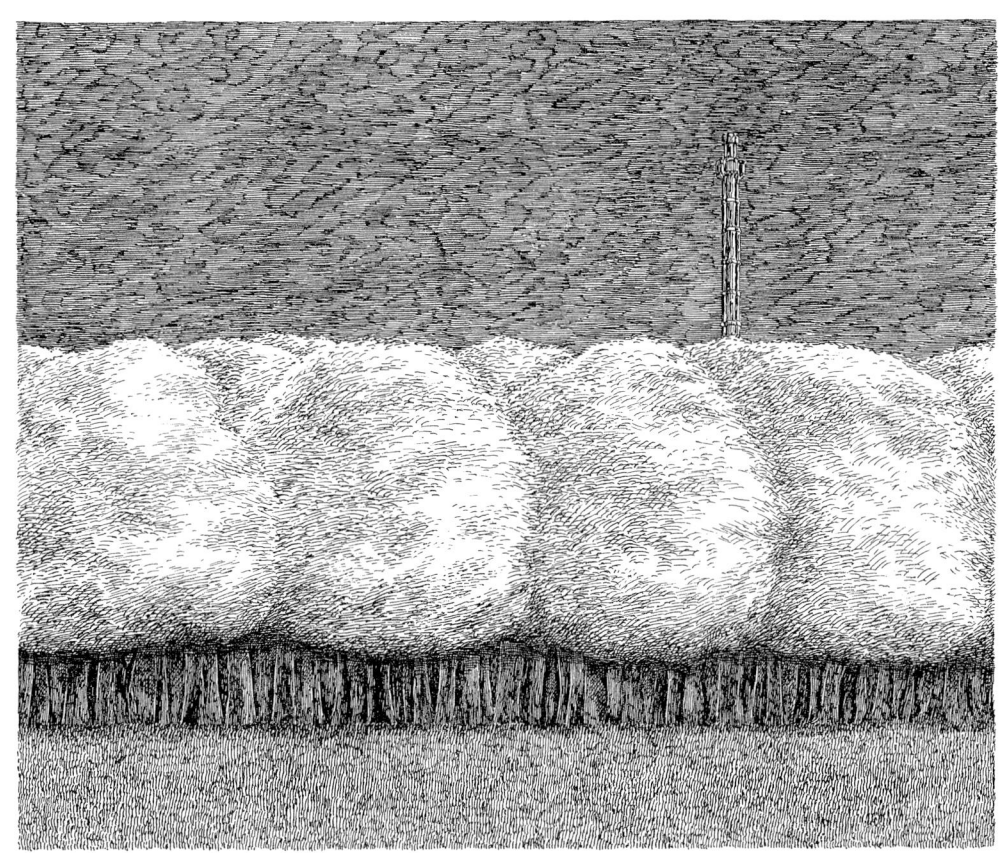

70. *A sudden gust of wind came up from nowhere and rushed through the trees.*

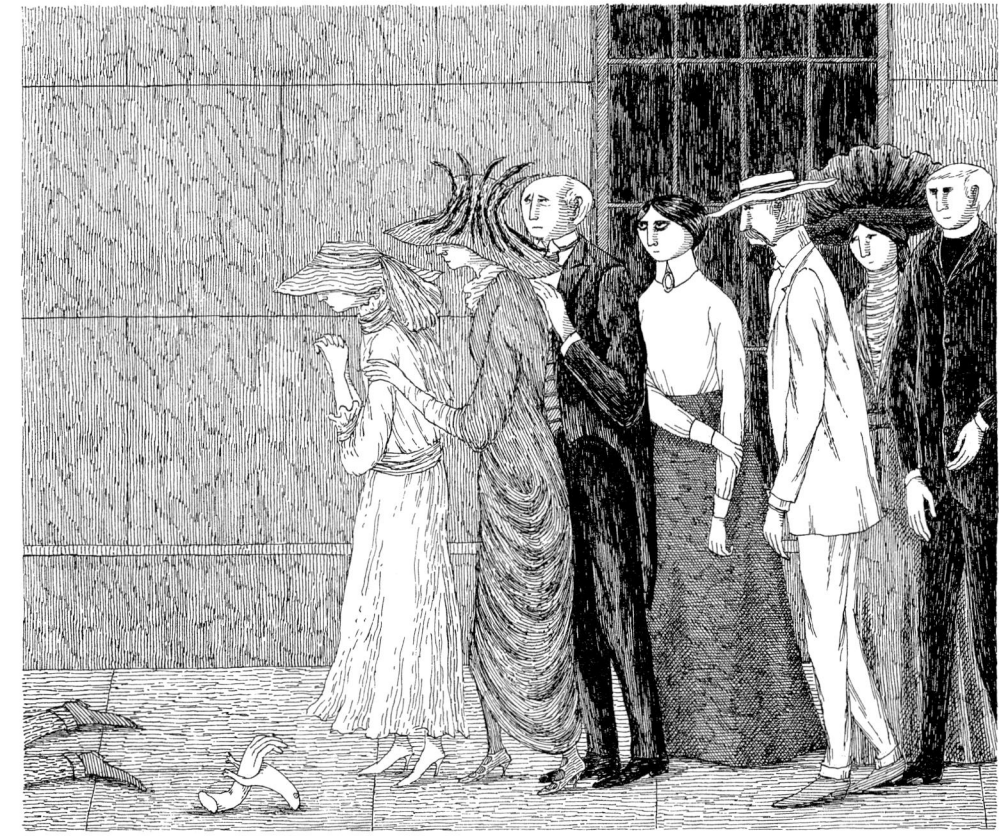

71. *After it had passed, Lord Wherewithal was found crushed beneath a statue blown down from the parapet.*

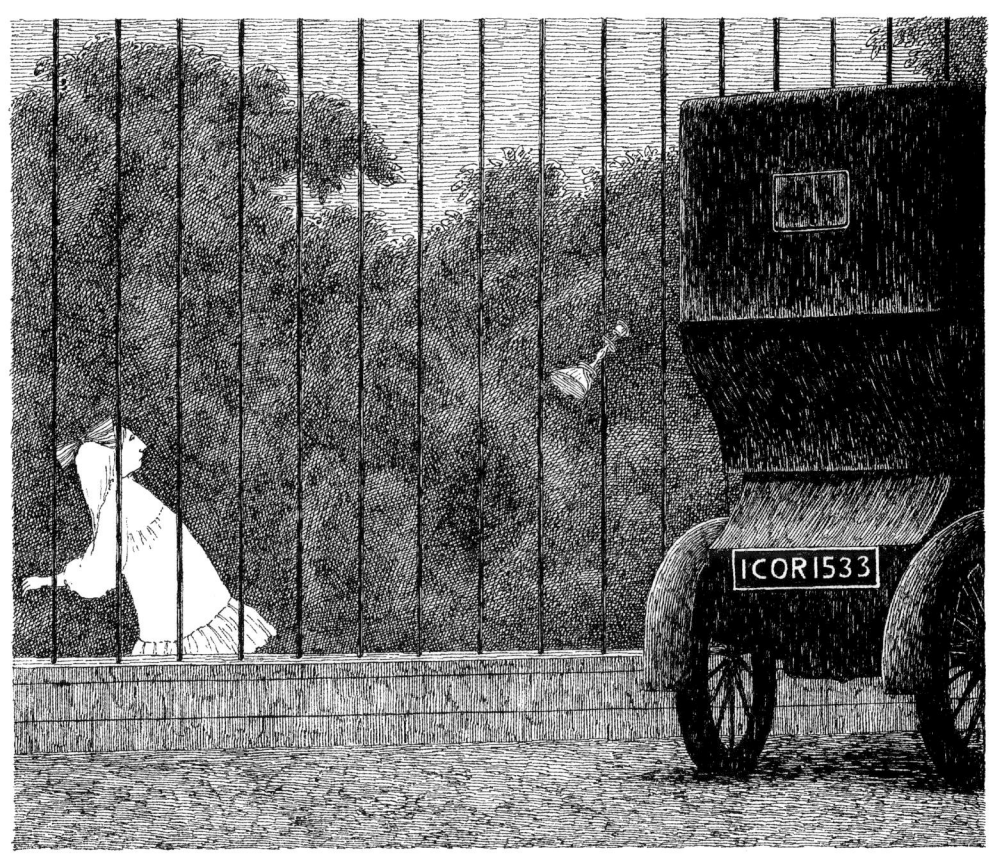

72. *Emily, helping her brother look for his twisby, saw a candlestick mounted on a horse's hoof thrown from a limousine as it drove away.*

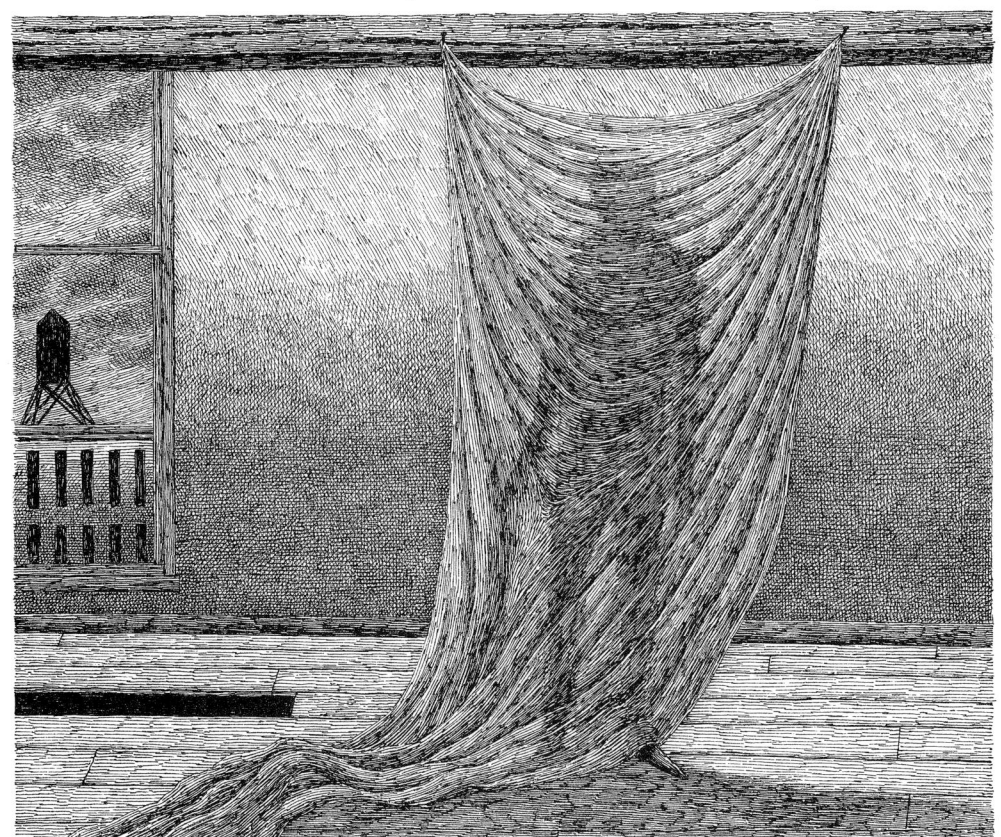

73. *Lord Wherewithal had been murdered, said Dr Belgravius, to gain possession of it.*

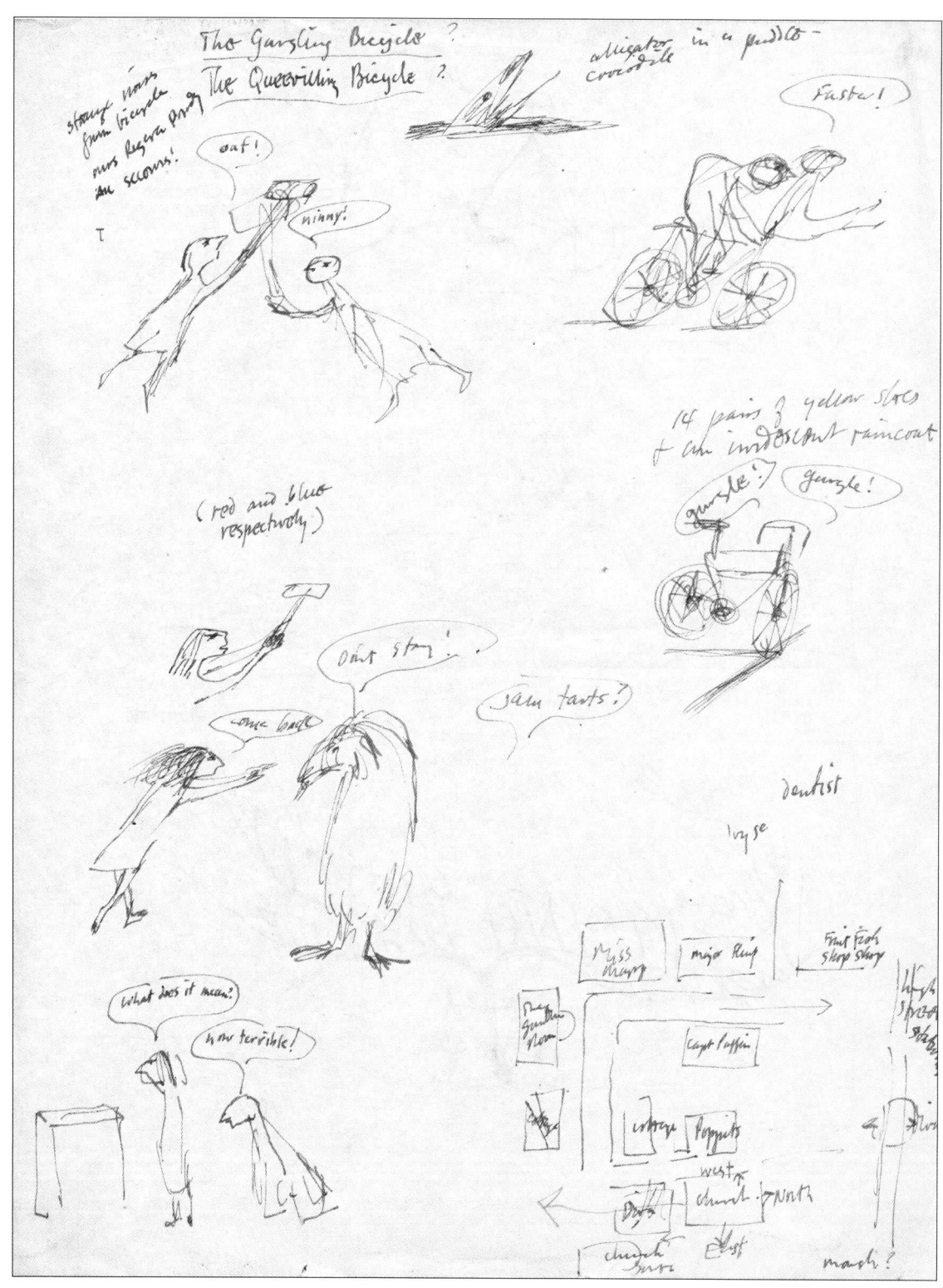

74. Page of studies

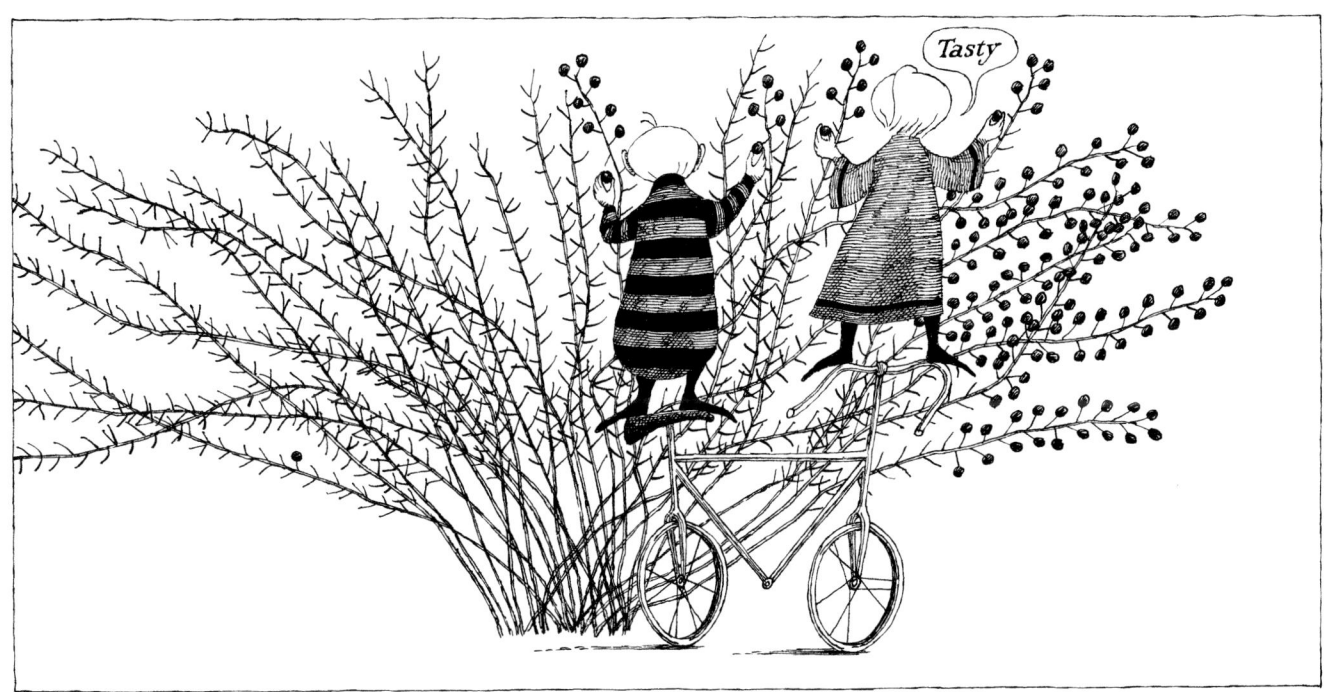

75. *off which they rapidly ate a quantity of berries.*

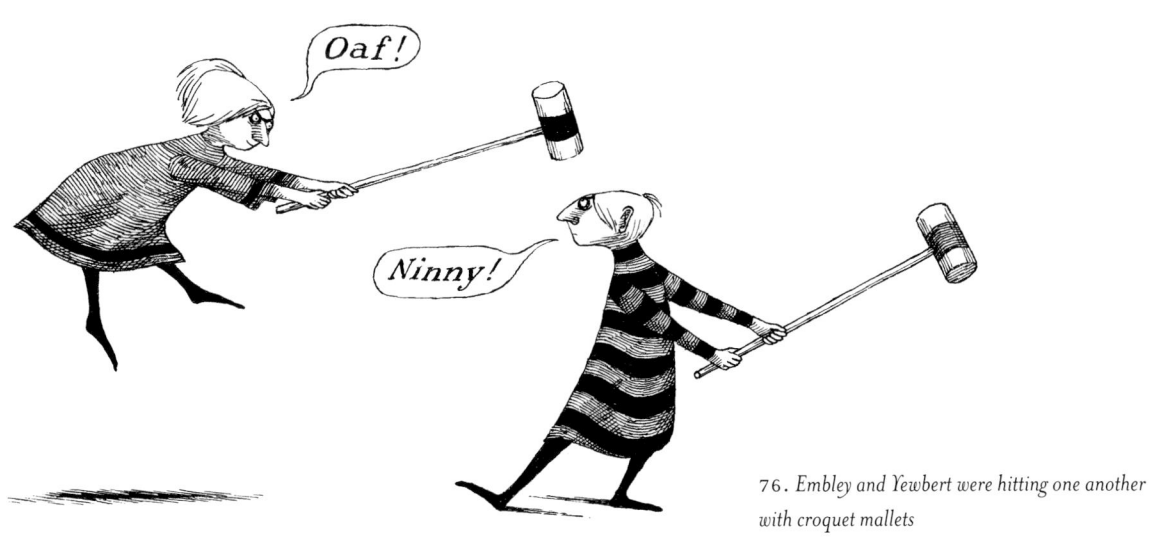

76. *Embley and Yewbert were hitting one another with croquet mallets*

THE IRON TONIC:
OR, A WINTER AFTERNOON IN LONELY VALLEY, 1969

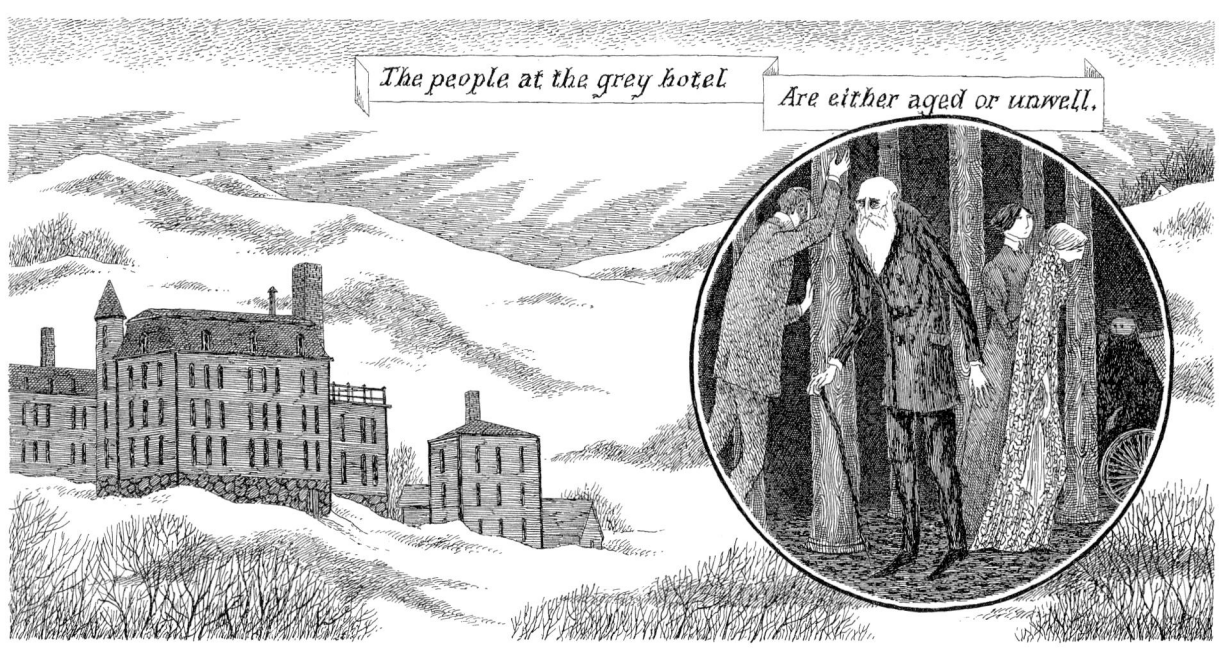

The people at the grey hotel *Are either aged or unwell.*

77.

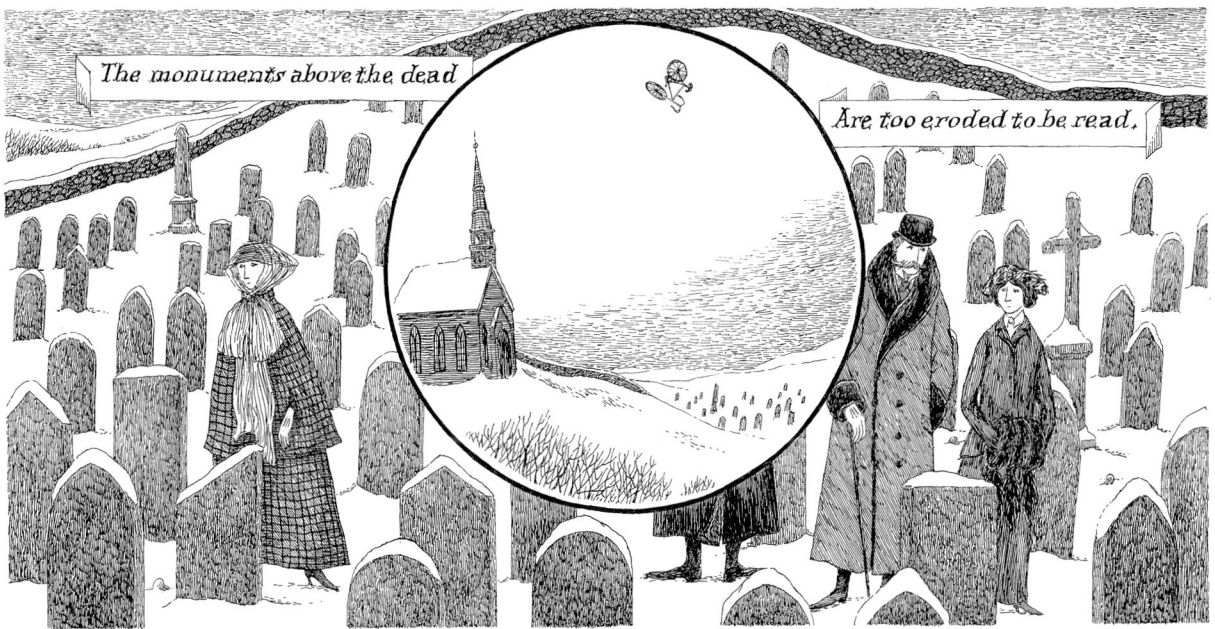

78.

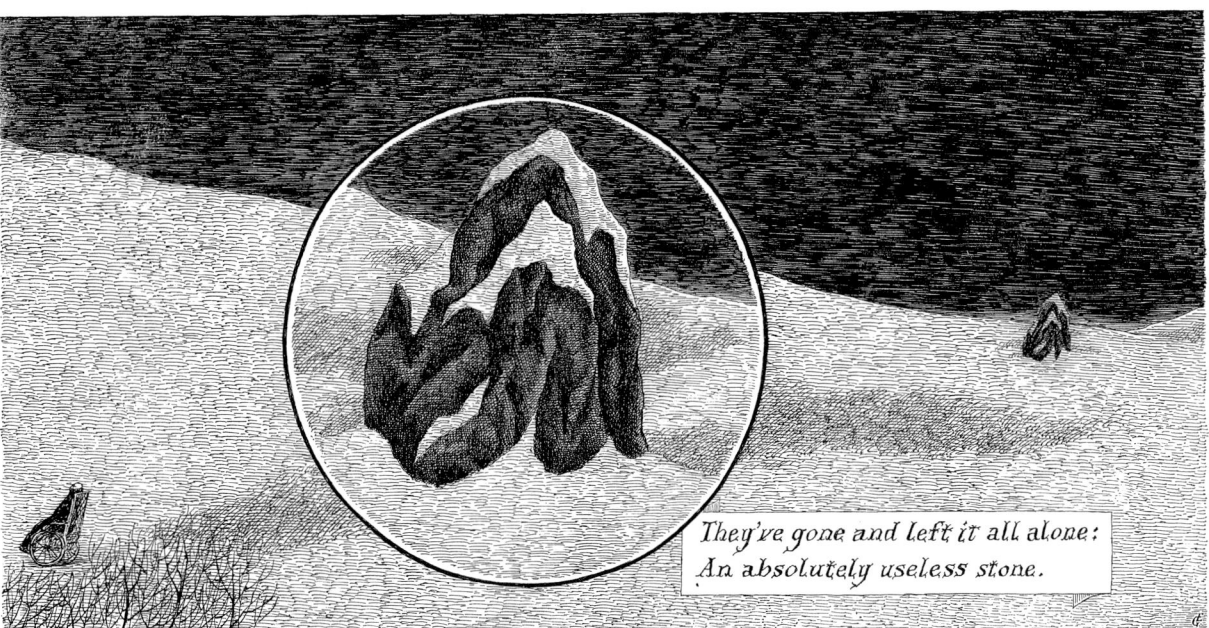

79.

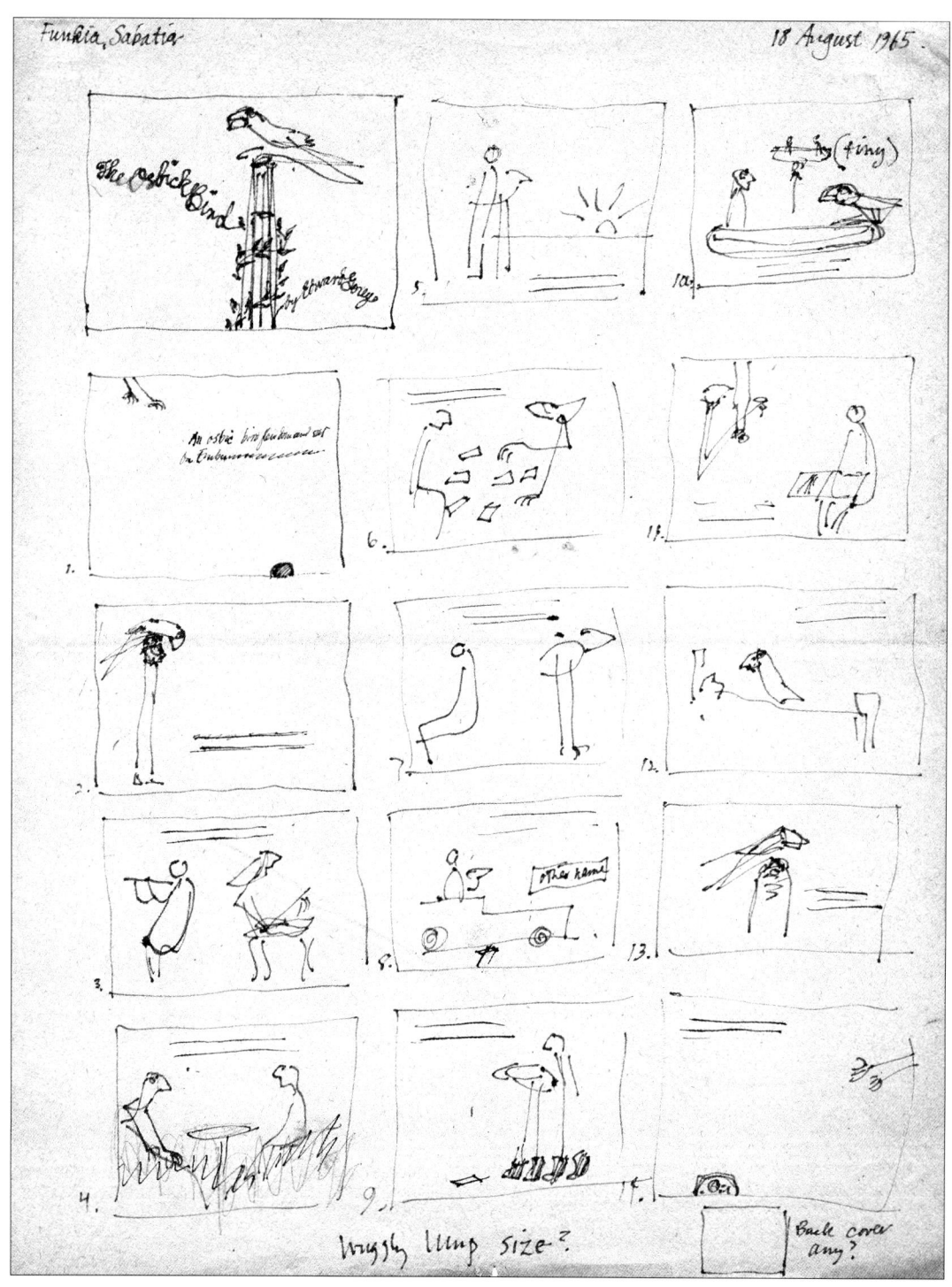

82. Page of studies

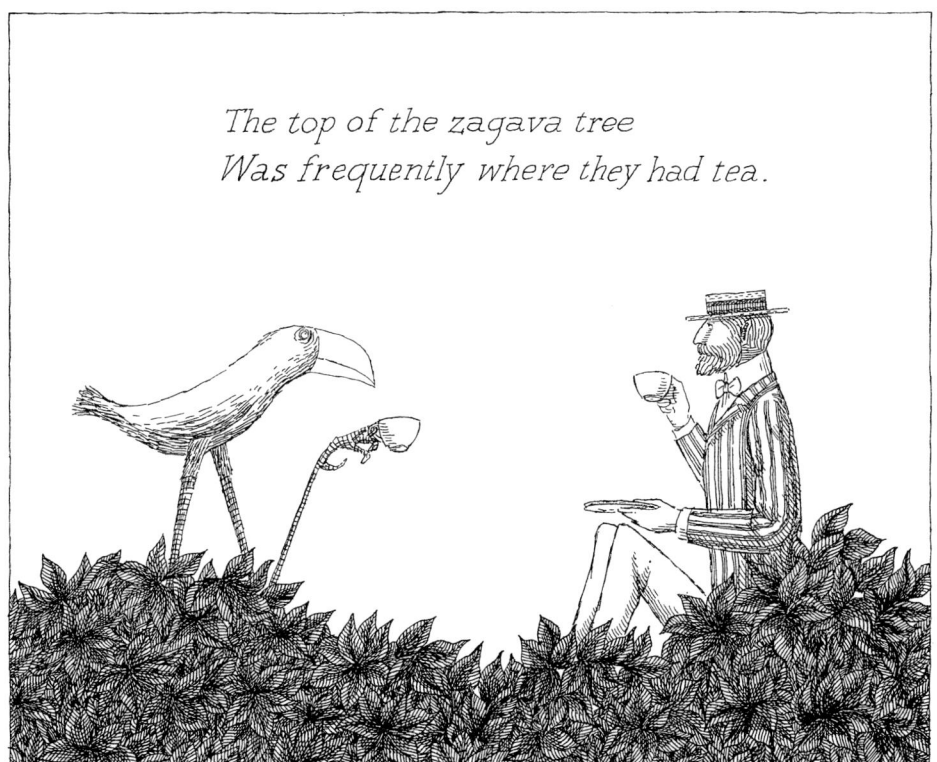

The top of the zagava tree
Was frequently where they had tea.

84.

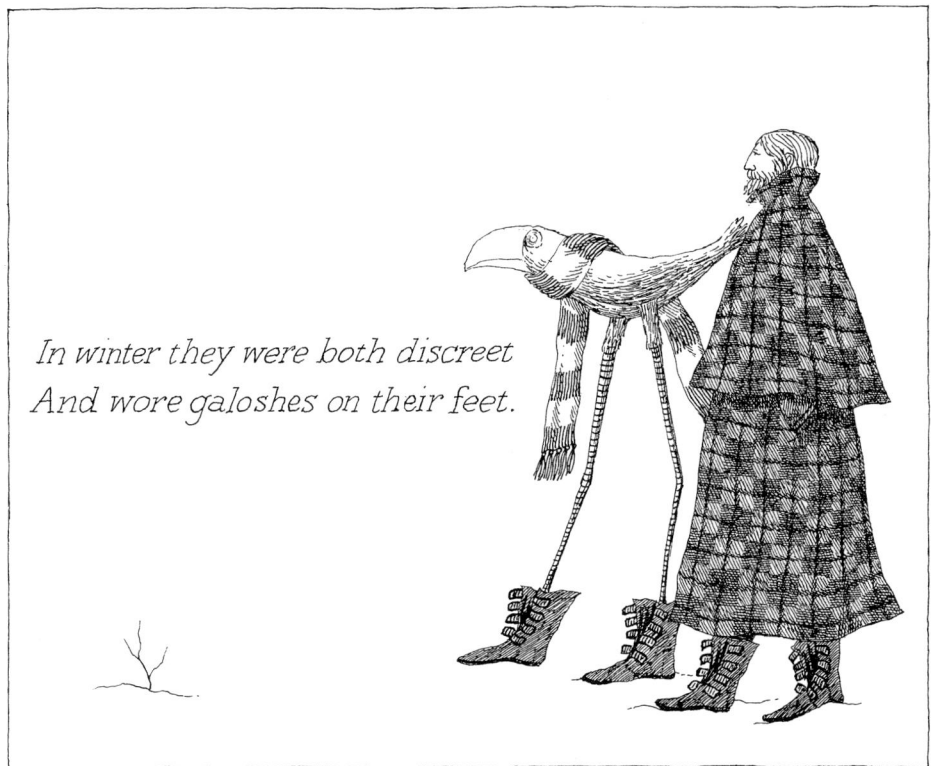

In winter they were both discreet
And wore galoshes on their feet.

85.

And when at last poor Emblus died
The osbick bird was by his side.

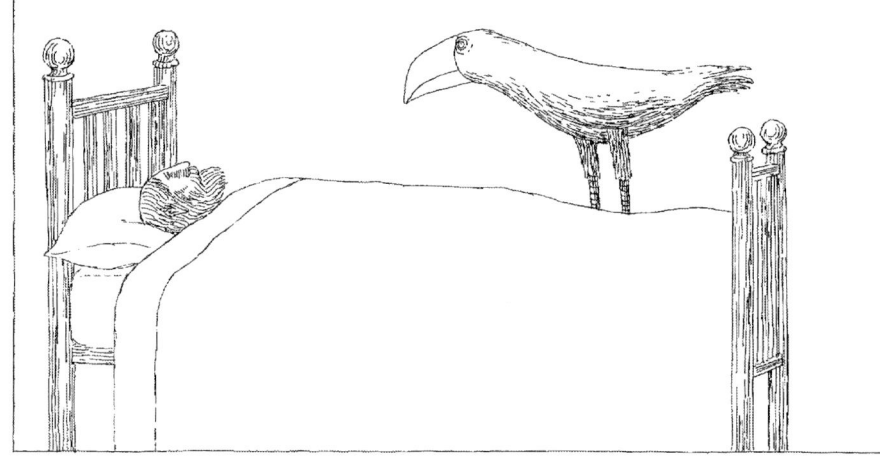

86.

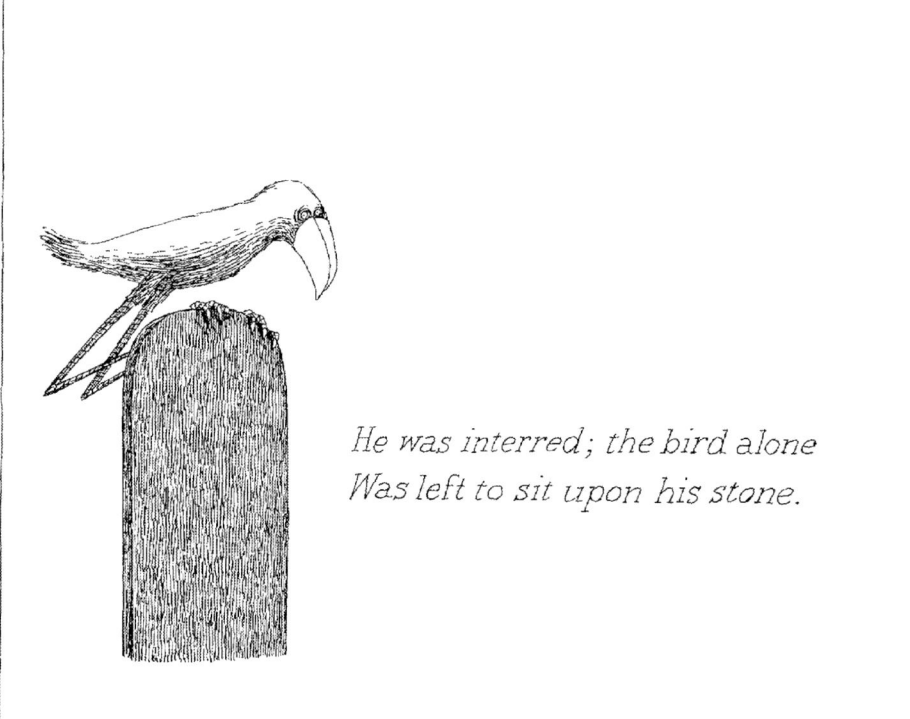

He was interred; the bird alone
Was left to sit upon his stone.

87.

THE DERANGED COUSINS; OR, WHATEVER, 1971

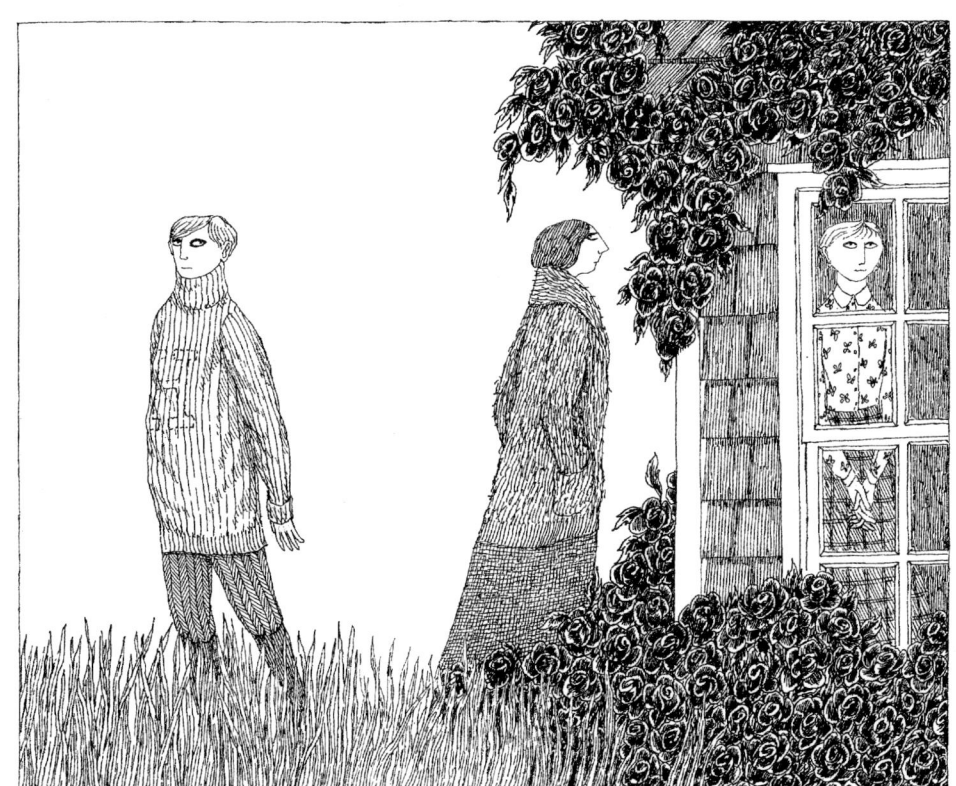

89. *They lived in a house covered with roses on the edge of a marsh.*

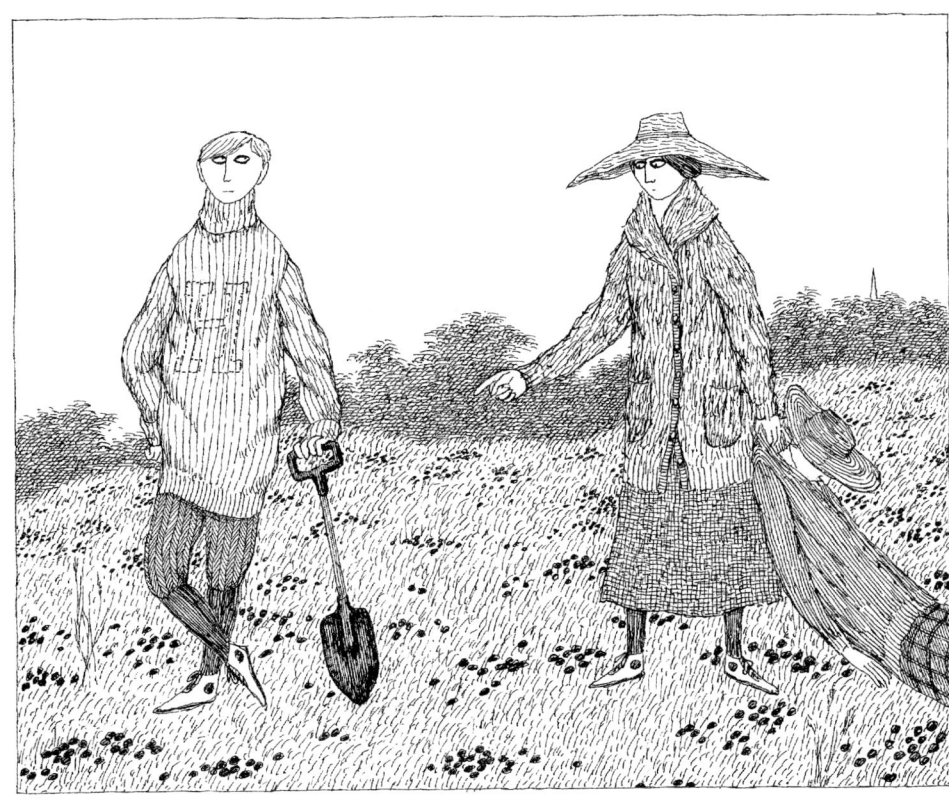

91. *She had Marsh bury her in a field known as the Rabbits' Restroom.*

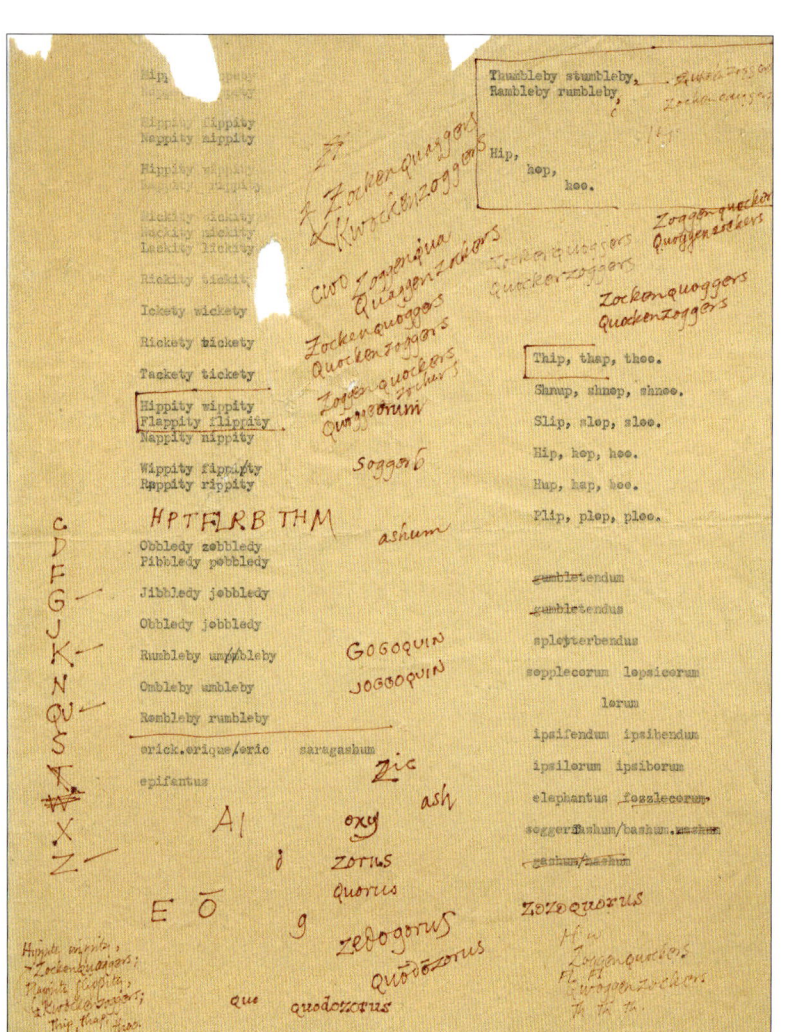

[THE UNTITLED BOOK]

1971

93. Working draft of text with annotations

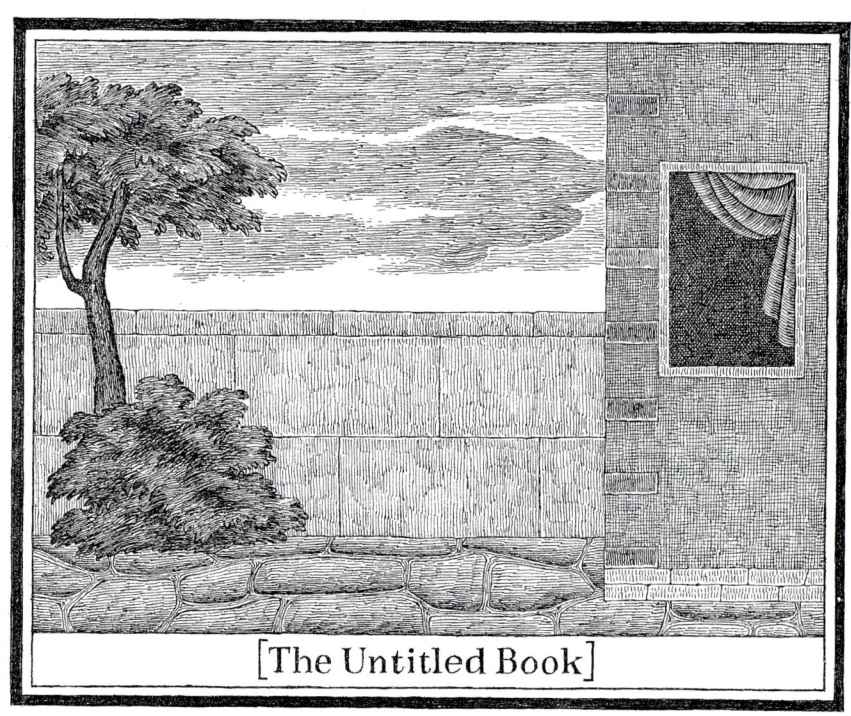

[The Untitled Book]

94. Cover

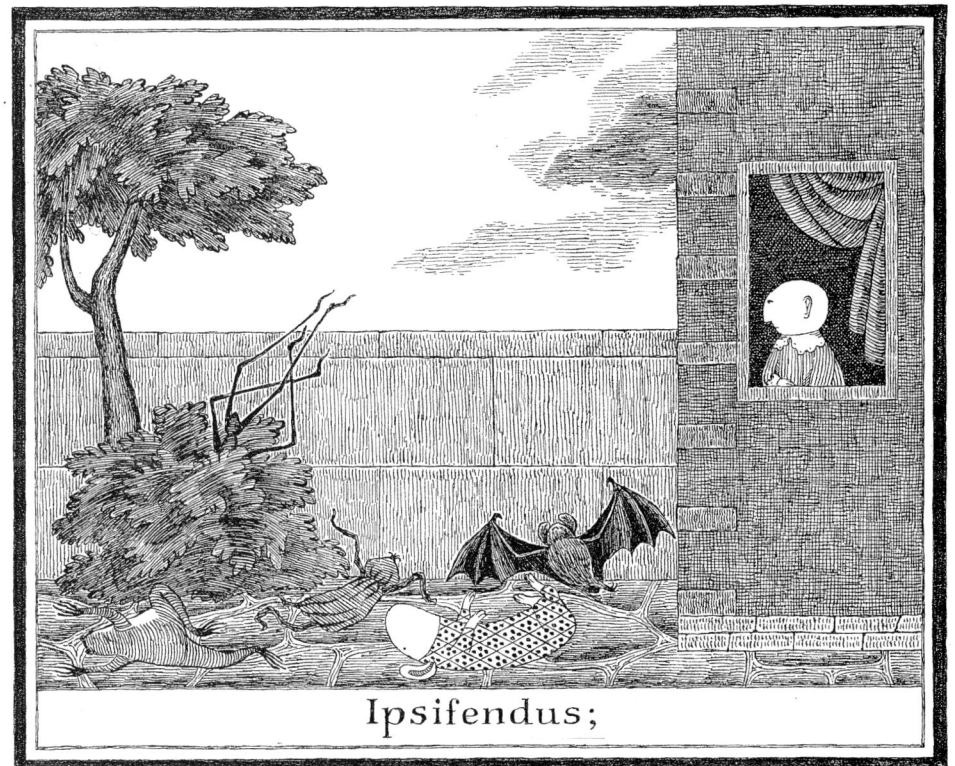

Ipsifendus;

95.

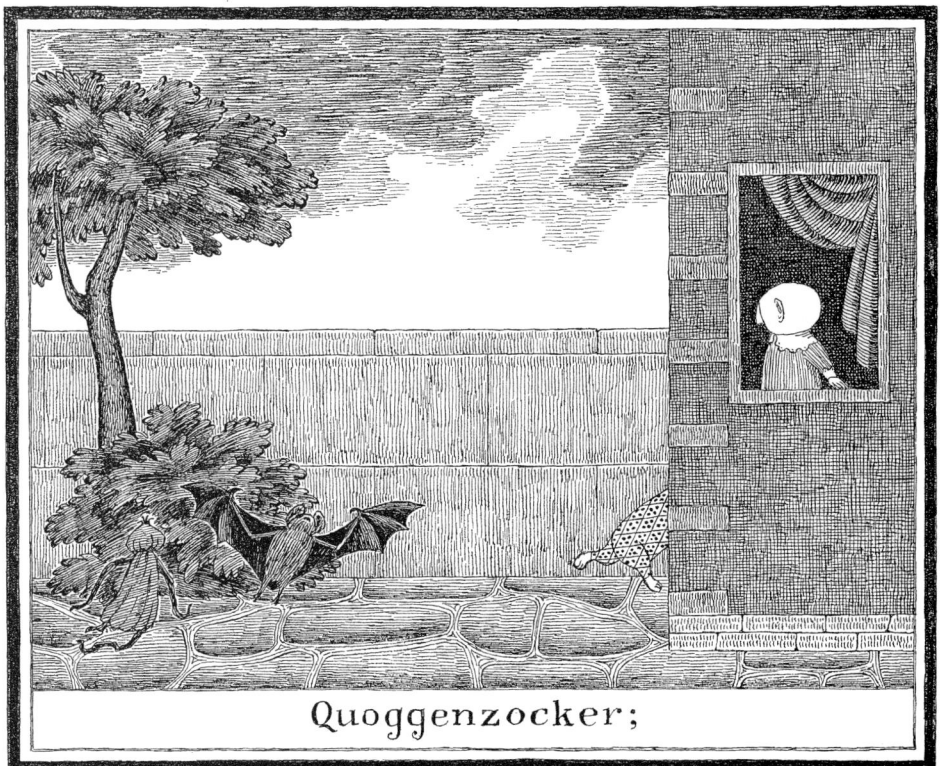

Quoggenzocker;

96.

A Limerick, 1973

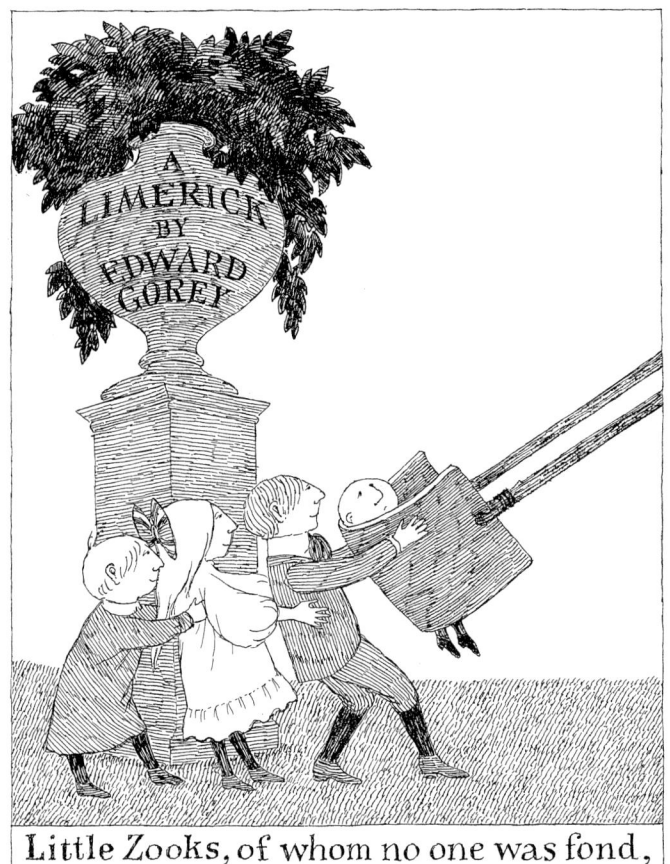

Little Zooks, of whom no one was fond,

99.

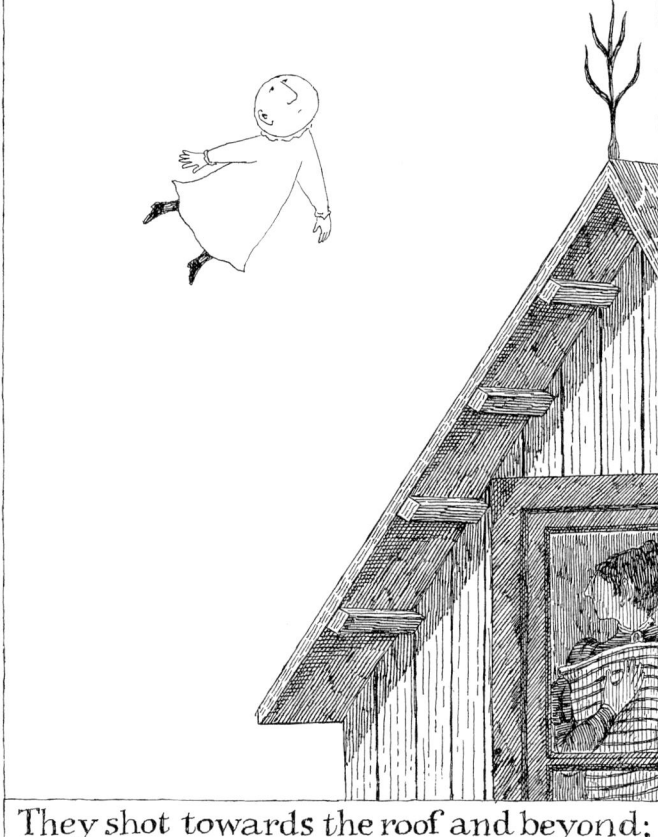

They shot towards the roof and beyond;

100.

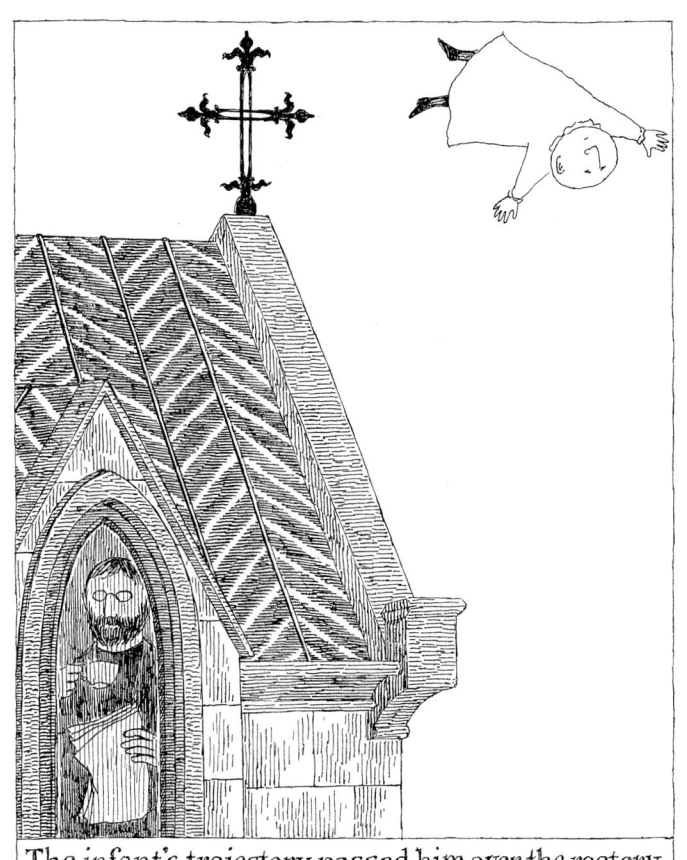

The infant's trajectory passed him over the rectory,

101.

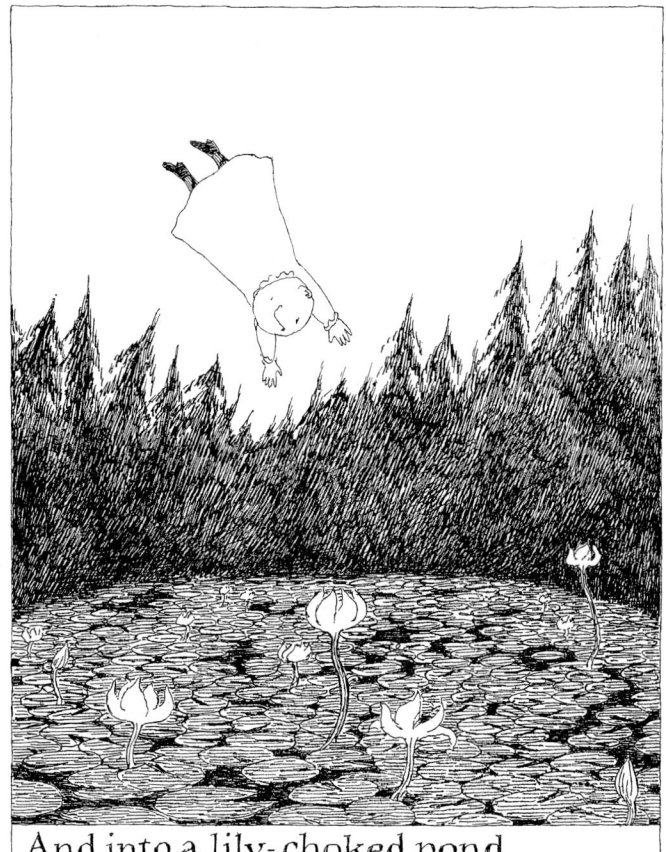

And into a lily-choked pond.

102.

The Lost Lions; or, Having Opened the Wrong Envelope, 1973

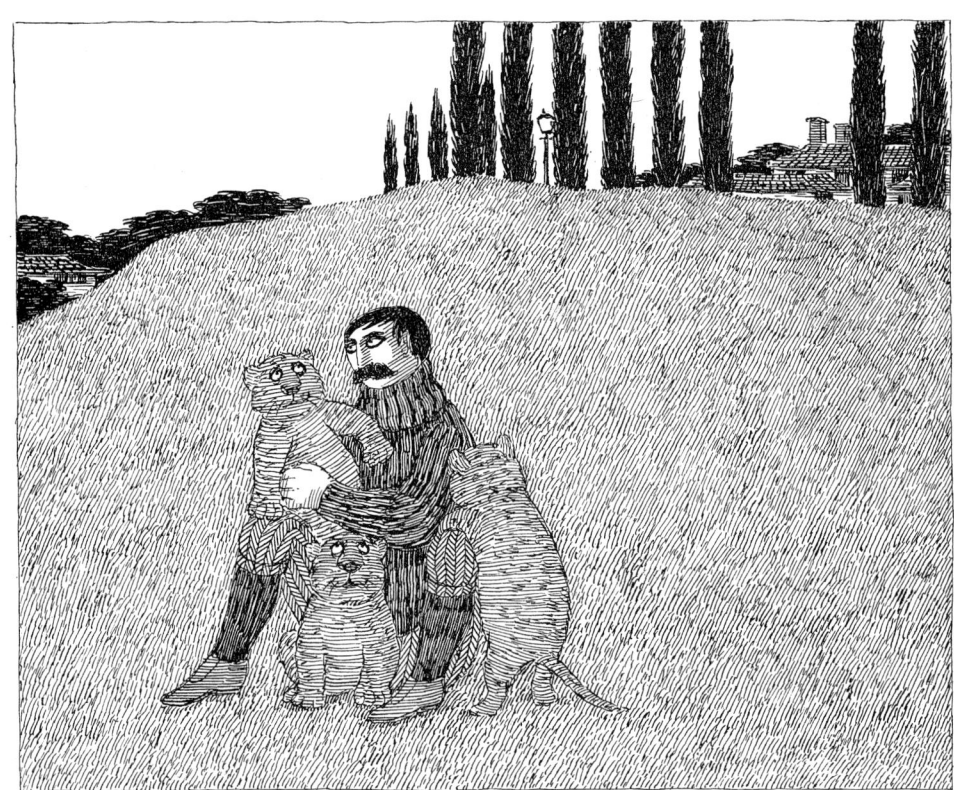

103. With his sudden wealth he bought a stylish house in extensive grounds, and began to raise lions.

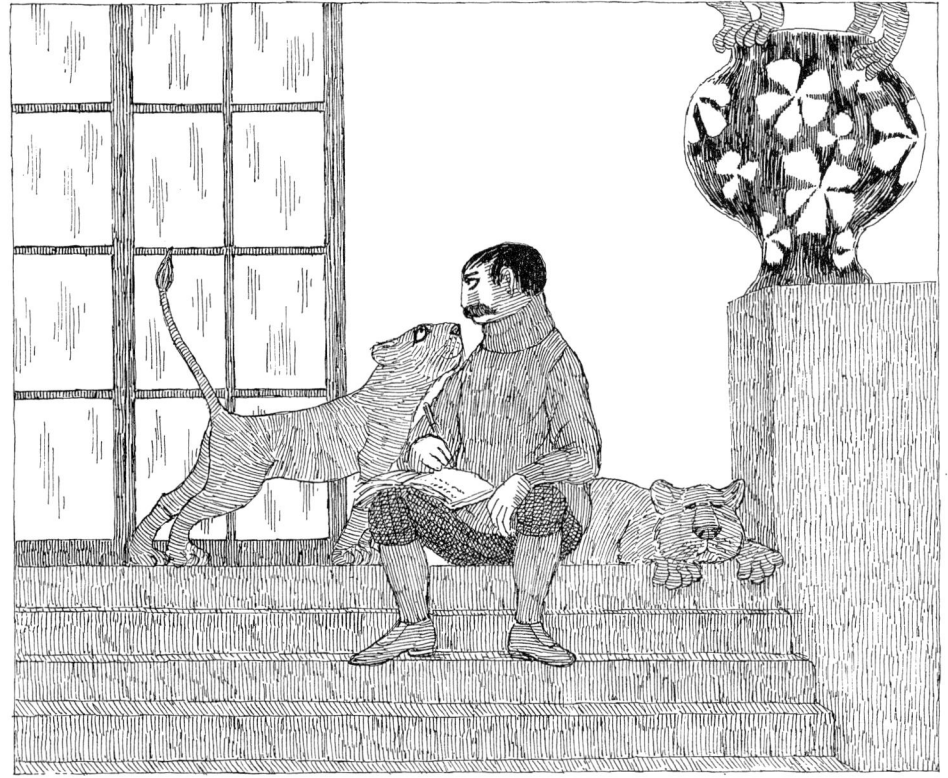

104. He devoted himself to raising more lions and working at his diaries.

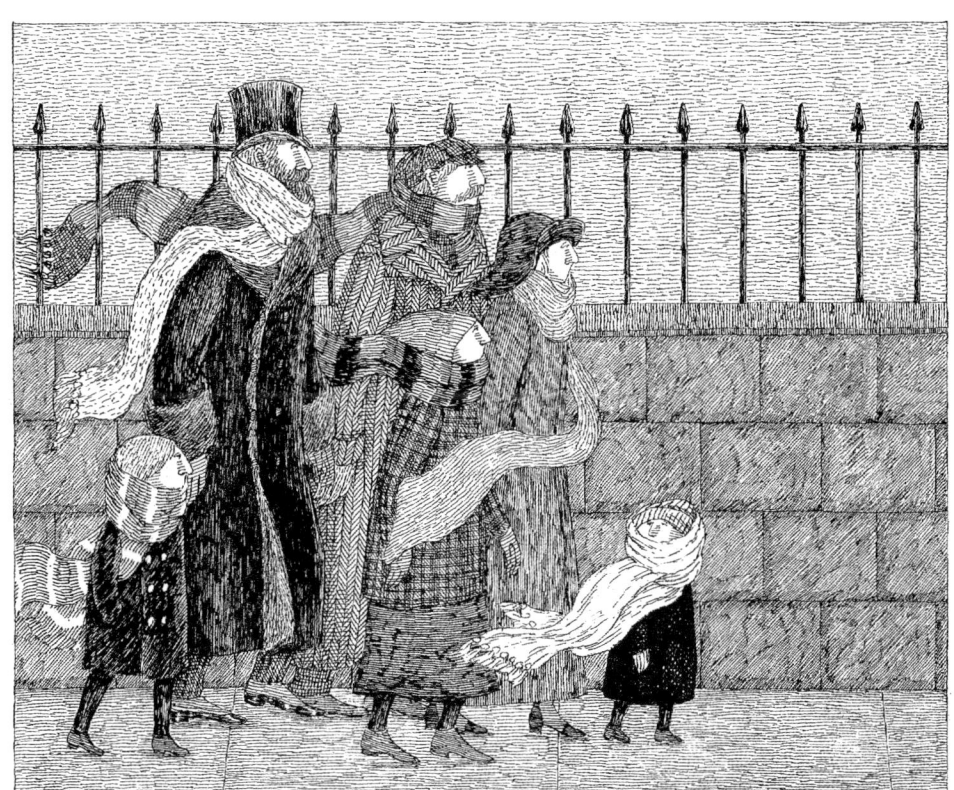

105. *She knitted mufflers Endlessly.*

106. *They searched the cellars Fruitlessly.*

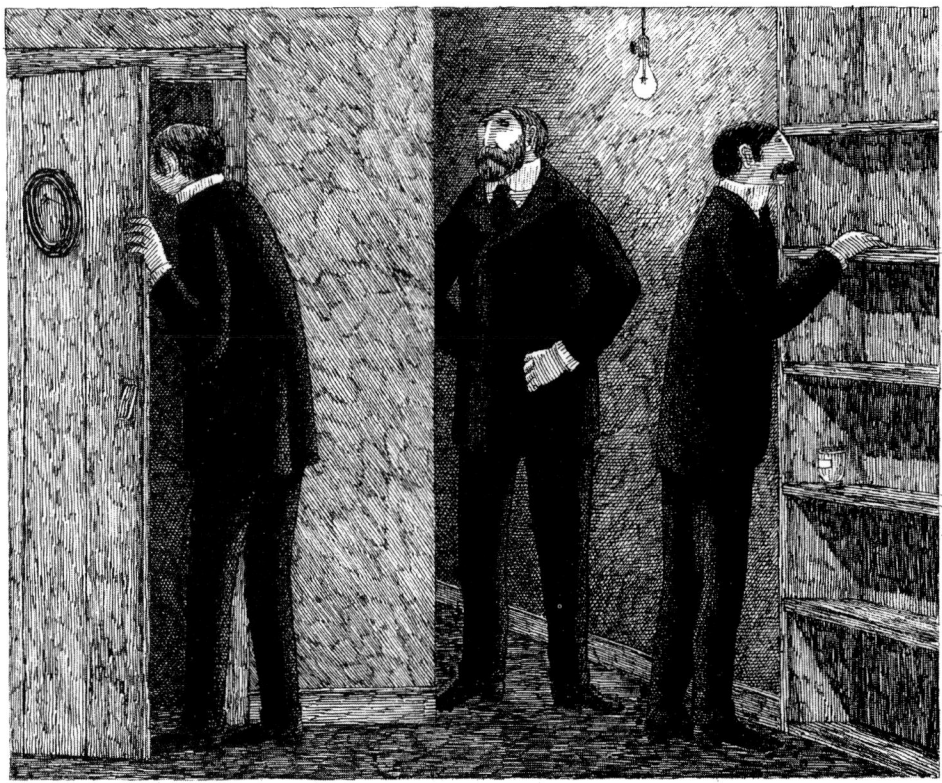

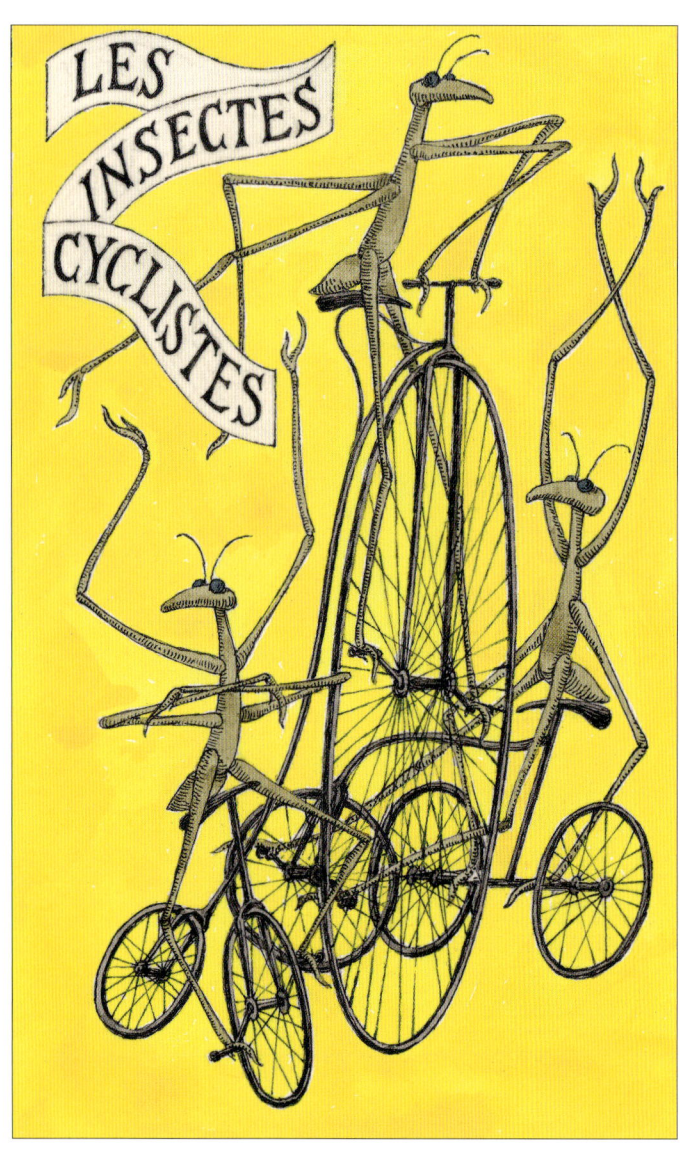

111. *Les Insectes Cyclistes*

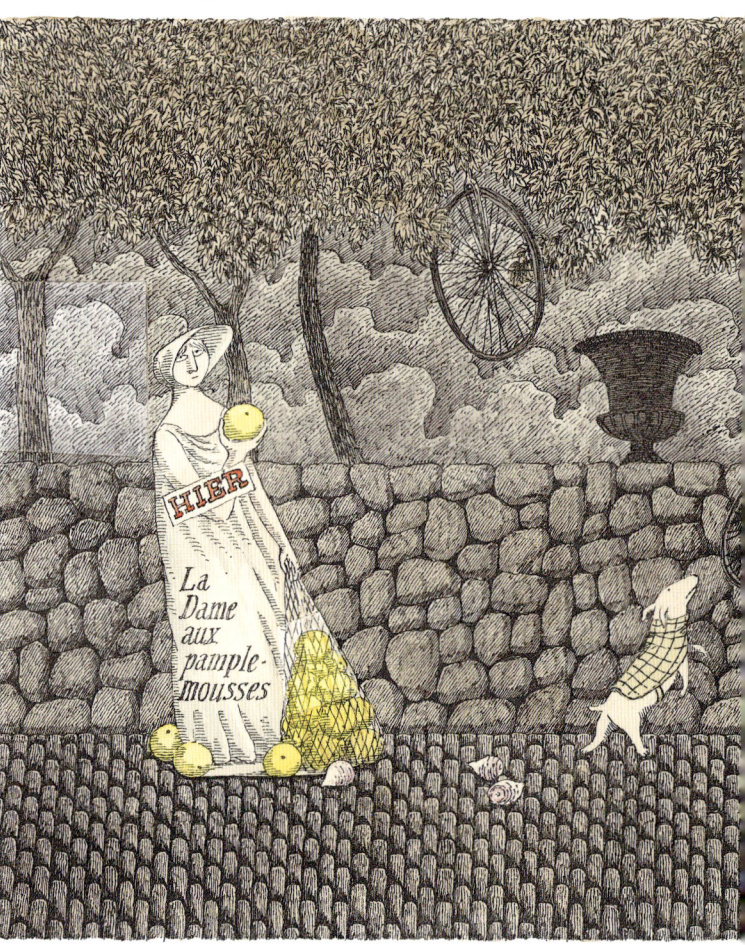

110. Wrap-around cover for *The Broken Spoke*

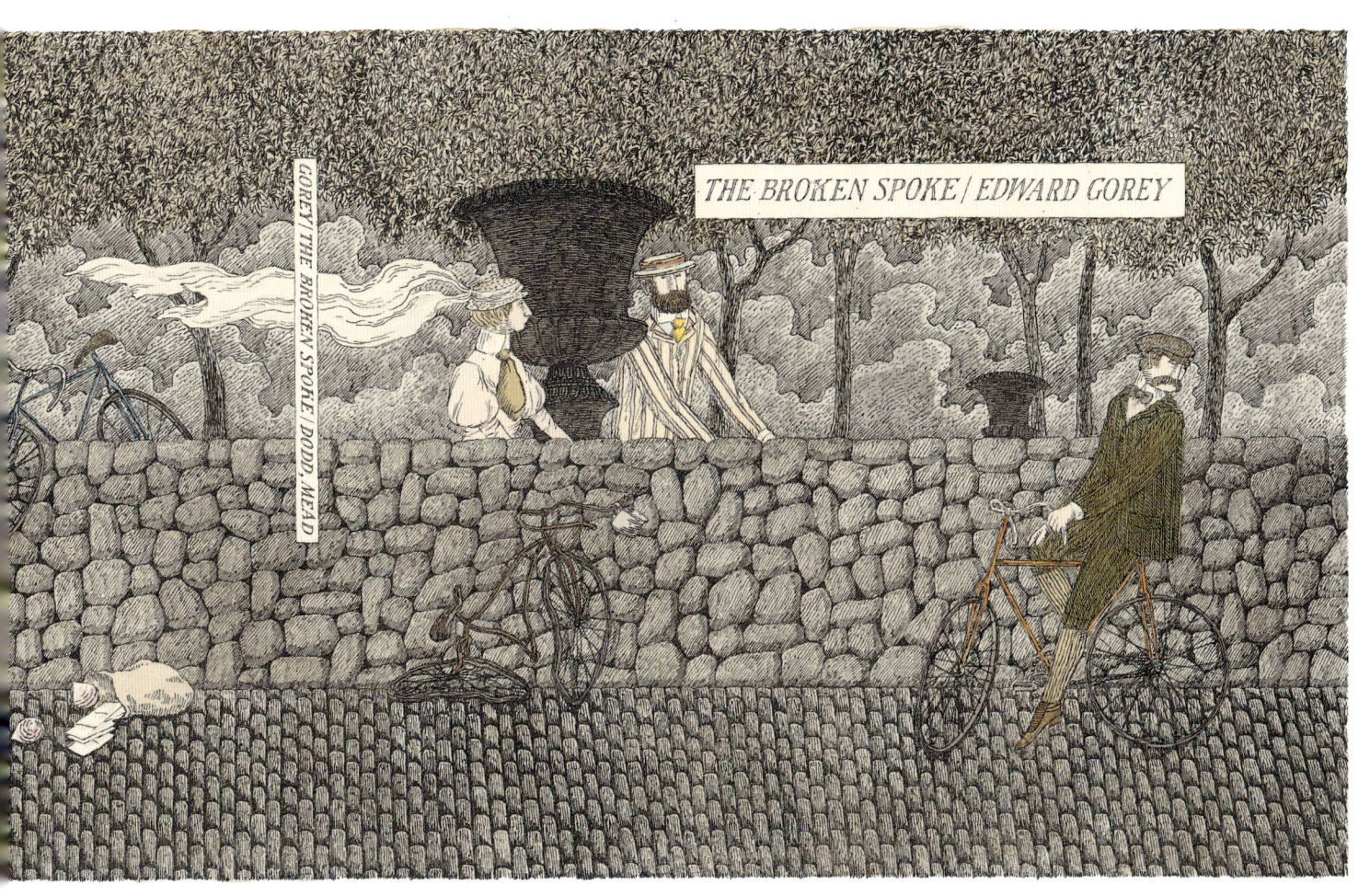

THE BROKEN SPOKE / EDWARD GOREY

GOREY / THE BROKEN SPOKE / DODD, MEAD

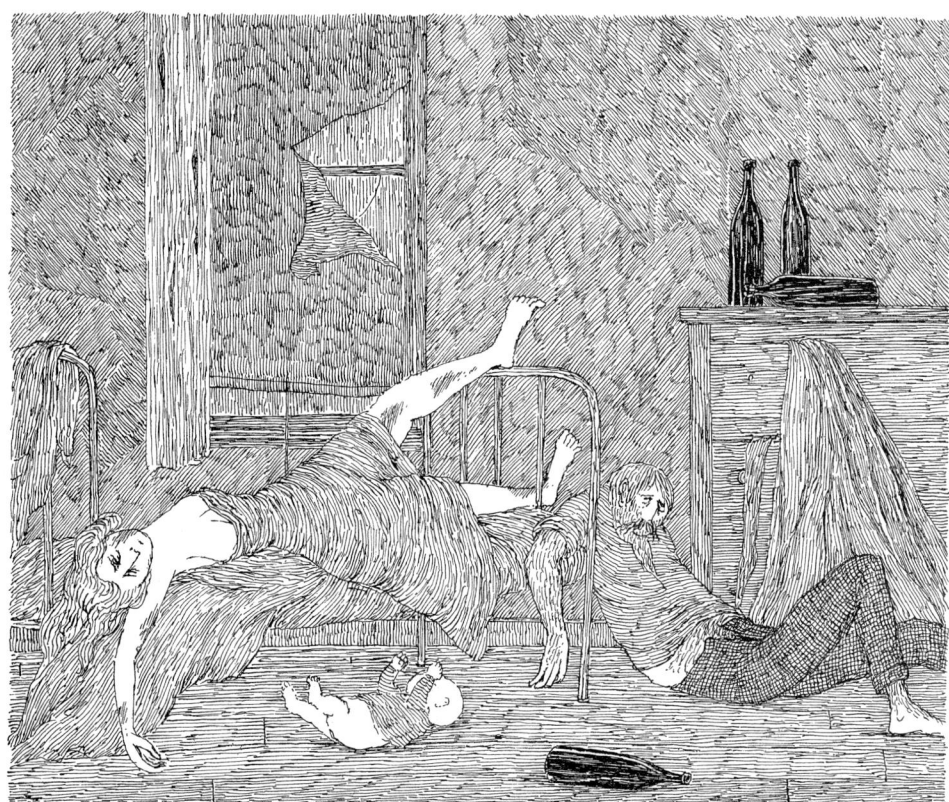

112. *That year Mona Gritch was born to a pair of drunkards.*

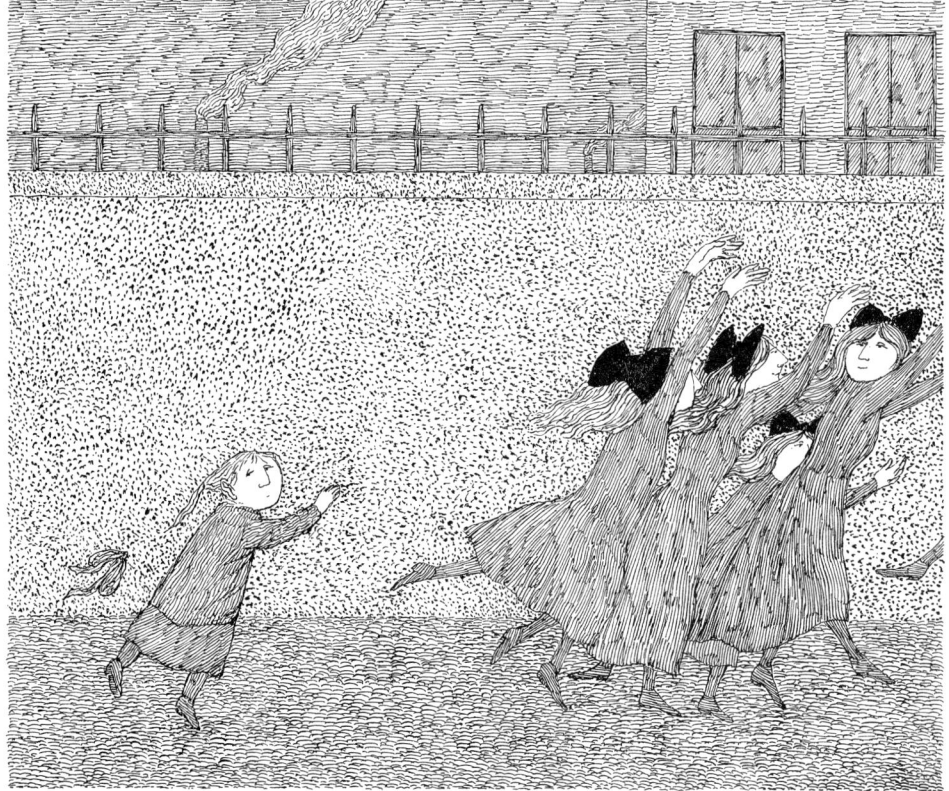

114. *As a child Mona already had thick ankles and thin hair.*

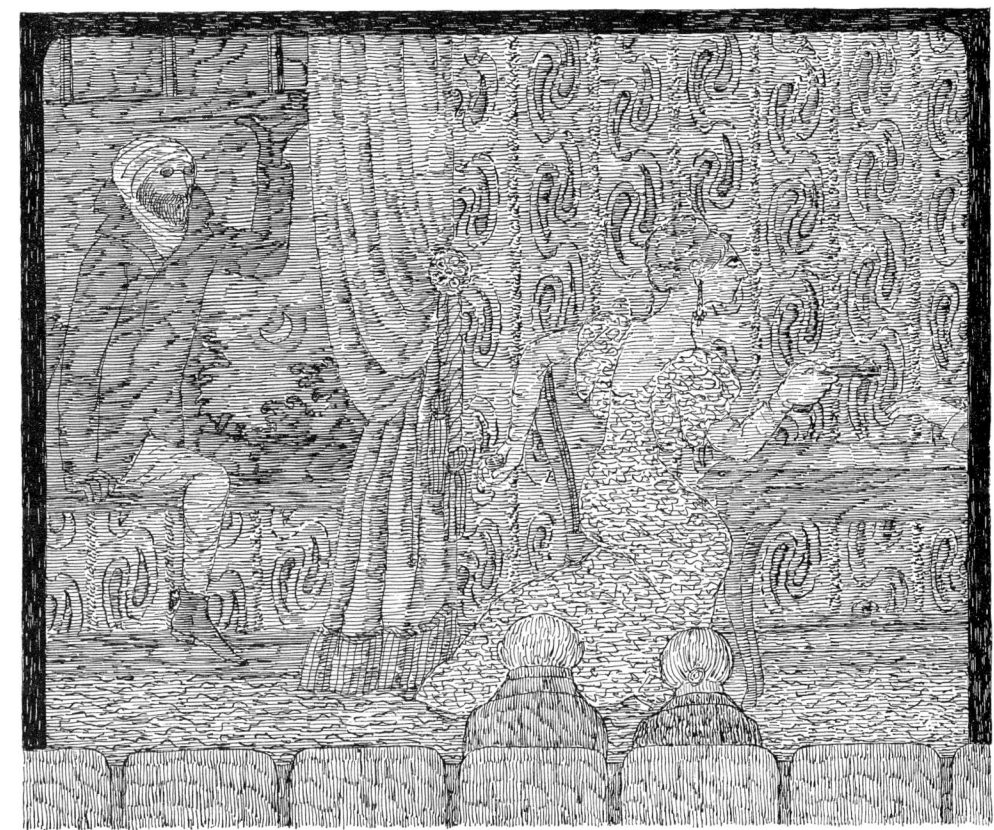

115. *They went to the local cinema whenever there was a crime film playing.*

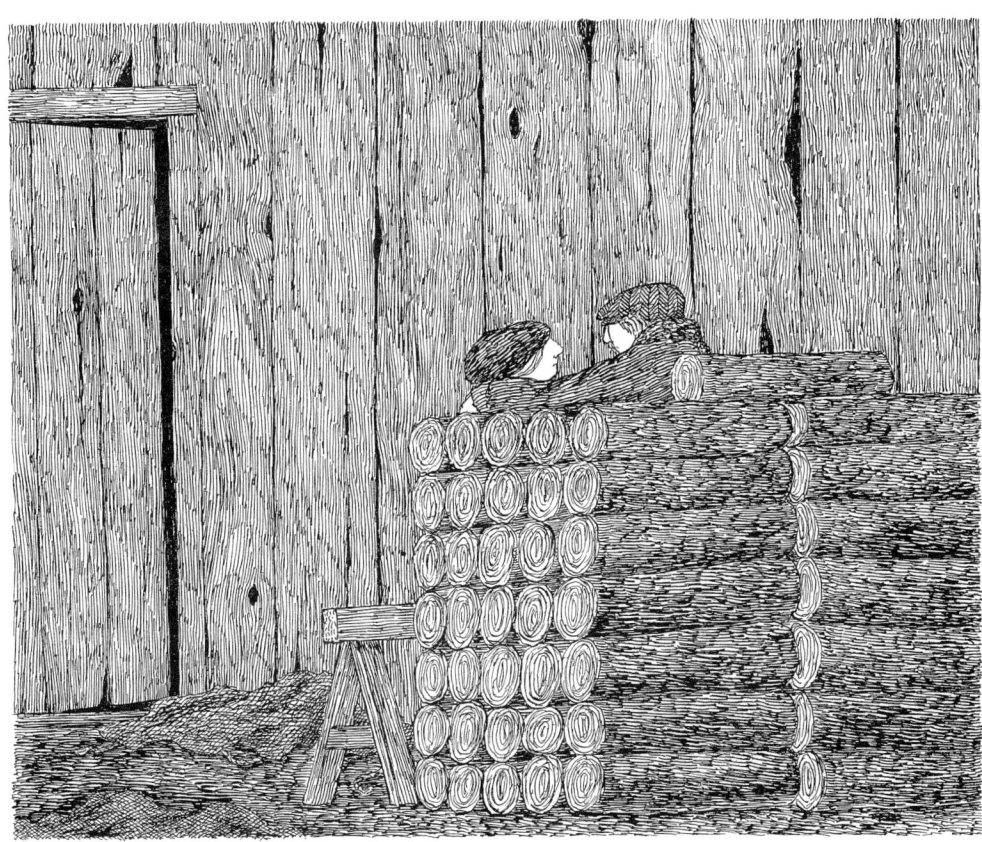

116. *Following one particularly exciting one, they fumbled with each other in a cold woodshed.*

LES URNES UTILES, 1980

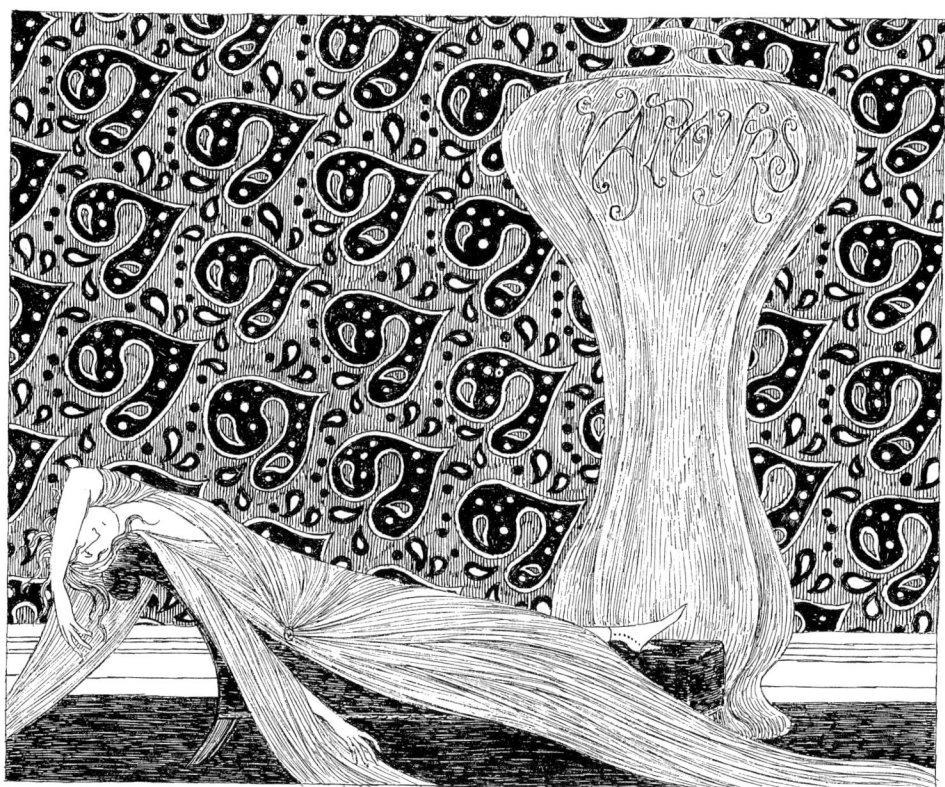

117. *Vapours*

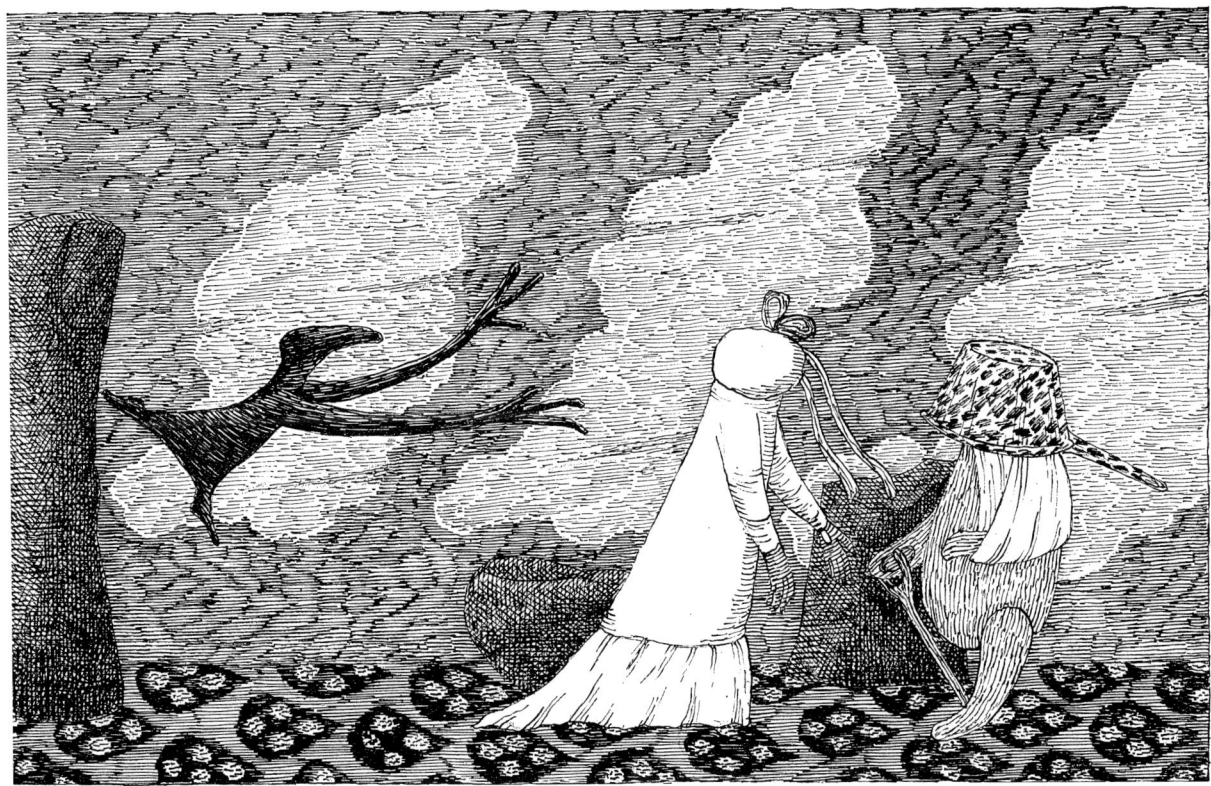

118. *No. 12—Figbash emerged from the woodwork before Naeelah and Hooglyboo. If this does not upset you unduly, turn to 16. If you wish to be morally improved, turn to 18.*

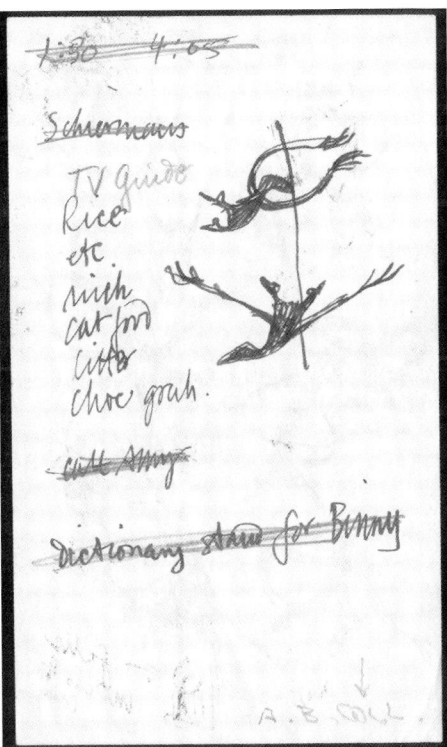

120. Sketches of Figbash

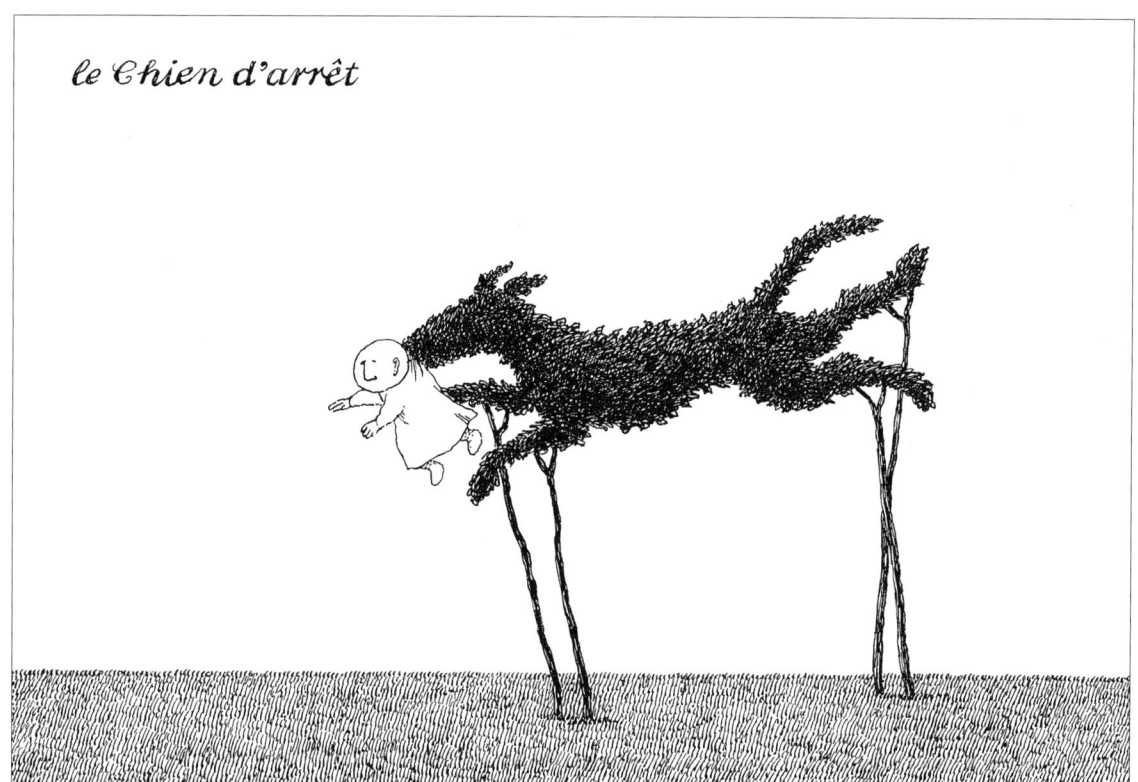

le Chien d'arrêt

122.

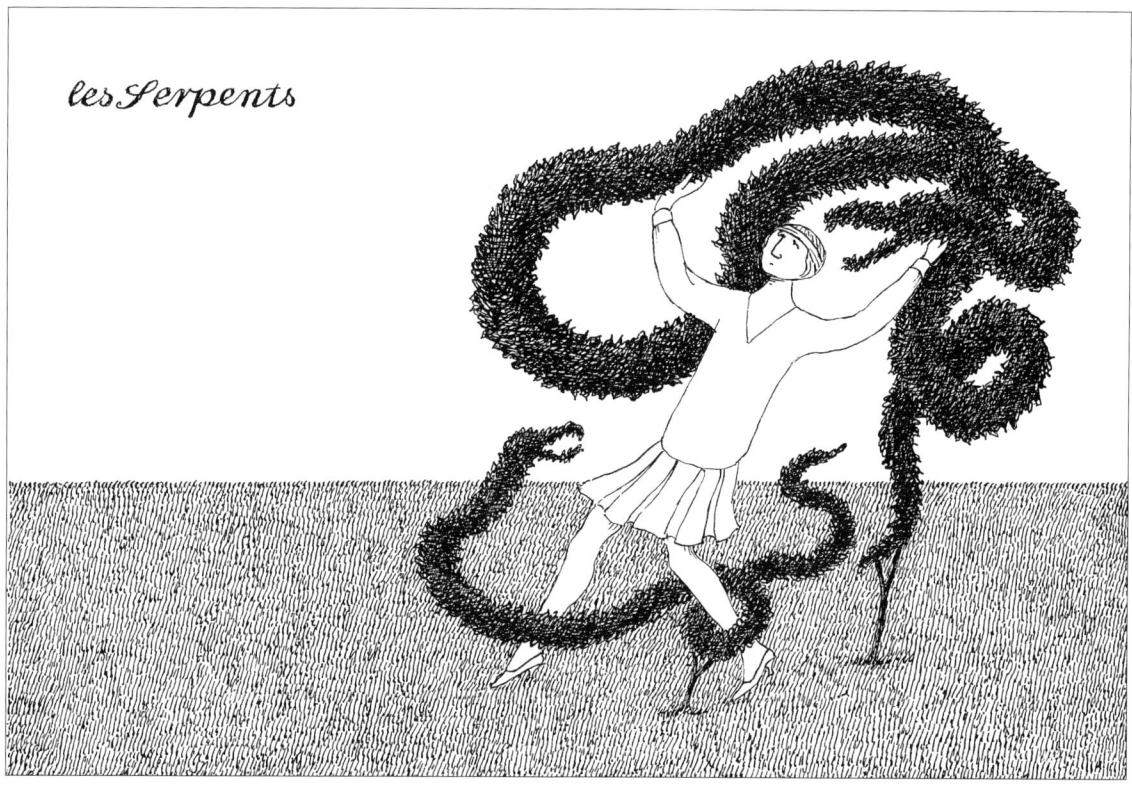

les Serpents

123.

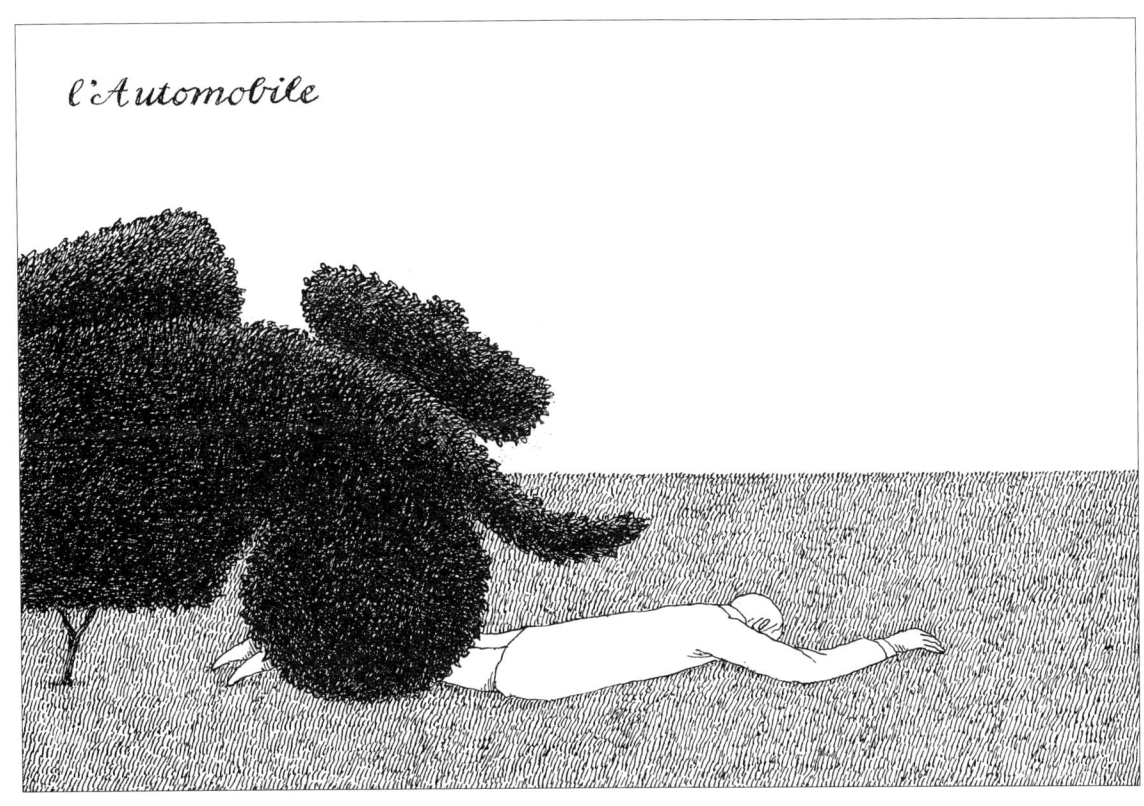

l'Automobile

124.

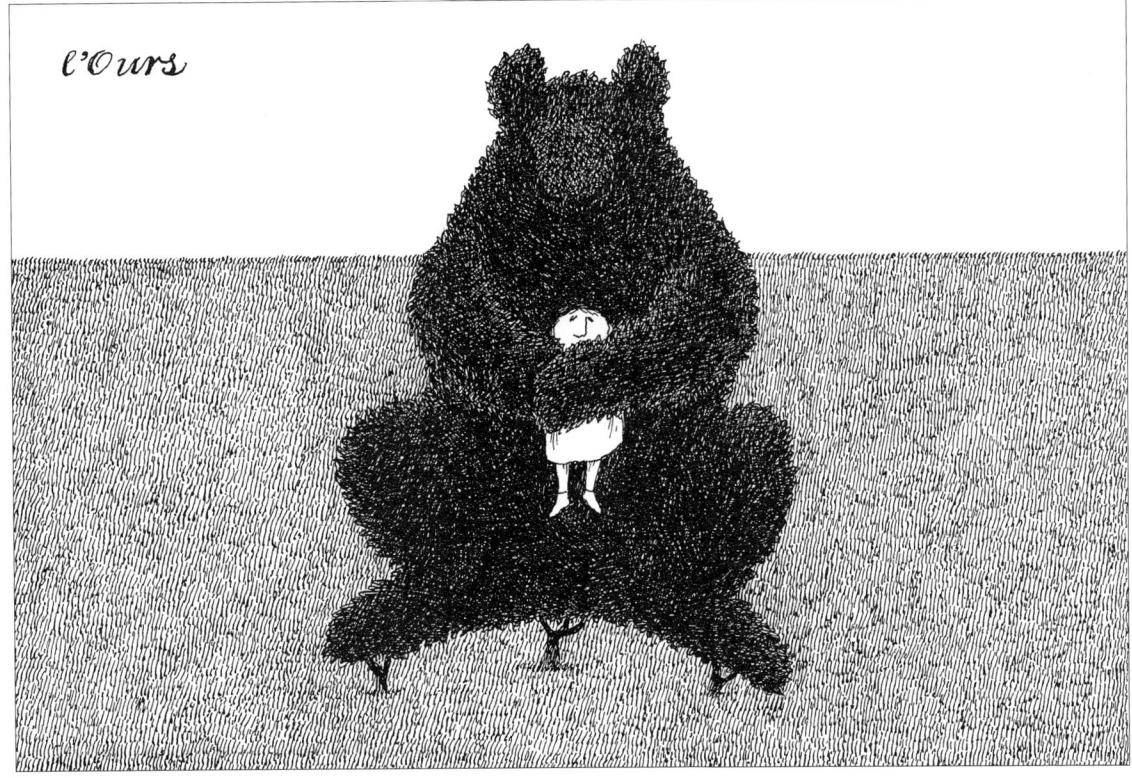

l'Ours

125.

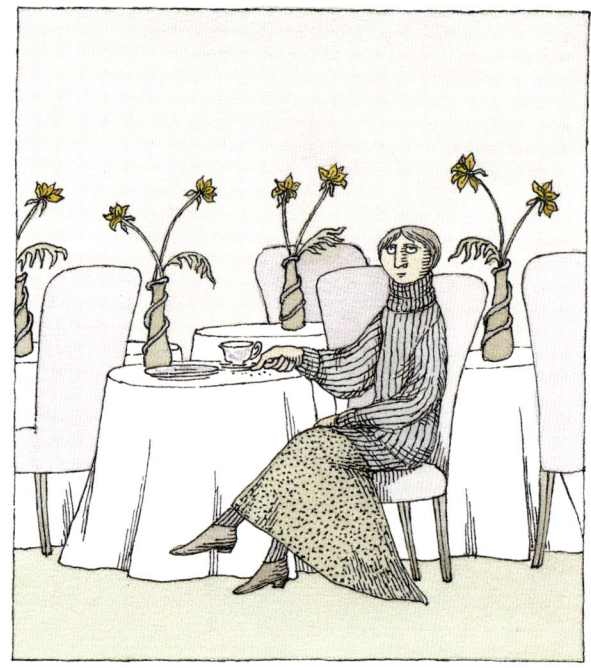

127.

It's possible to pick up crumbs
By pressing on them with the thumbs.

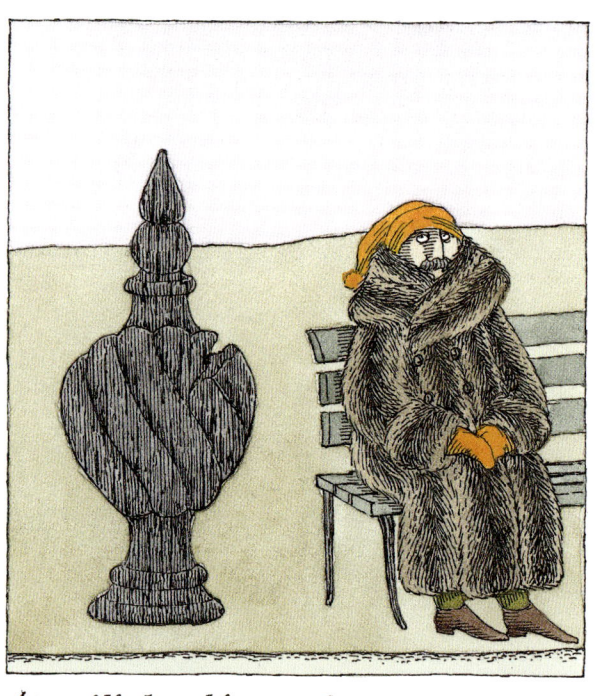

129.

At twilight objects often start
To make odd sounds and fall apart.

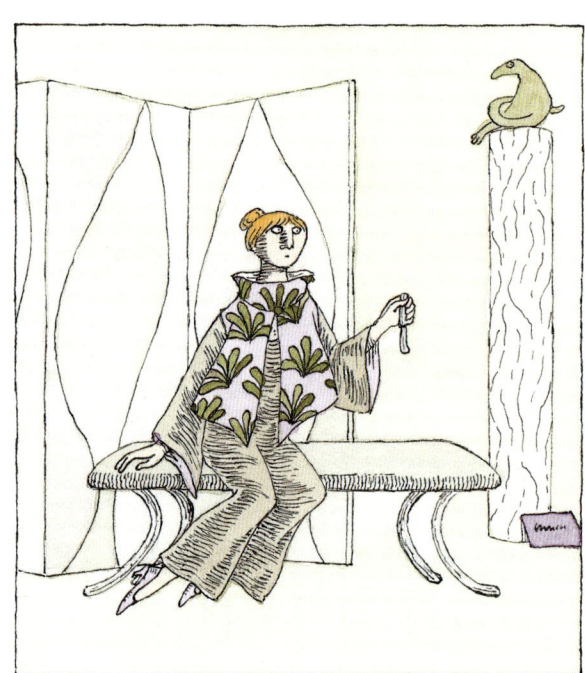

130.

One cannot hope to end one's life
With nothing but a butter knife.

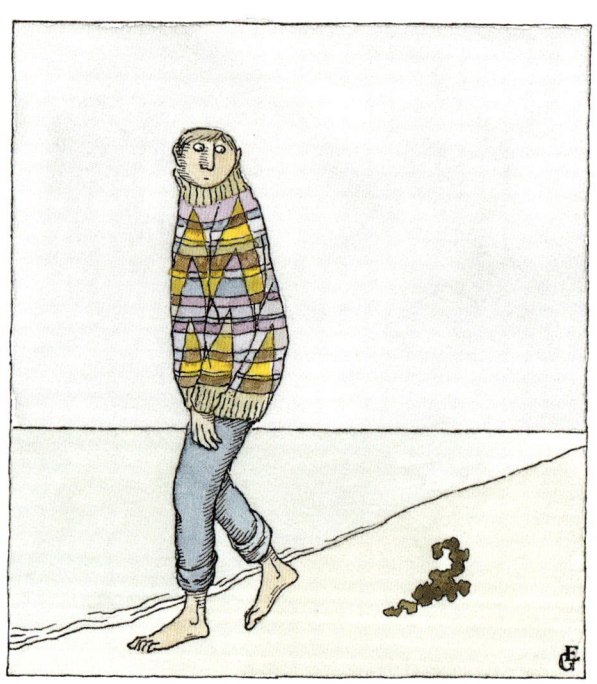

131.

The seaweed on the shore cries out,
But only it knows what about.

BOOKS BY
OTHER AUTHORS

The Jumblies,
by Edward Lear, 1968

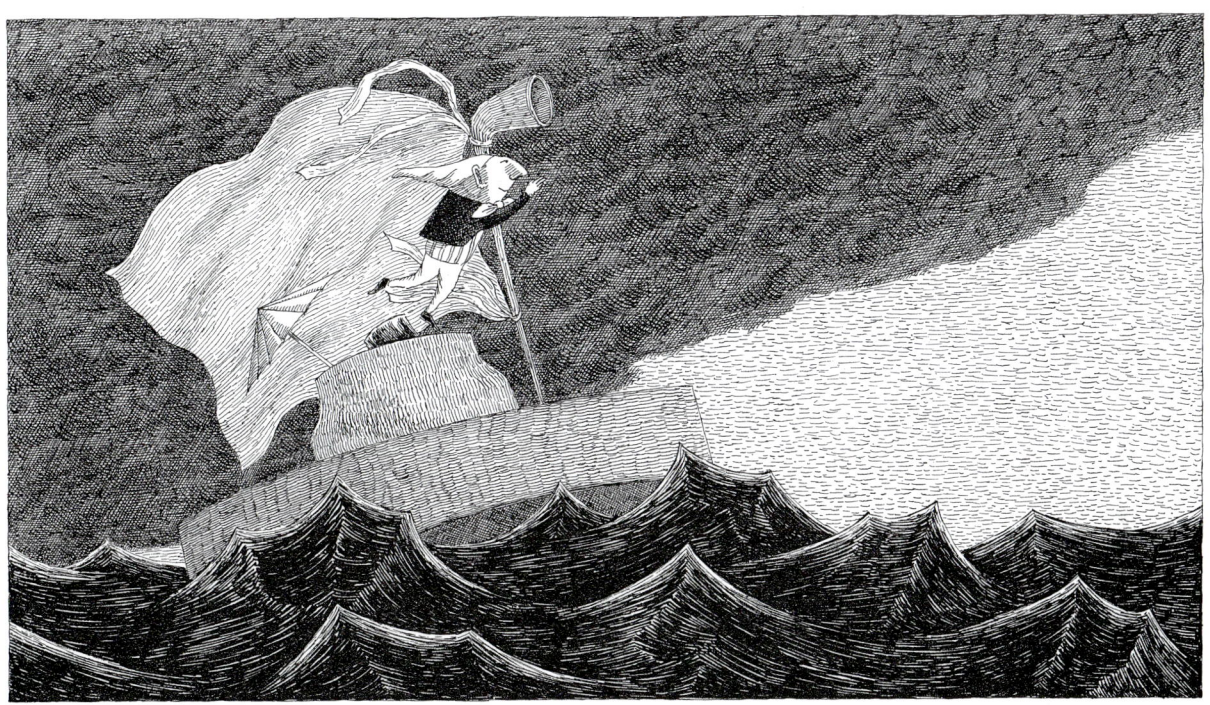

135.

And they passed the night in a crockery-jar,
And each of them said, 'How wise we are!
Though the sky be dark, and the voyage be long,
Yet we never can think we were rash or wrong,
While round in our Sieve we spin!'

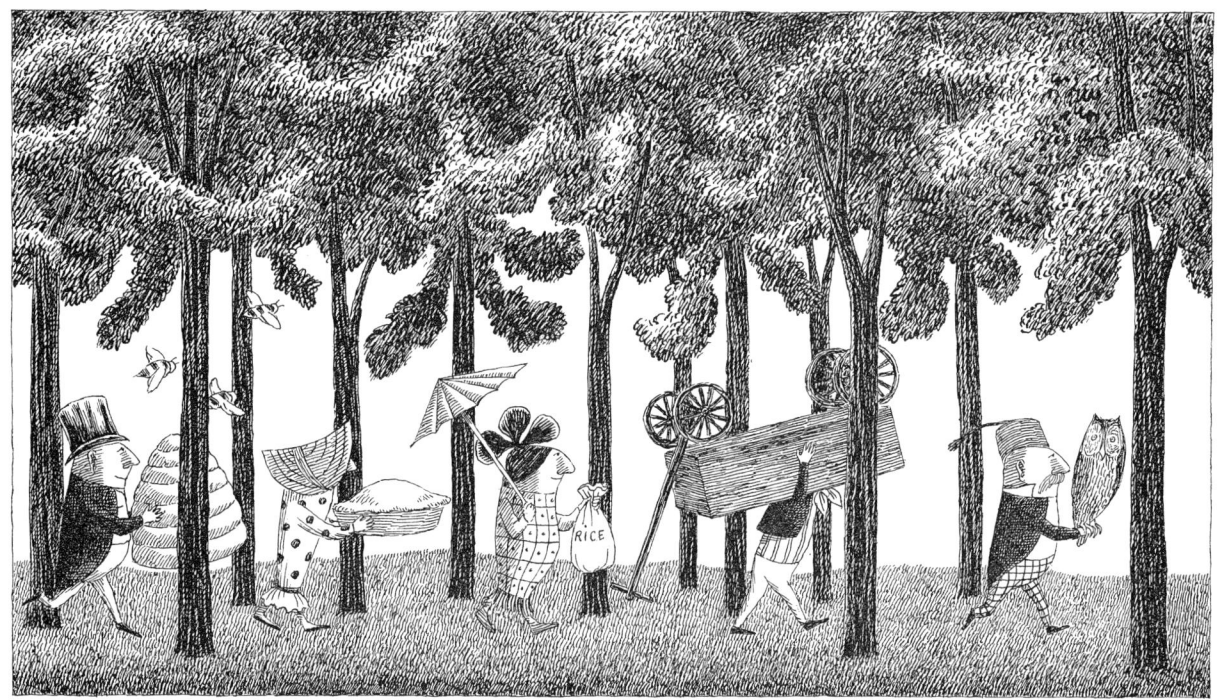

136.

They sailed to the Western Sea, they did,
To a land all covered with trees,
And they bought an owl, and a useful Cart,
And a pound of Rice, and a Cranberry Tart,
And a hive of silvery Bees.

137.

And they bought a Pig, and some green Jack-daws,
And a lovely Monkey with lollipop paws,
And forty bottles of Ring-Bo-Ree,
And no end of Stilton Cheese.

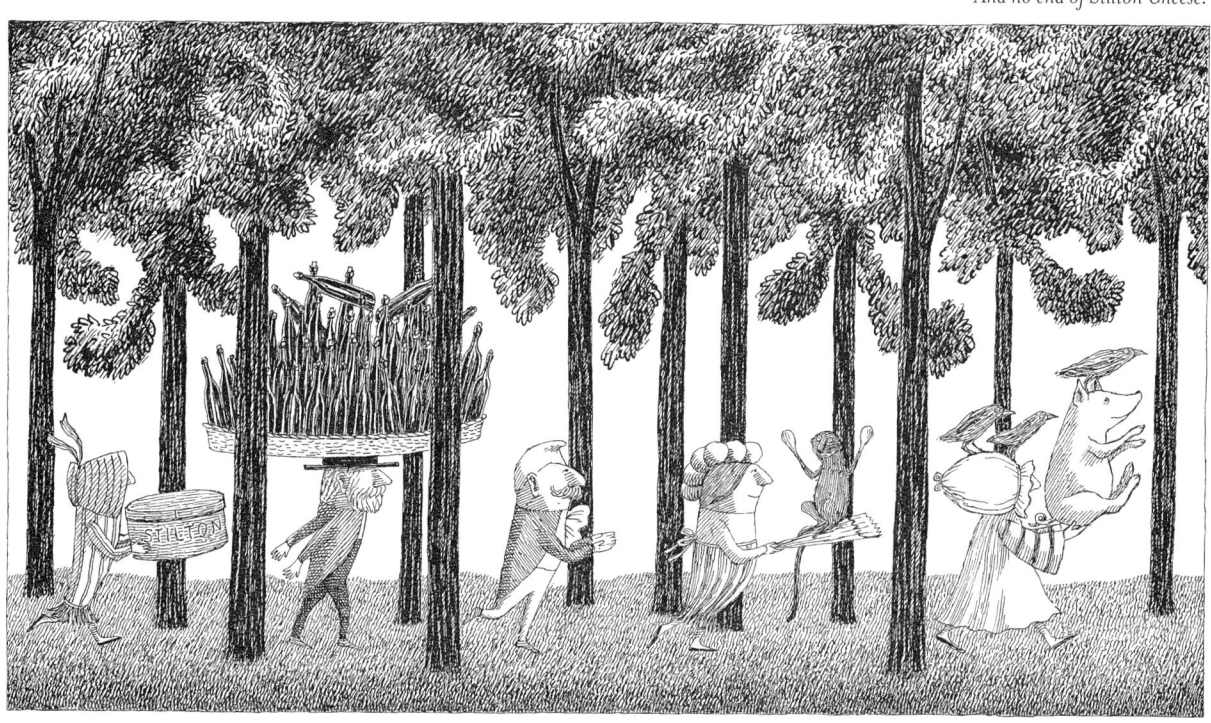

The Dong with a Luminous Nose,
by Edward Lear, 1969

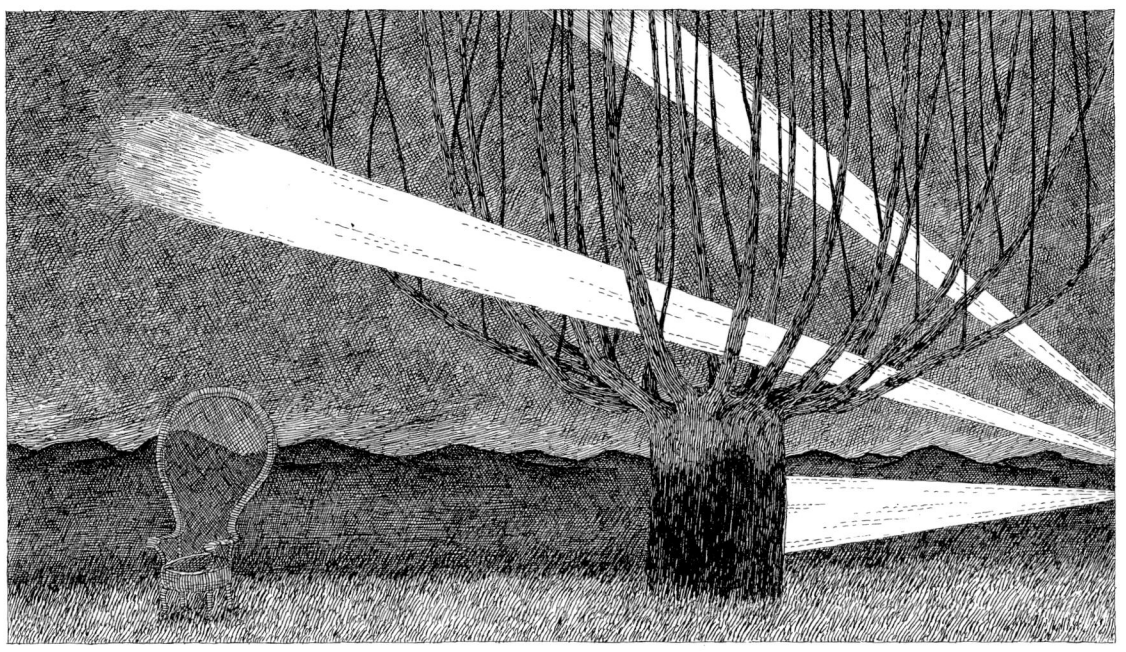

139. *Slowly it wanders,—pauses,—creeps,— / Anon it sparkles,—flashes and leaps; / And ever as onward it gleaming goes / A light on the Bong-tree stems it throws.*

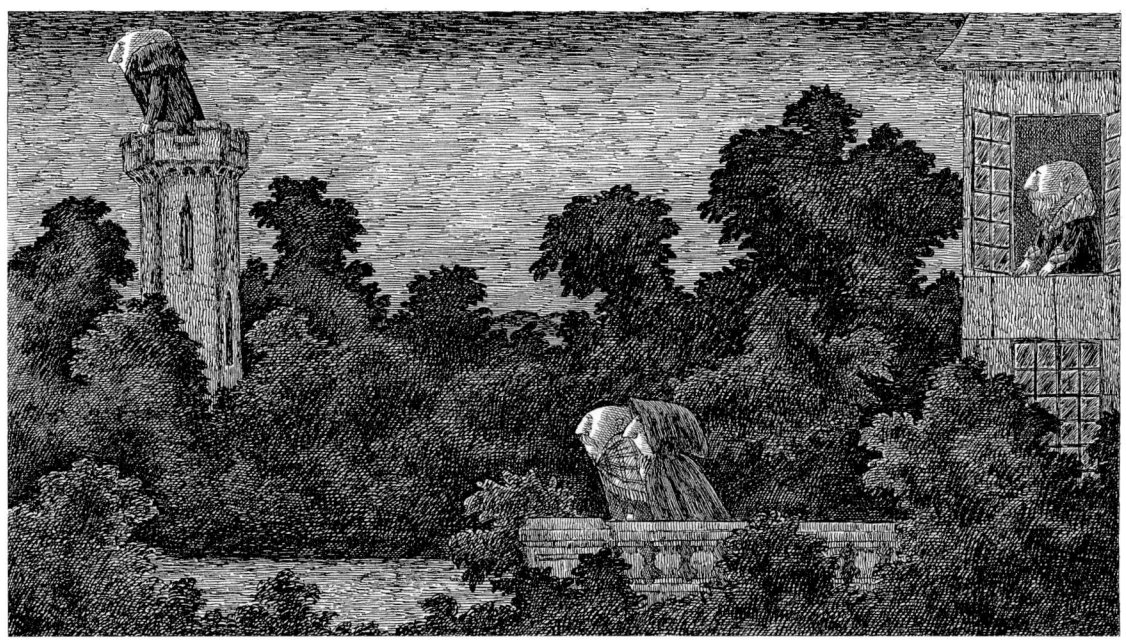

140. *And those who watch at that midnight hour / From Hall or Terrace, or lofty Tower, / Cry, as the wild light passes along, —/ 'The Dong!—the Dong! / 'The wandering Dong through the forest goes! / 'The Dong! the Dong! / 'The Dong with a luminous Nose!'*

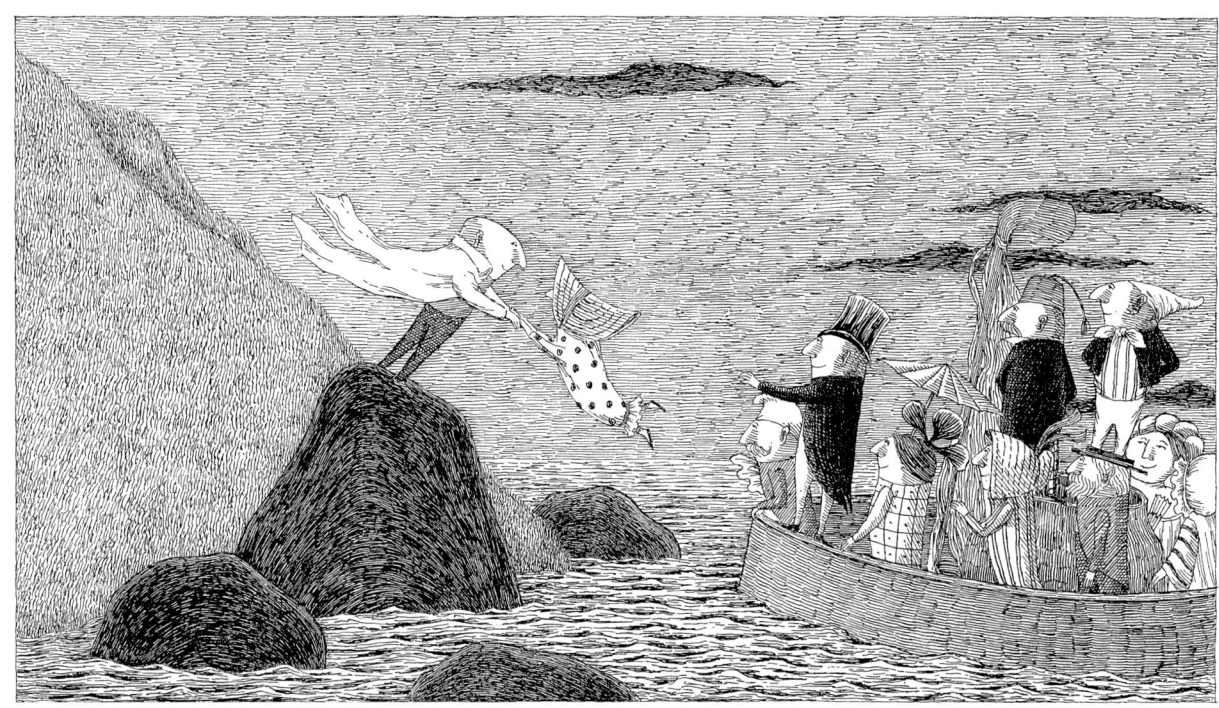

141. *For the Jumblies came in a sieve, they did, —/ Landing at eve near the Zemmery Fidd / Where the Oblong Oysters grow, / And the rocks are smooth and gray. / And all the woods and the valleys rang / With the Chorus they daily and nightly sang,—*

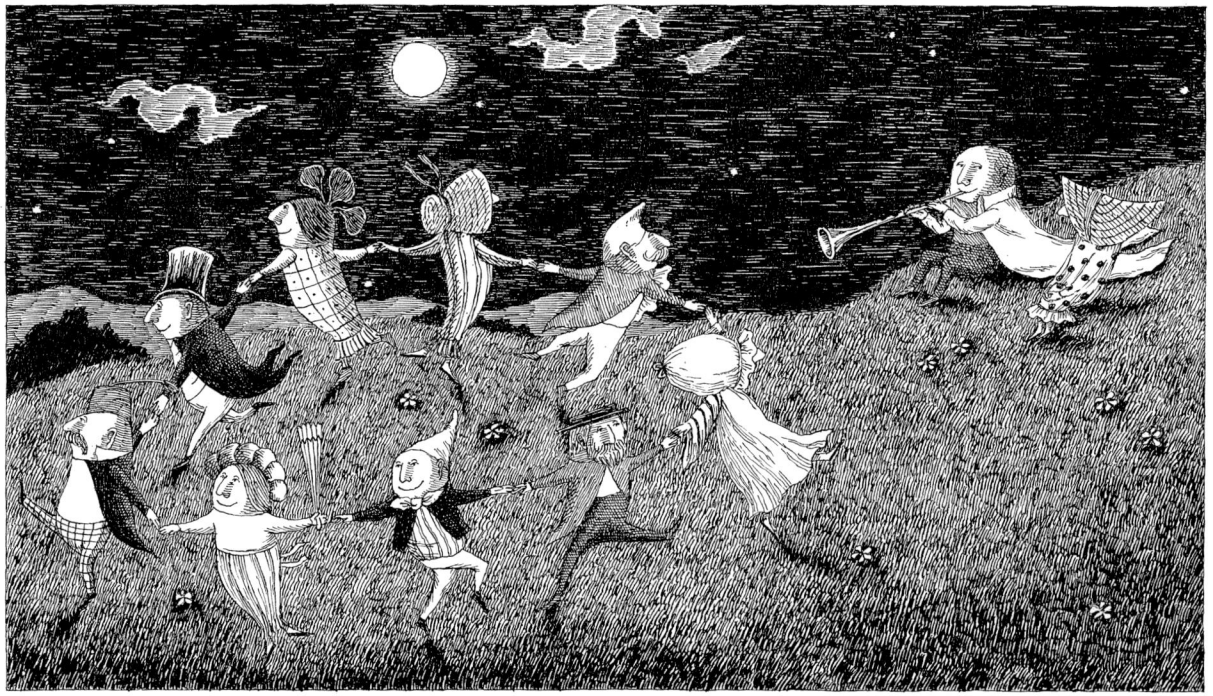

142. *Happily, happily passed those days! / While the cheerful Jumblies staid; / They danced in circlets all night long, / To the plaintive pipe of the lively Dong, / In moonlight, shine, or shade. / For day and night he was always there / By the side of the Jumbly Girl so fair, / With her sky-blue hands, and her sea-green hair.*

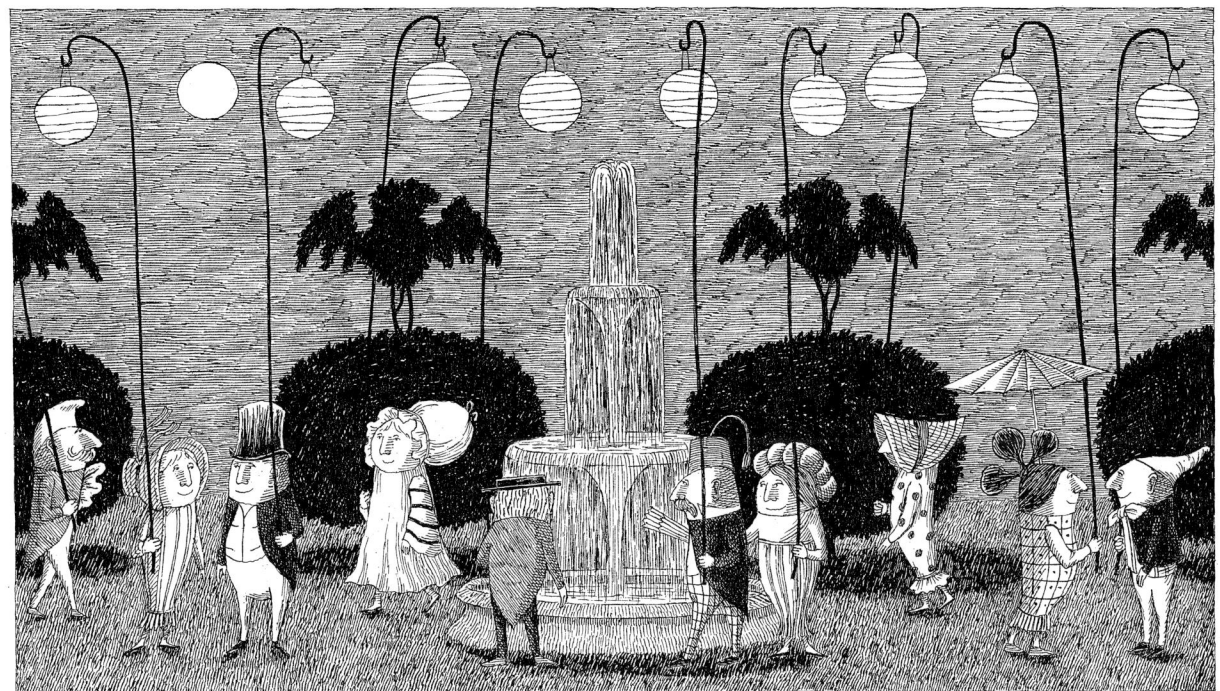

143. *'Far and few, far and few, / Are the lands where the Jumblies live; / Their heads are green, and their hands are blue, / And they went to sea in a sieve.'*

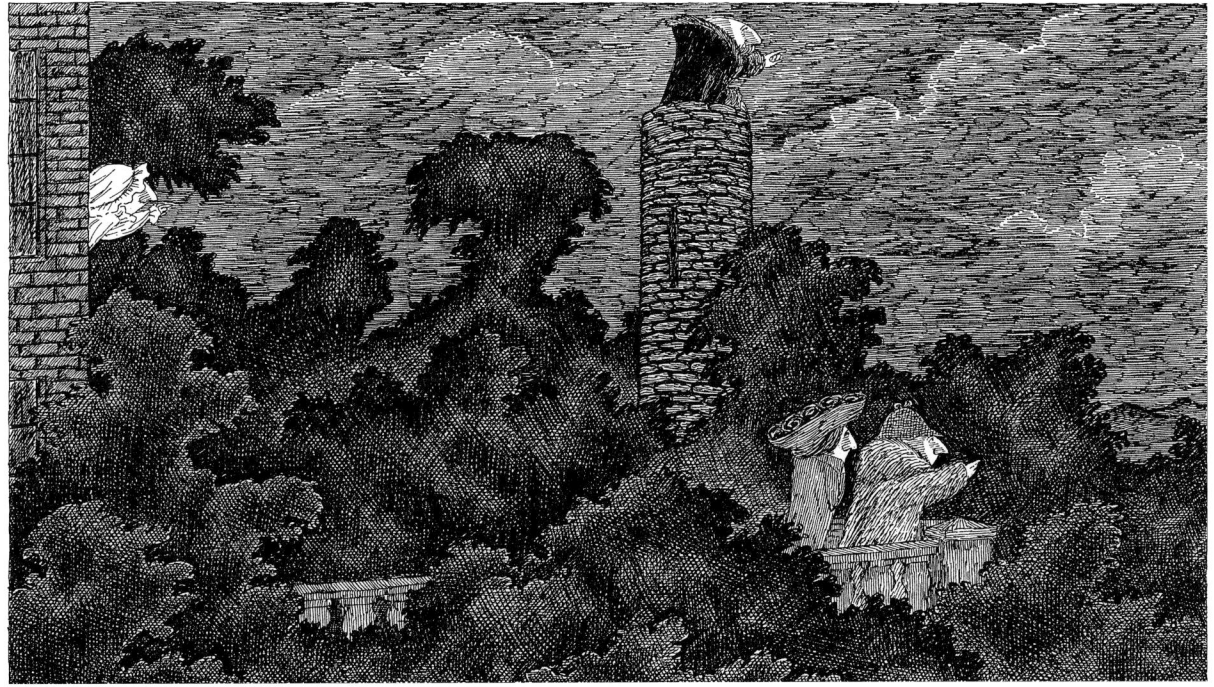

144. *And all who watch at the midnight hour, / From Hall or Terrace, or lofty Tower, / Cry, as they trace the Meteor bright, / Moving along through the dreary night,—*

OLD POSSUM'S BOOK OF PRACTICAL CATS, BY T. S. ELIOT, 1982

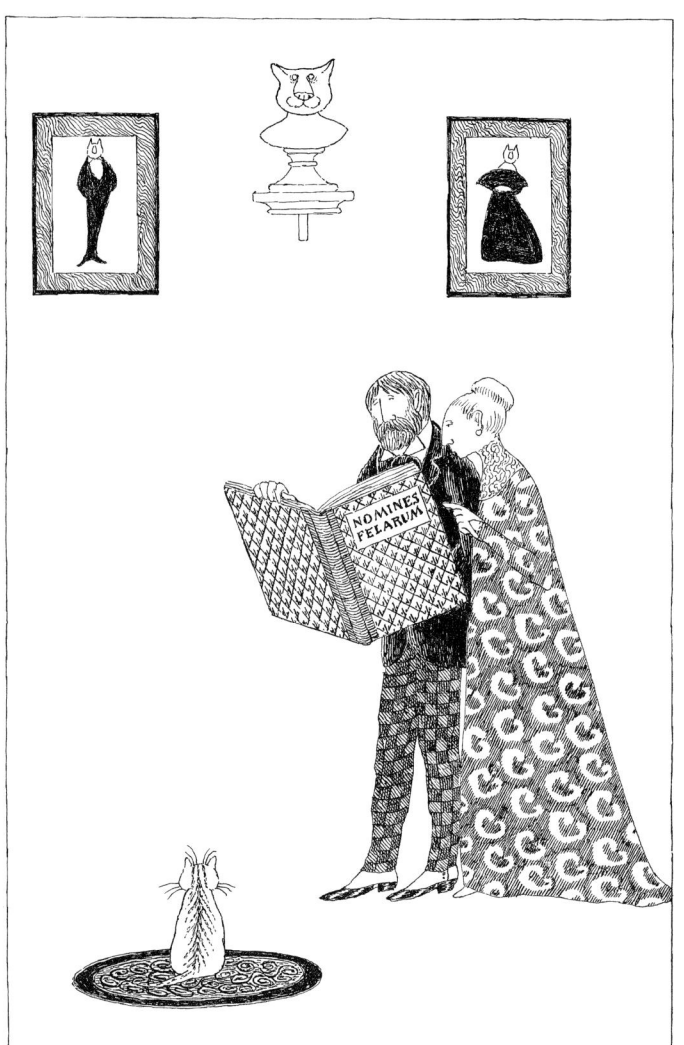

146. *The Naming of Cats*

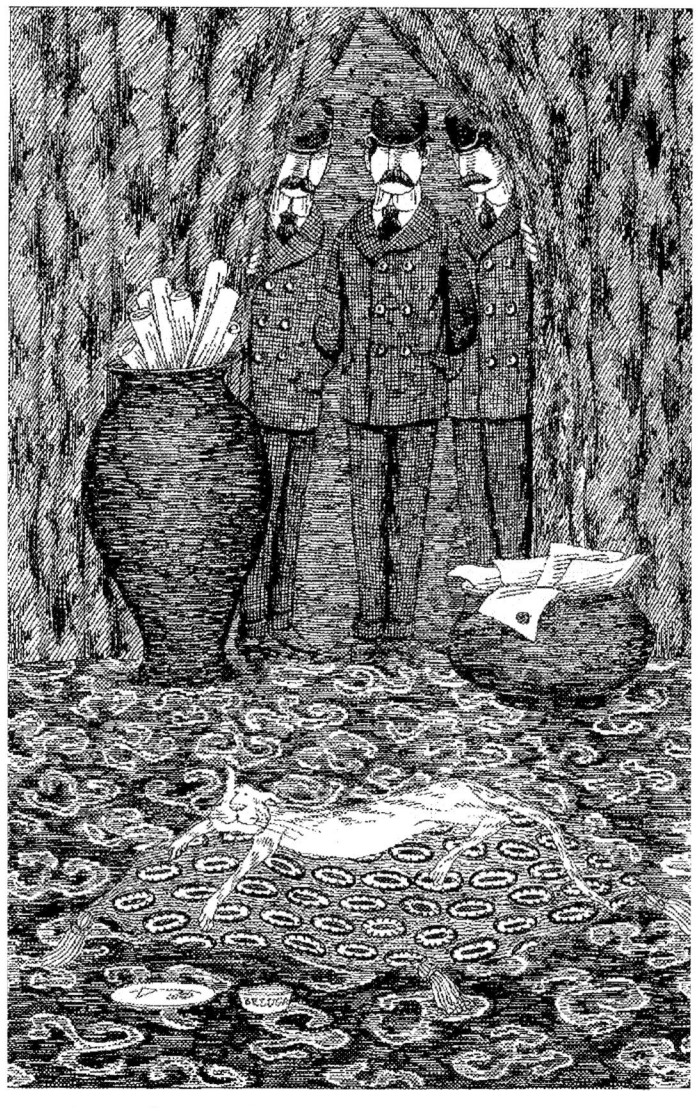

147. *Macavity: The Mystery Cat*

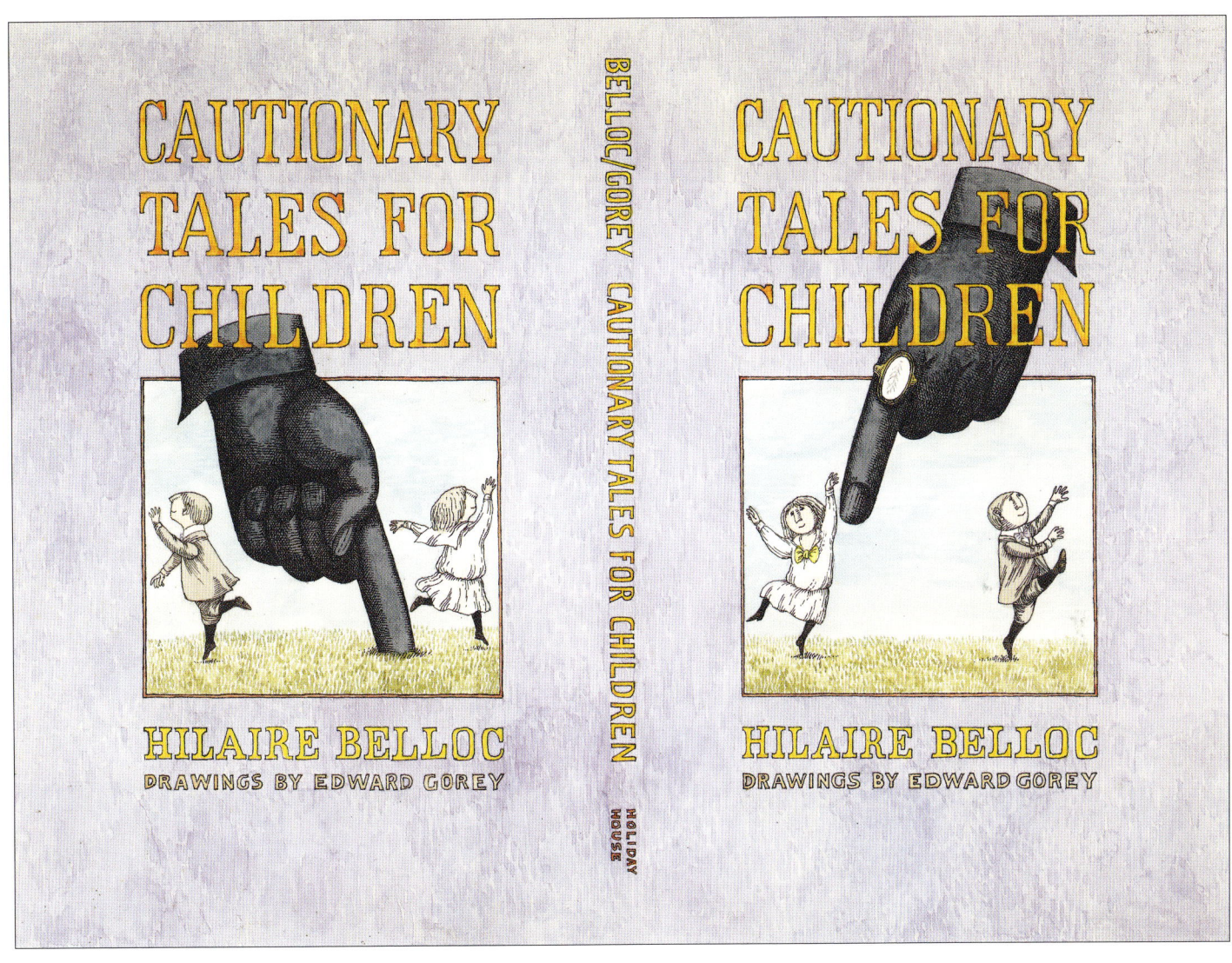

148. Front and back covers

Algernon,

Who played with a Loaded Gun,
and, on missing his Sister, was
reprimanded by his Father.

Jim,

Who ran away from his Nurse,
and was eaten by a Lion.

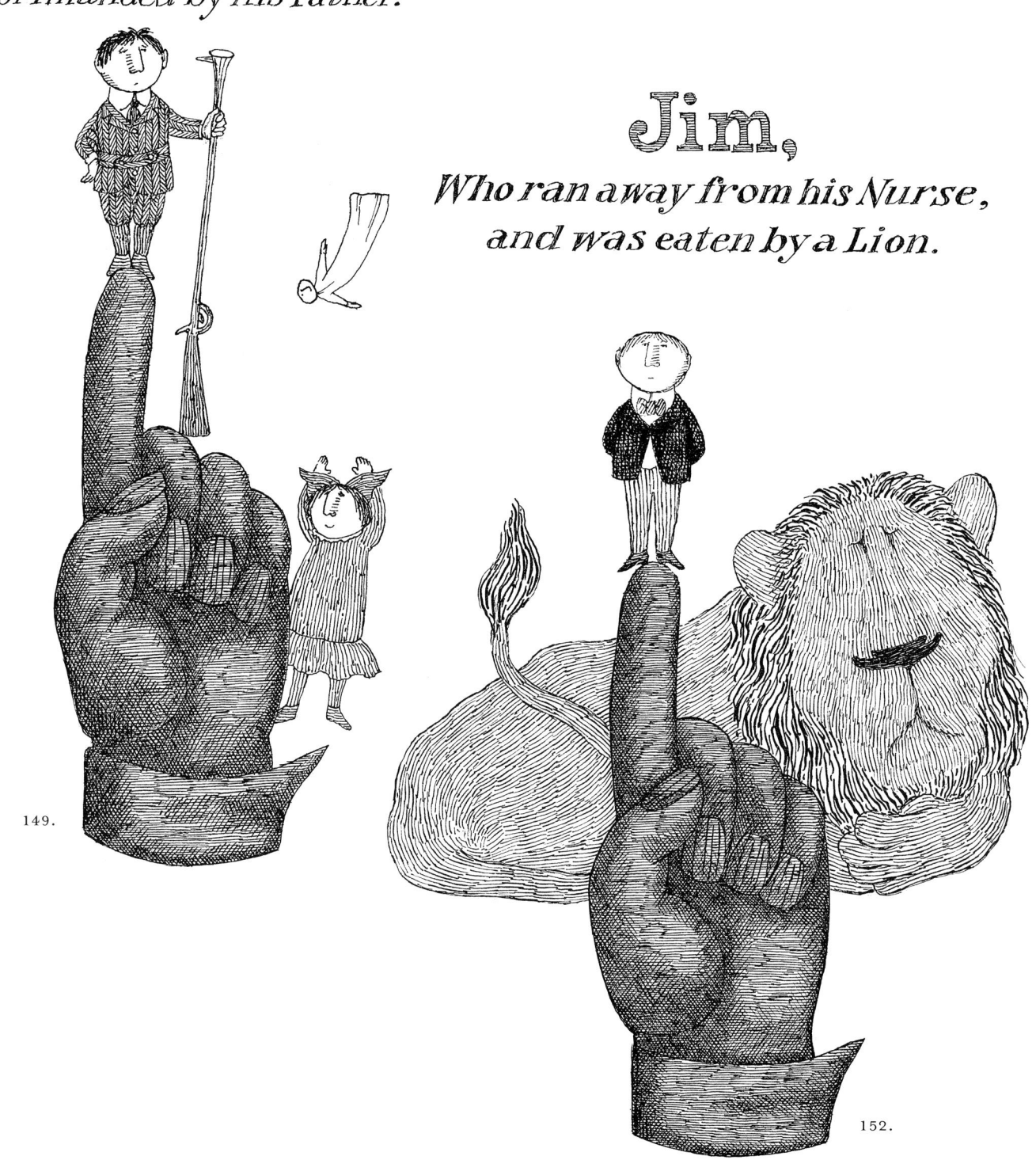

149.

152.

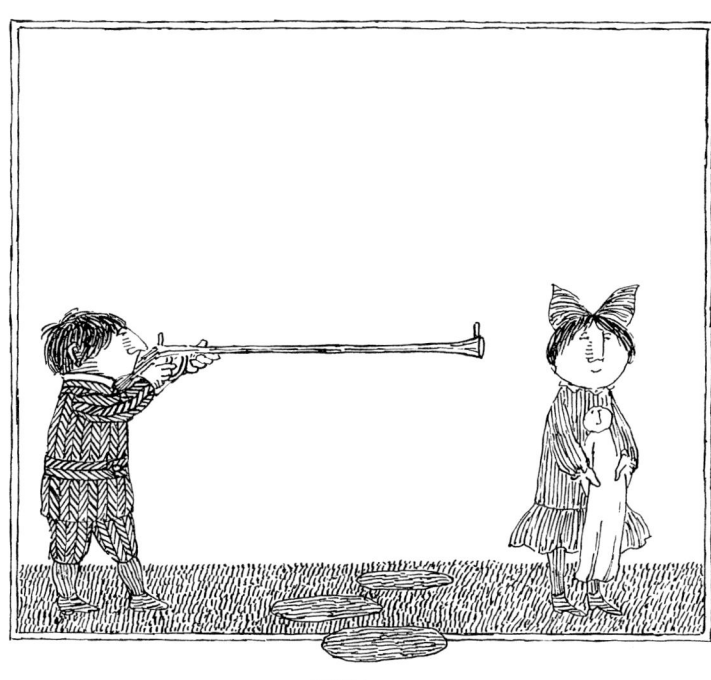

150.

Young Algernon, the Doctor's Son,
Was playing with a Loaded Gun.
He pointed it towards his sister,
Aimed very carefully, but Missed her!

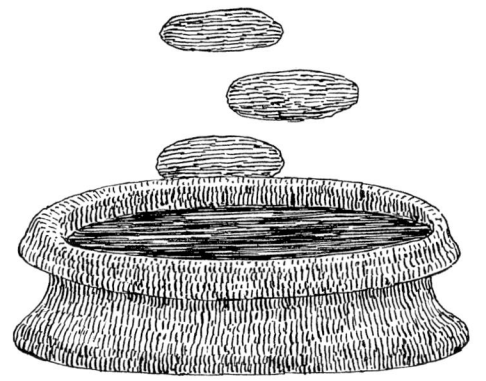

151.

His Father, who was standing near,
The Loud Explosion chanced to Hear,
And reprimanded Algernon
For playing with a Loaded Gun.

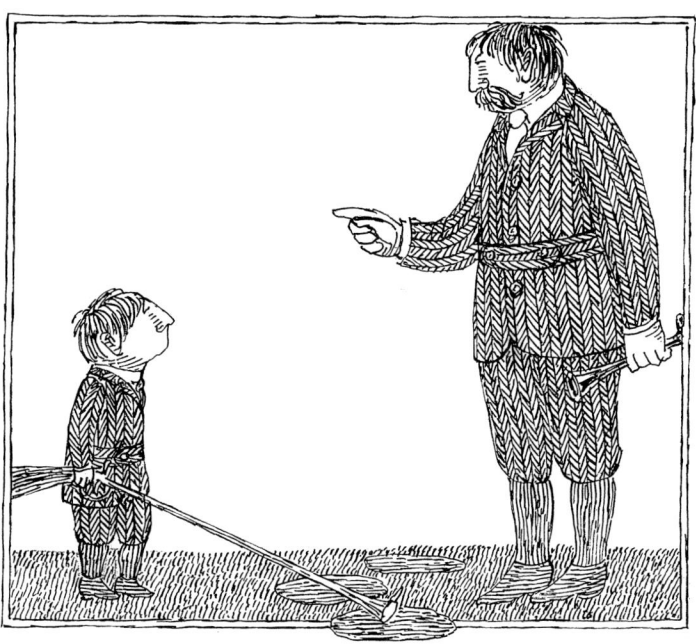

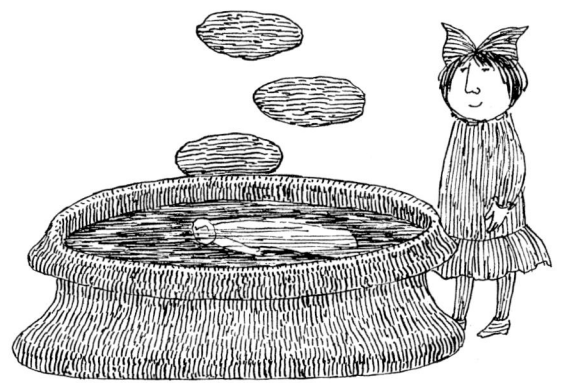

103

MISCELLANEOUS ARTWORKS

ILLUSTRATED ENVELOPES, 1948

Writing to his mother while at Harvard in 1948, Gorey decorated his envelopes with scenes and figures that are harbingers of his mature style. This is especially noticeable in the human figures that bear a striking resemblance to Mr Earbrass, the main character from his first publication, *The Unstrung Harp* (see pages 38–40). The envelope images are published here for the first time.

—LW

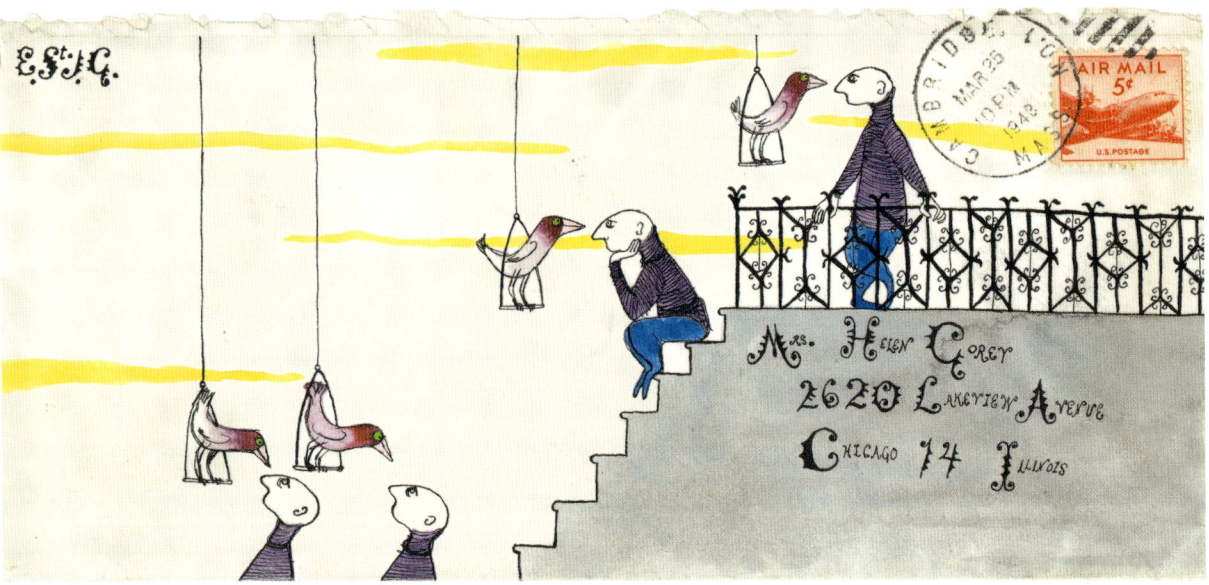

153.

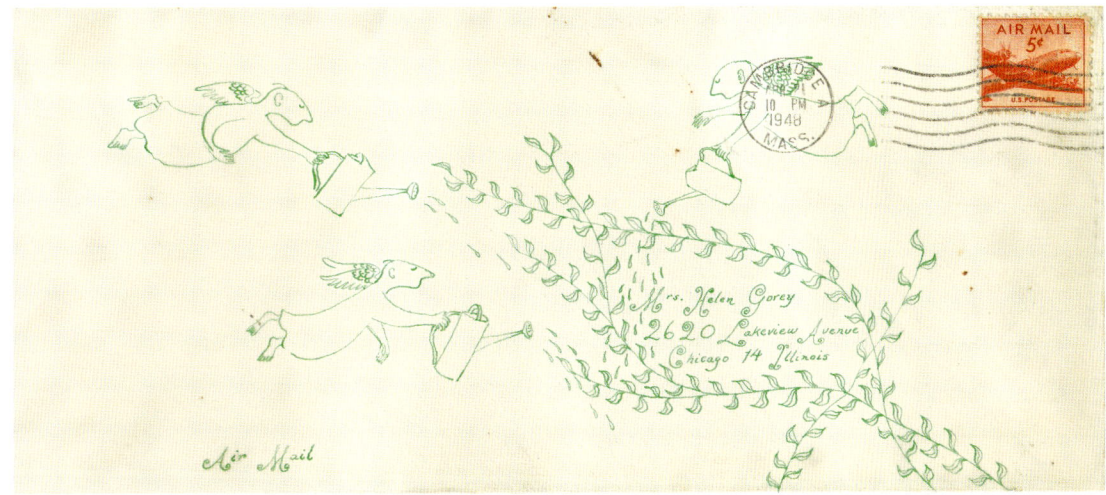

154.

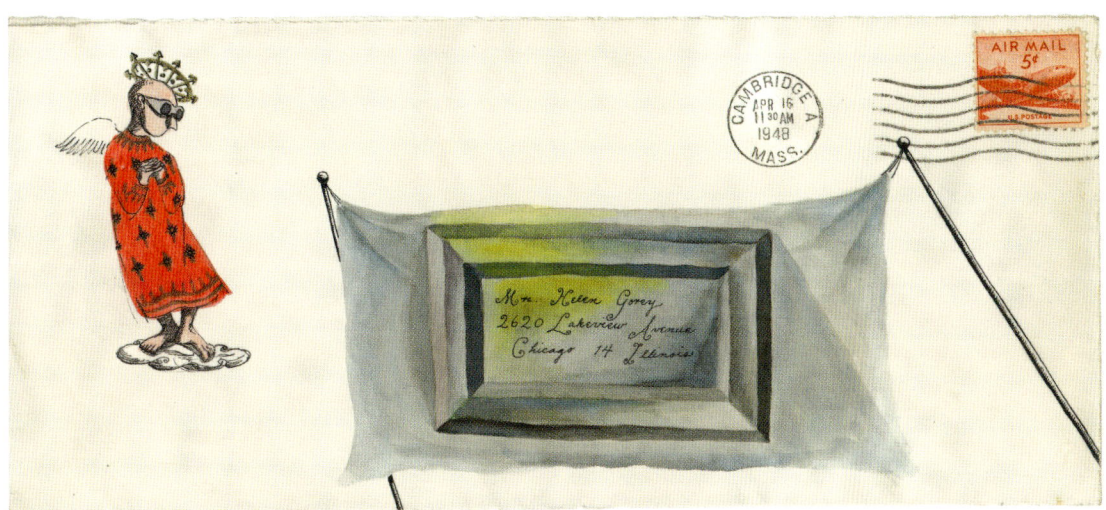

155.

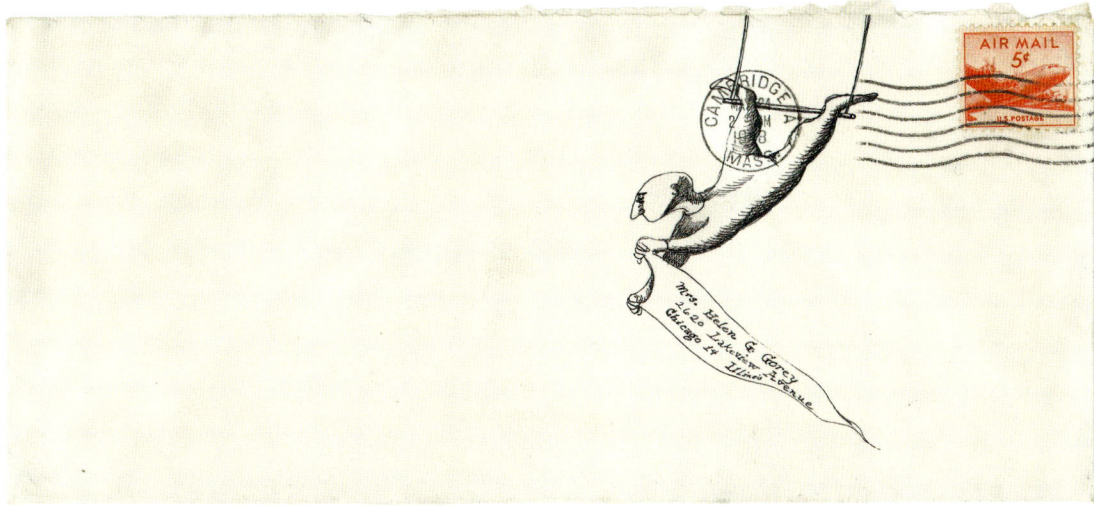

156.

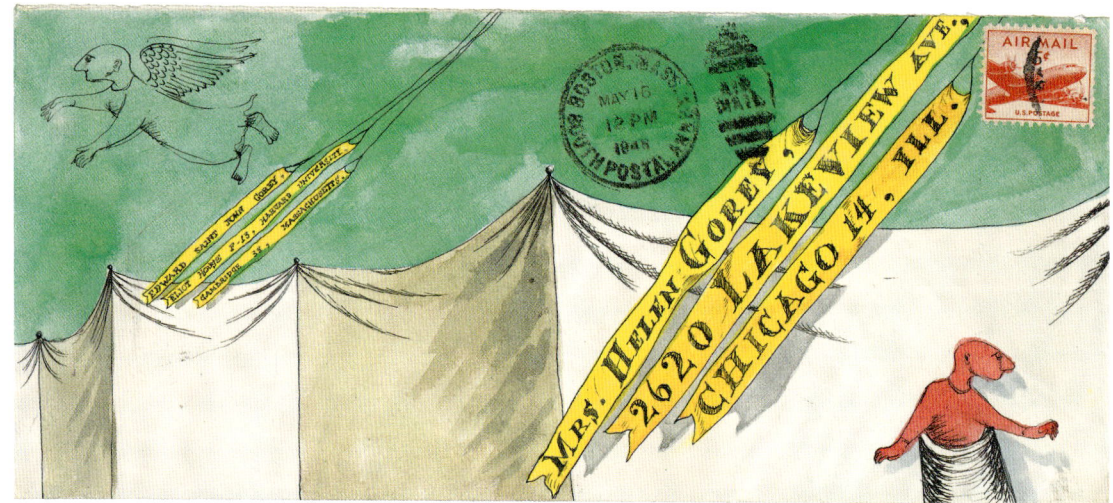

157.

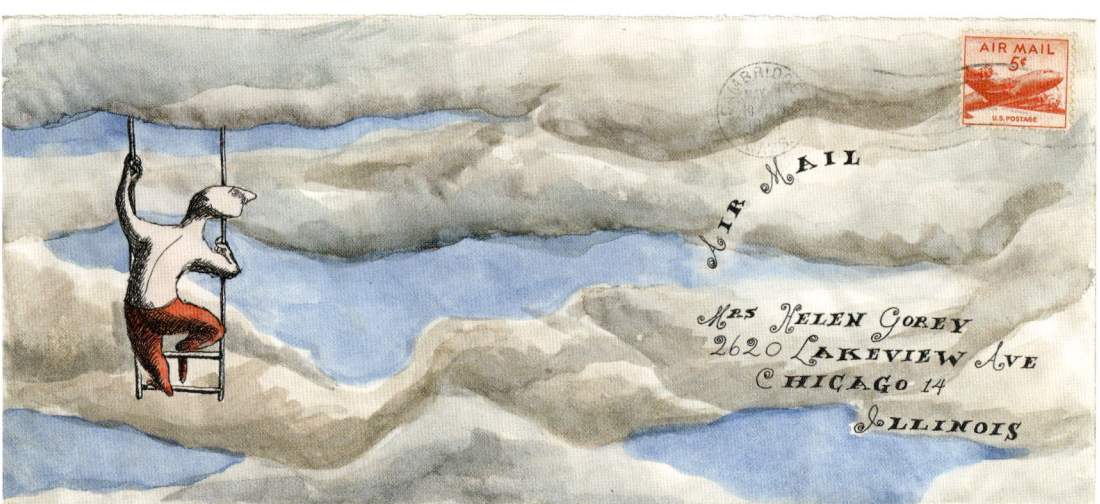

158.

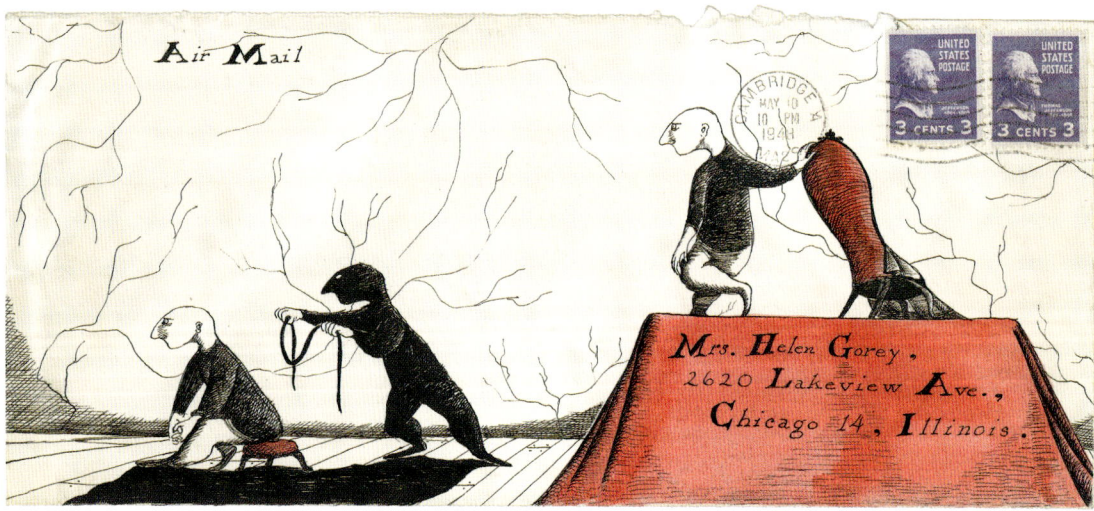

159.

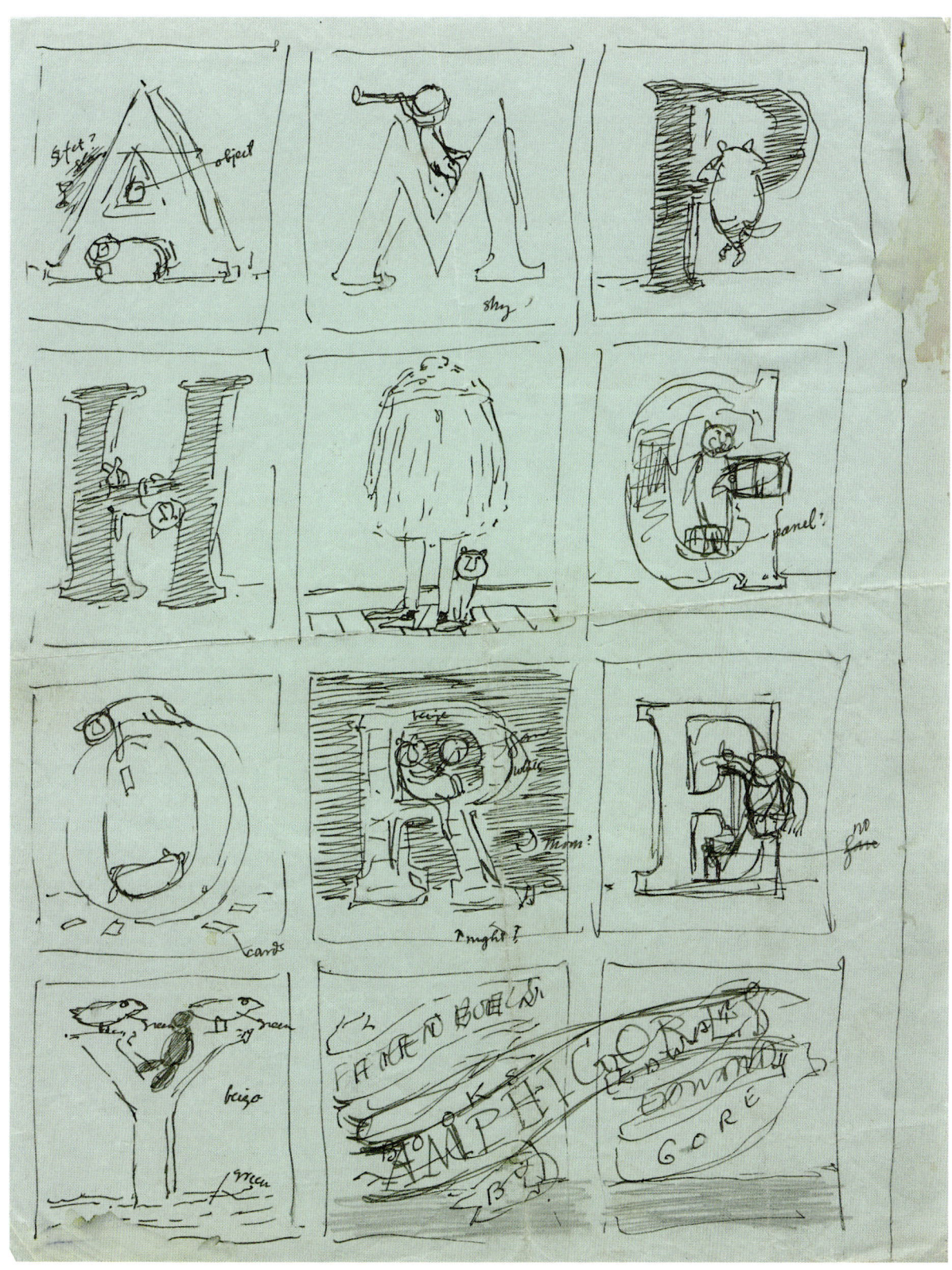

163. Study for the cover for *Amphigorey*, 1972

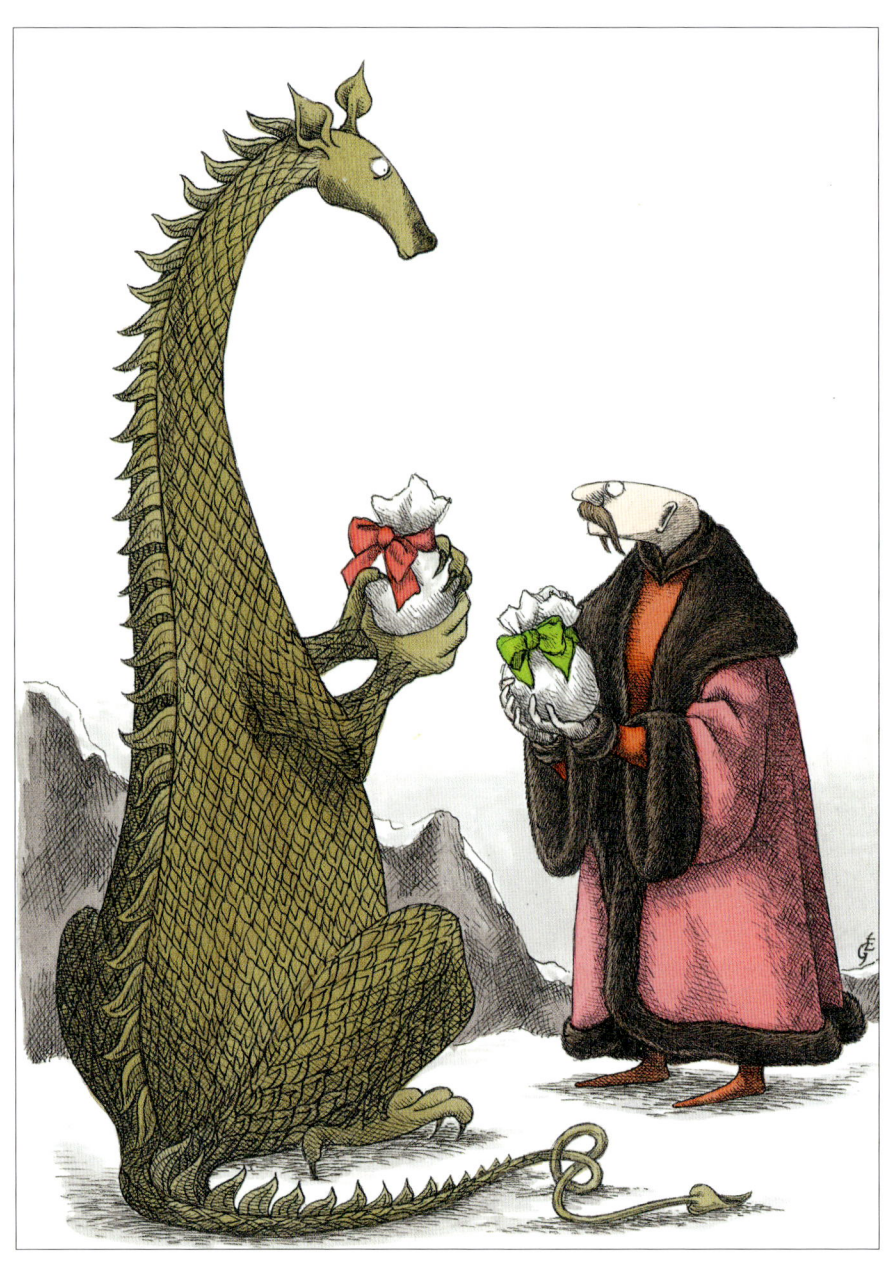

160. *Dragon and Man Exchange Gifts,* circa 1950

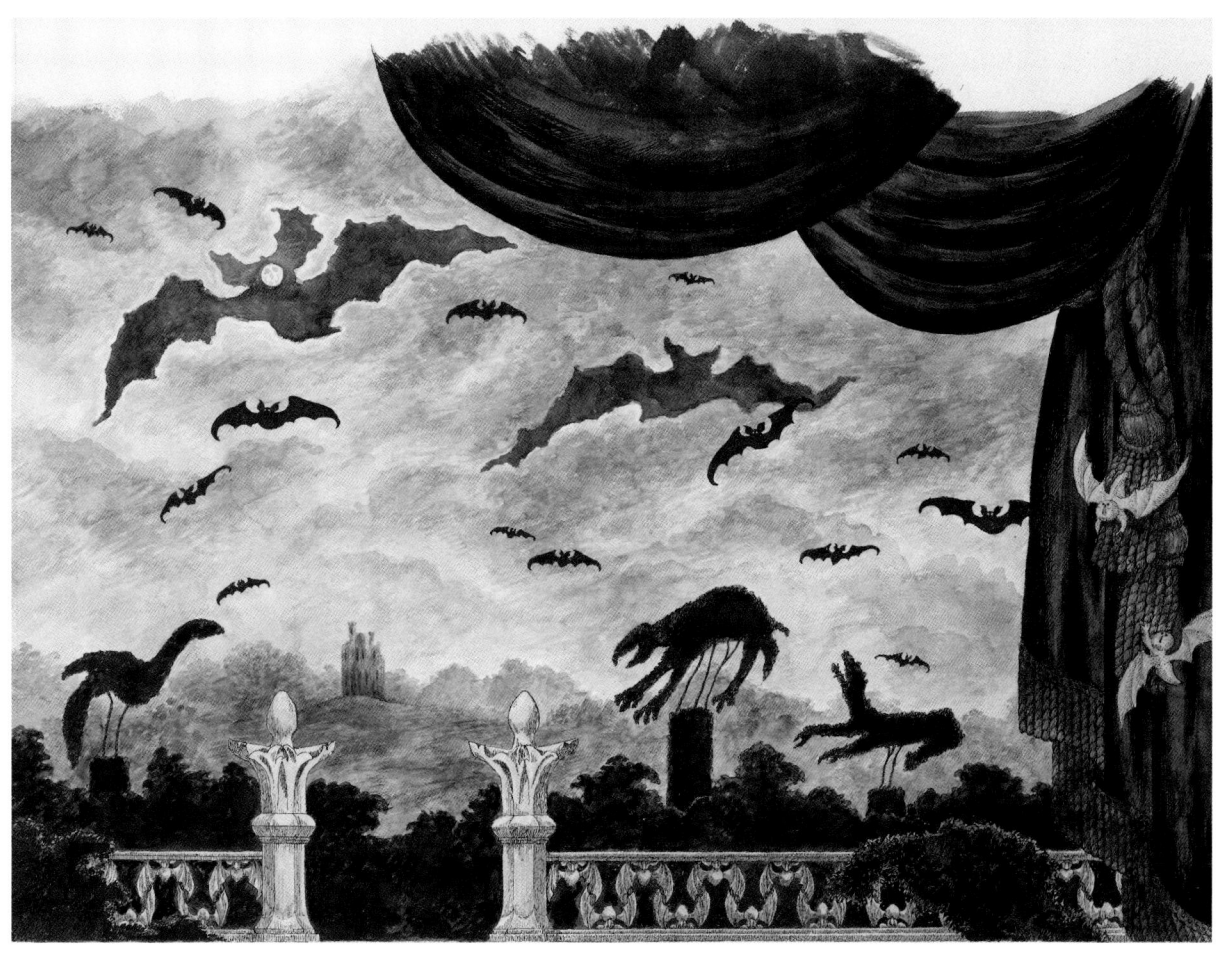

165. Design for drop curtain for *Dracula*, 1977

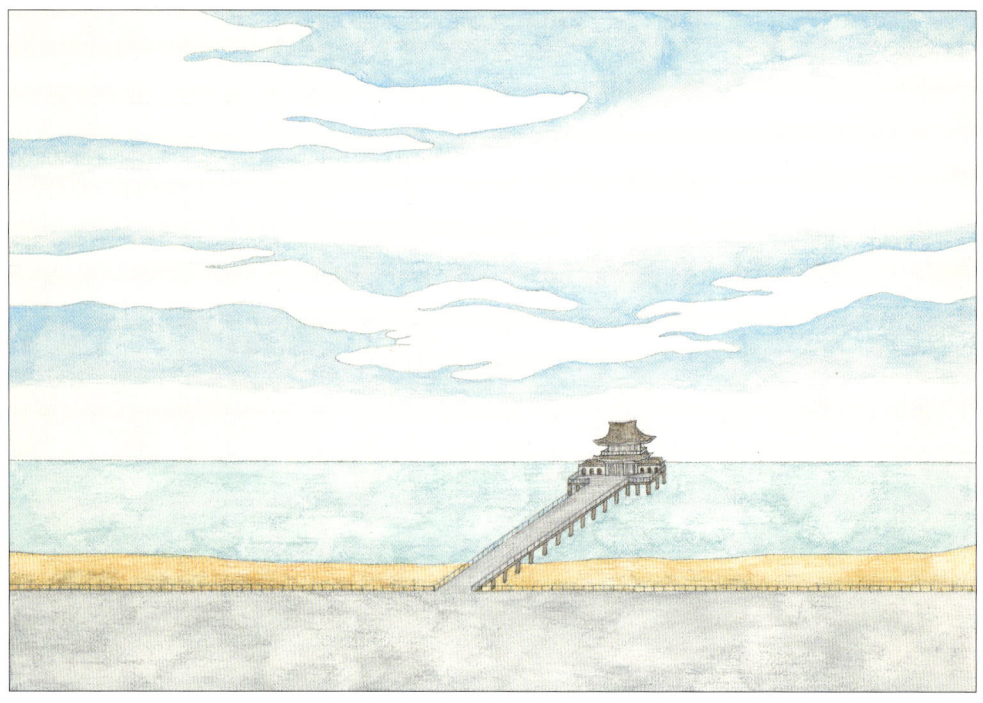

167. Set design

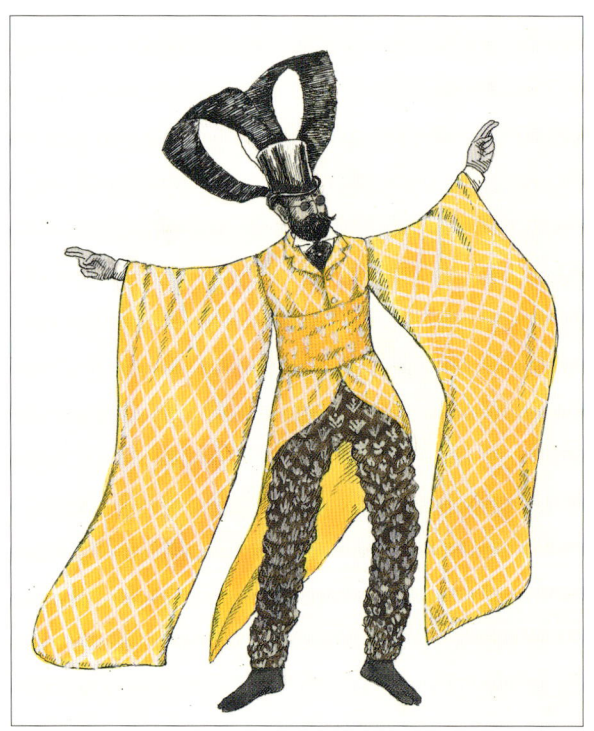

169. *The Mikado*

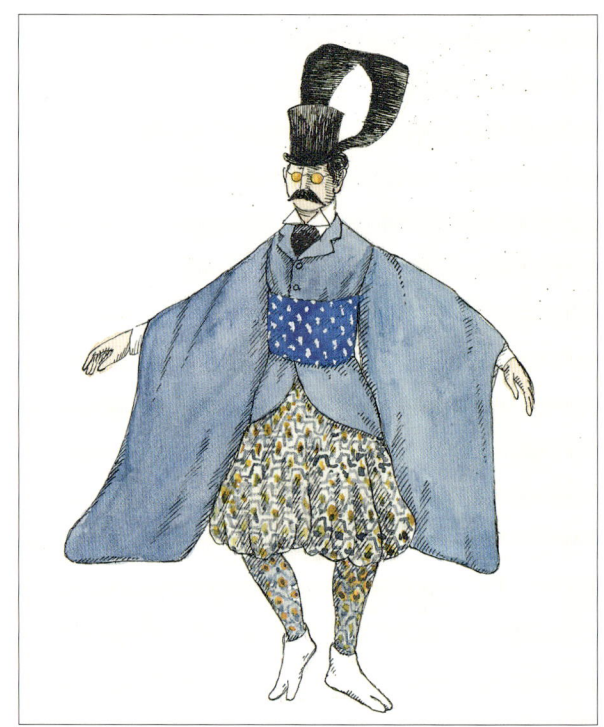

170. *Pishtush*

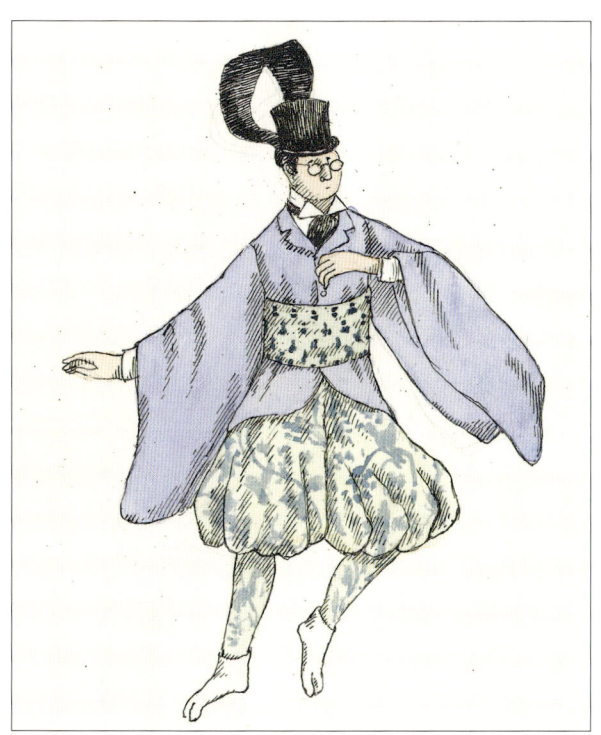

171. *Koko*

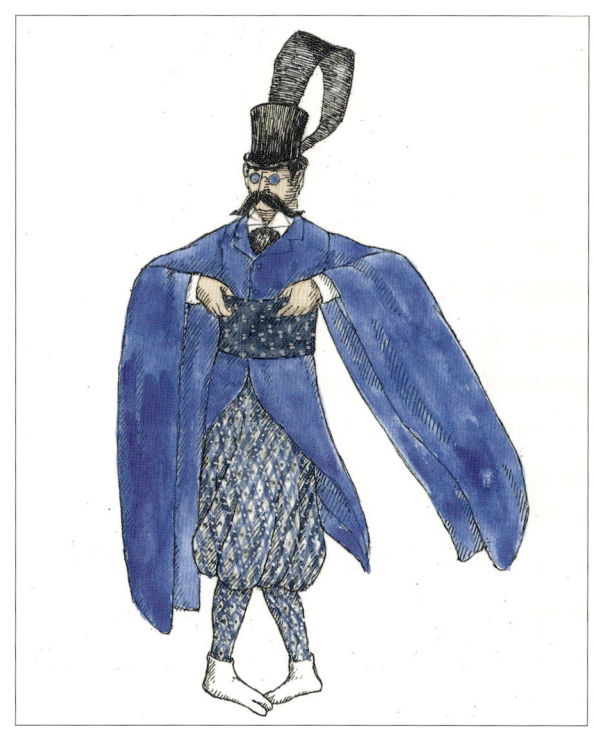

172. *Poohbah*

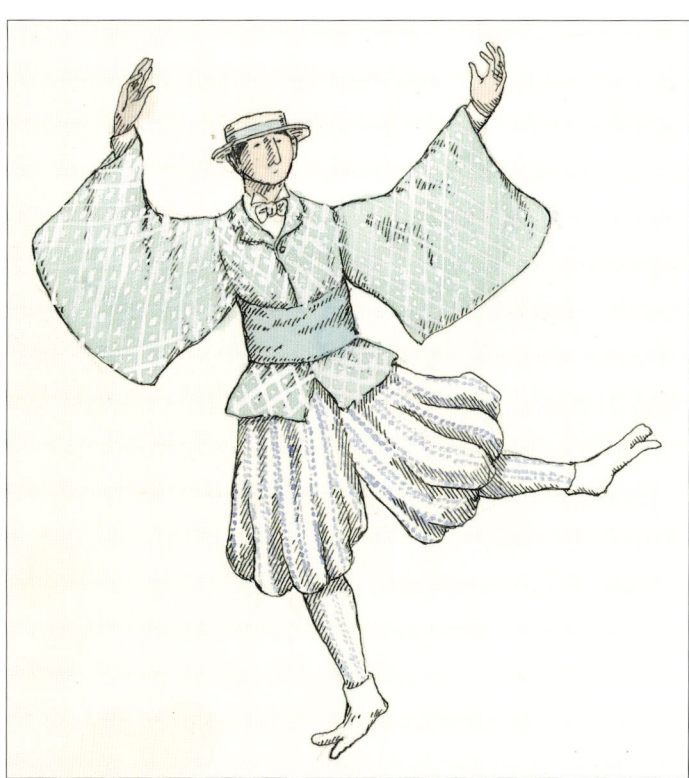

173. *Nankipoo*

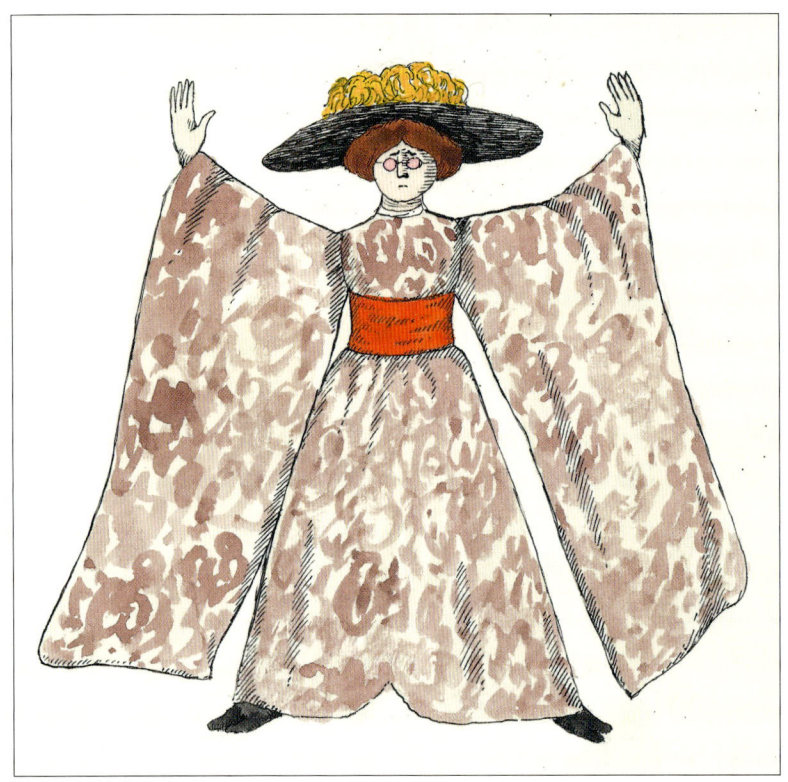

174. *Katisha*

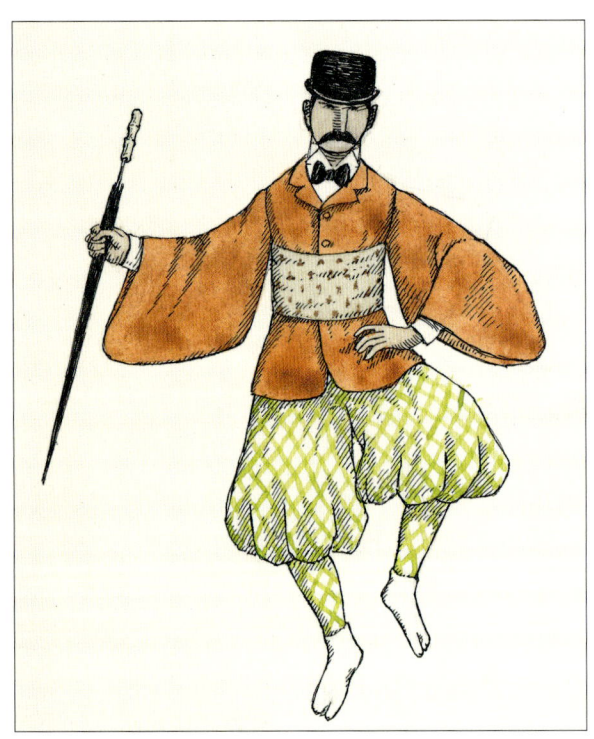

175. *Chorus Man*

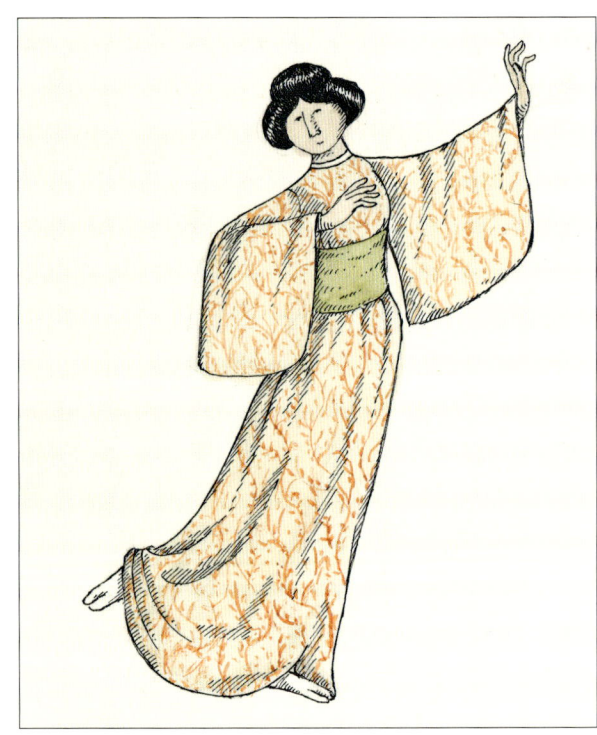

176. *Chorus Woman*

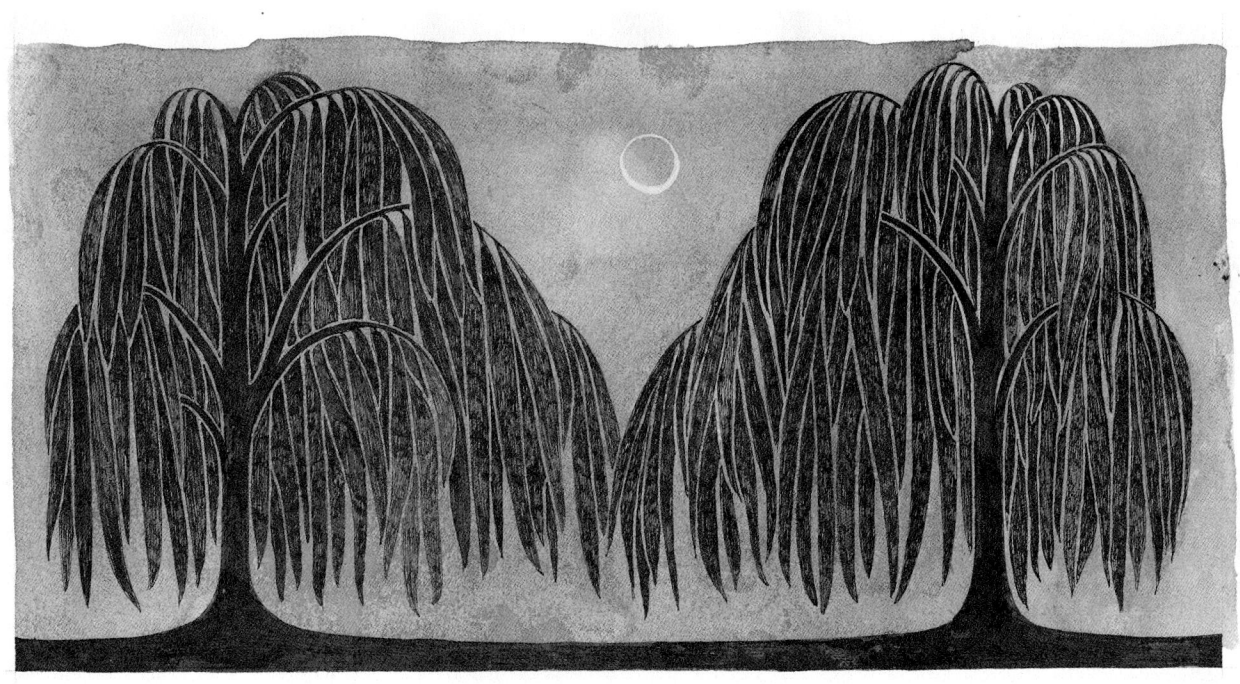

178. Set design for *Giselle*, Act II, 1994

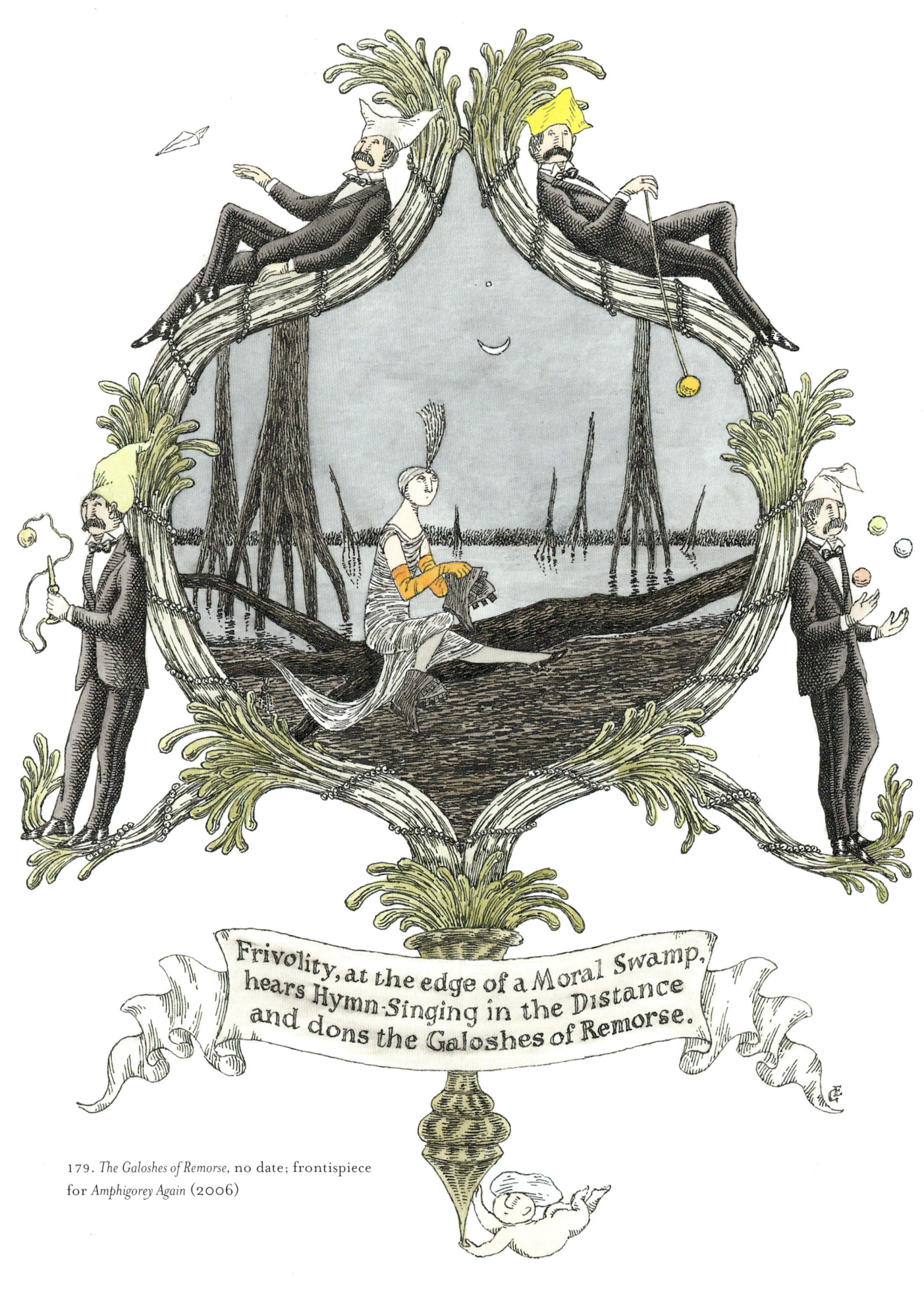

179. *The Galoshes of Remorse*, no date; frontispiece
for *Amphigorey Again* (2006)

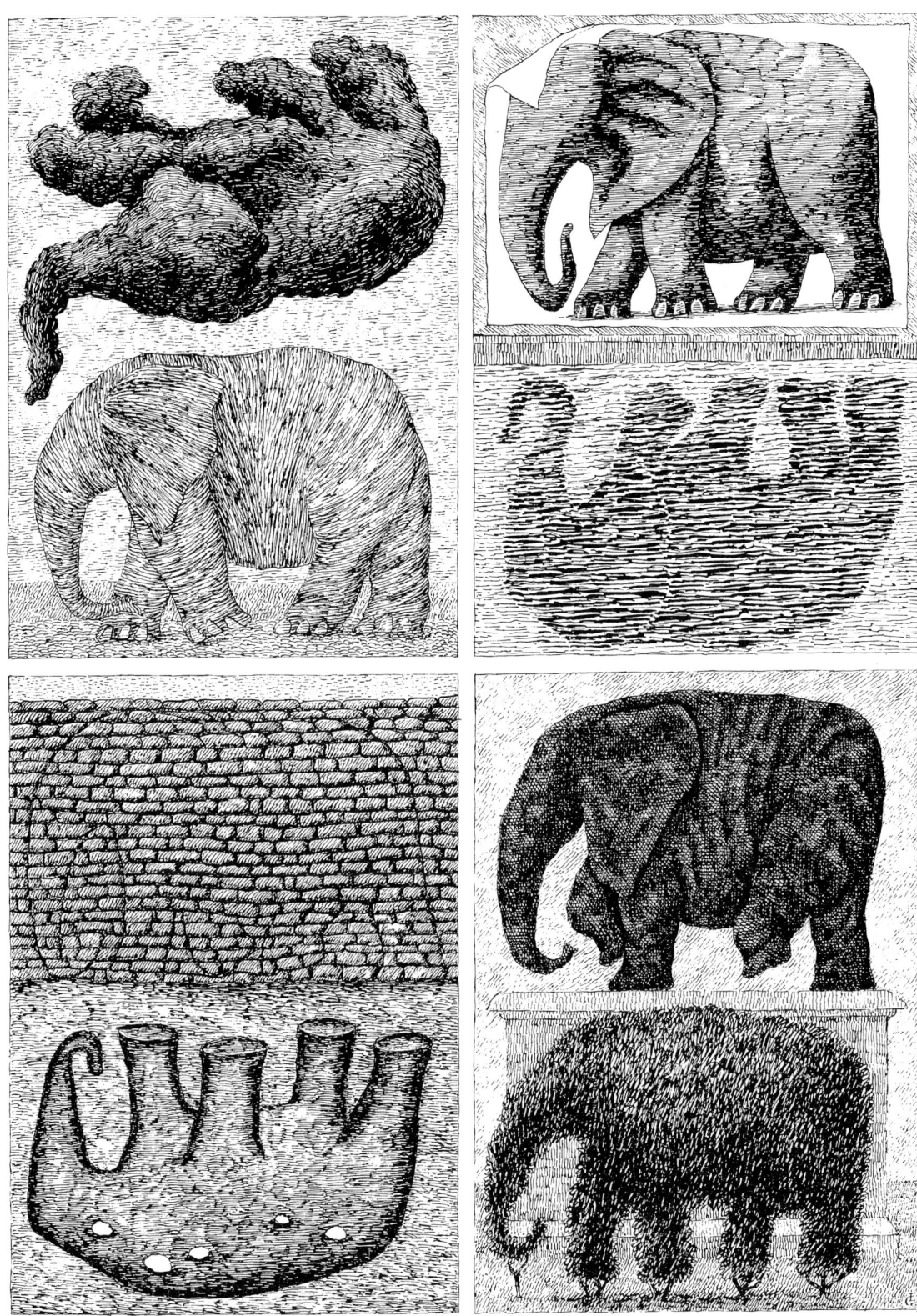

180. *Creativity*, published in *Amphigorey Again* (2006)

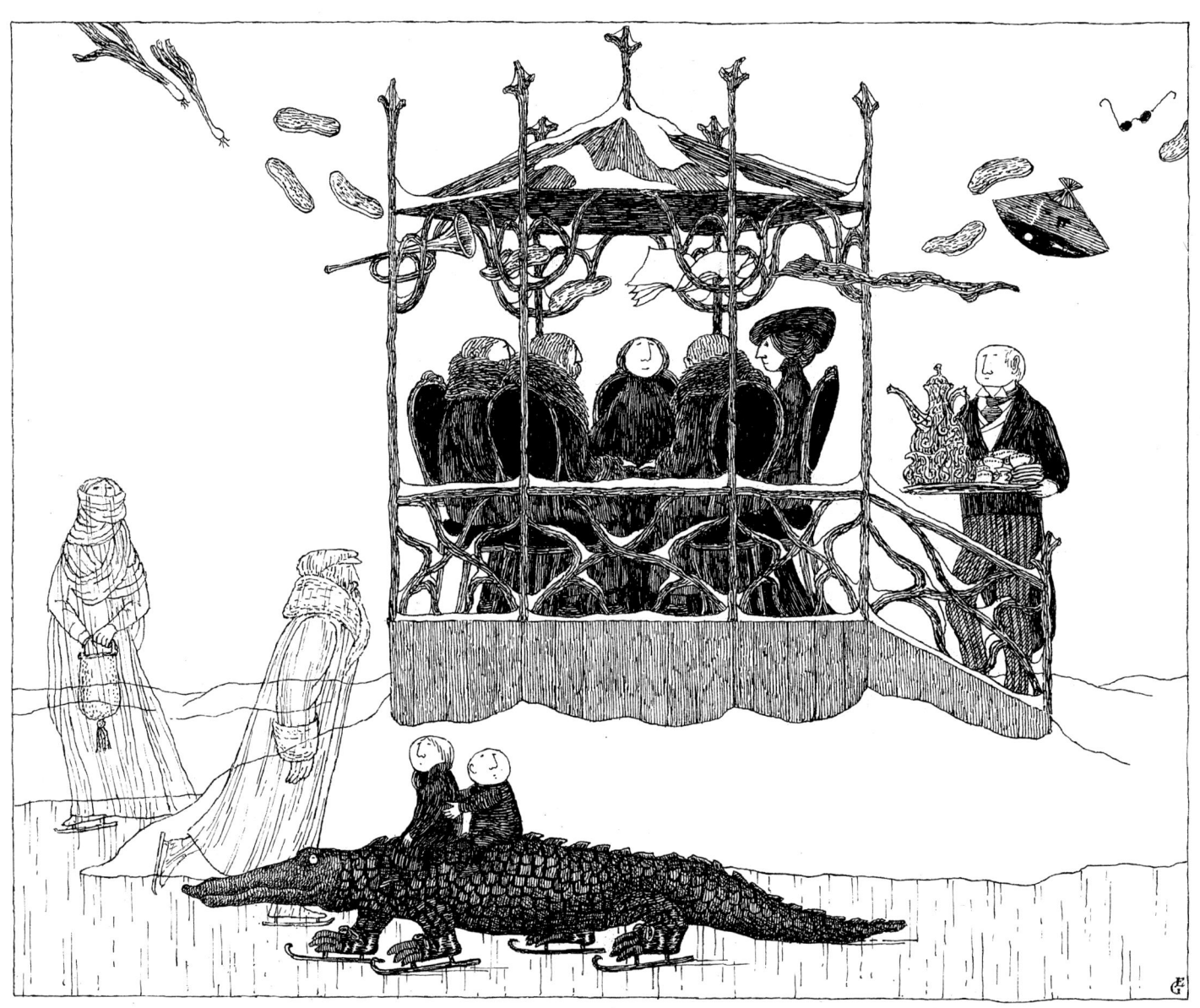

181. *Gazebo,* no date

CATALOGUE of the EXHIBITION

The catalogue checklist and the captions for the illustrations within
replicate Gorey's usage of punctuation.

BOOKS BY EDWARD GOREY

THE UNSTRUNG HARP; OR, MR EARBRASS WRITES A NOVEL
New York: Duell, Sloan
& Pearce, 1953

1. Study for the cover for
    The Unstrung Harp
    Pen and ink on colored paper,
    7⅝ x 5½ in. (n.i.)

2. Study for the cover for
    The Unstrung Harp
    Pen and ink on orange and
    white paper, 7 x 4¾ in. (p. 38)

3. Mr C(lavius) F(rederick)
    Earbrass is, of course, the
    well-known novelist. Of his
    books, *A Moral Dustbin, More
    Chains Than Clank, Was It Likely?,*
    and the Hipdeep trilogy are,
    perhaps, the most admired. Mr
    Earbrass is seen on the croquet
    lawn of his home, Hobbies
    Odd, near Collapsed Pudding
    in Mortshire. He is studying a
    game left unfinished at the end
    of summer.
    Pen and ink, 4½ x 3½ in.
    (p. 39)

4. Mr Earbrass was virtually
    asleep when several lines of
    verse passed through his mind
    and left it hopelessly awake.
    Here was the perfect epigraph
    for *TUH: A horrid ?monster has been
    [something] delay'd / By your/their
    indiff'rence in the dank brown shade /*

Below the garden. . . His mind's
eye sees them quoted on the
bottom third of a right-hand
page in a (possibly) olive-
bound book he read at least
five years ago. When he does
find them, it will be a great
nuisance if no clue is given to
their authorship.
Pen and ink, 4½ x 3½ in.
(p. 39)

5. Some weeks later, with
    pen, ink, scissors, paste, a
    decanter of sherry, and a vast
    reluctance, Mr Earbrass begins
    to revise *TUH.* This means,
    first, transposing passages, or
    reversing the order of their
    paragraphs, or crumpling them
    up furiously and throwing
    them in the waste-basket. After
    that there is rewriting. This
    is worse than merely writing,
    because not only does he have
    to think up new things just the
    same, but at the same time try
    not to remember the old ones.
    Before Mr Earbrass is through,
    at least one third of *TUH* will
    bear no resemblance to its
    original state.
    Pen and ink, 4½ x 3½ in.
    (p. 40)

THE LISTING ATTIC
New York: Duell, Sloan
& Pearce, 1954

6. Cover for *The Listing Attic*
    Pen and ink, 6½ x 4⅞ in.
    (p. 41)

7. There's a rather odd couple in
    Herts / Who are cousins (or
    so each asserts) / Their sex is
    in doubt / For they're never
    without / Their moustaches
    and long, trailing skirts.
    Pen and ink, 2⅞ x 3⅜ in.
    (p. 41)

THE DOUBTFUL GUEST
Garden City, N.Y.: Doubleday, 1957

8. Title page for *The Doubtful Guest*
    Pen and ink, 4½ x 6½ in.
    (p. 17)

9. Then they saw something
    standing on top of an urn, /
    Whose peculiar appearance
    gave them quite a turn.
    Pen and ink, 2⅝ x 3⅛ in.
    (p. 42)

10. It joined them at breakfast and
    presently ate / All the syrup
    and toast, and a part of a plate.
    Pen and ink, 2⅝ x 3½ in.
    (p. 43)

11. In the night through the house
    it would aimlessly creep, / In
    spite of the fact of its being
    asleep.
    Pen and ink, 2⅝ x 3½ in.
    (p. 43)

THE OBJECT-LESSON
Garden City, N.Y.: Doubleday, 1958

12. Unpublished cover for
    The Object-Lesson
    Pen and ink, 6 x 8 in. (p. 44)

13. Cover for *The Object-Lesson*
    Pen and ink, 6 x 8 in. (p. 44)

14. On the shore a bat, or possibly
    an umbrella,
    Pen and ink, 3 x 7½ in.
    (p. 45)

15. disengaged itself from the
    shrubbery,
    Pen and ink, 3 x 7½ in.
    (p. 45)

16. causing those nearby to
    recollect the miseries of
    childhood.
    Pen and ink, 3 x 7½ in.
    (p. 45)

THE FATAL LOZENGE
New York: Ivan Obolensky, 1960

17. Unpublished cover for
The Fatal Lozenge
Pen, ink, and watercolor,
5¹³⁄₁₆ x 5⅝ in. (p. 50)

18. Cover for *The Fatal Lozenge*
Pen and ink, 4½ x 3½ in.
(p. 50)

19. The Tourist huddles in the
station / While slowly night
gives way to dawn, / He finds
a certain fascination / In
knowing all the trains are
gone.
Pen and ink, 3 x 3½ in.
(p. 50)

THE HAPLESS CHILD
New York: Ivan Obolensky, 1961

20. There was once a little girl
named Charlotte Sophia.
Pen and ink, 3¾ x 4½ in.
(p. 46)

21. Her only other relative, an
uncle, was brained by a piece
of masonry.
Pen and ink, 3¾ x 4½ in.
(p. 24)

22. Charlotte Sophia was left in
the hands of the family lawyer.
Pen and ink, 3¾ x 4½ in.
(p. 46)

23. Every day he motored through
the streets searching for her.
Pen and ink, 3¾ x 4½ in.
(p. 47)

24. She was so changed, he did not
recognize her.
Reproduction, 3¾ x 4½ in.
(p. 24)

THE WILLOWDALE HANDCAR;
OR, THE RETURN OF THE
BLACK DOLL
Indianapolis, In.: Bobbs-Merrill,
1962

25. Page of studies for the cover
for *The Willowdale Handcar*
Pencil on paper, 11 x 8½ in.
(p. 48)

26. From the trestle over Peevish
Gorge they spied the wreck of
a touring car at the bottom.
'I don't see Dick's friend
anywhere,' said Harry.
Pen and ink, 3 x 4¼ in.
(p. 22)

27. Between West Elbow and
Penetralia they almost ran over
someone who was tied to the
track. It proved to be Nellie.
Pen and ink, 3 x 4¼ in.
(p. 49)

28. Some months went by, and
still they had not returned to
Willowdale.
Pen and ink, 3 x 4¼ in.
(p. 49)

29. At sunset they entered a tunnel
in the Iron Hills and did not
come out the other end.
Pen and ink, 3 x 4¼ in.
(p. 21)

THE GASHLYCRUMB TINIES; OR,
AFTER THE OUTING
New York: Simon & Schuster, 1963

30. Page of studies for front and
back covers
Pen and ink, 11 x 8½ in.
(p. 51)

31. A is for Amy who fell down the
stairs
Pen and ink, 2⅞ x 4 in.
(p. 52)

32. B is for Basil assaulted by bears
Pen and ink, 2⅞ x 4 in.
(p. 52)

33. M is for Maud who was swept
out to sea
Pen and ink, 2⅞ x 4 in.
(p. 18)

34. N is for Neville who died of
ennui
Reproduction, 2⅞ x 4 in.
(p. 18)

35. Cover for slipcase (front, top,
side, and bottom panels) for
*The Vinegar Works: Three Volumes of
Moral Instruction*, 1963
Pen and ink, 9½ x 8½ in.
(p. 53)

36. U is for Una who slipped down
a drain
Pen and ink, 2⅞ x 4 in. (n.i.)

37. V is for Victor squashed under
a train
Pen and ink, 2⅞ x 4 in. (n.i.)

THE WEST WING
New York: Simon & Schuster, 1963

38. Title page for *The West Wing*
Pen and ink, 4½ x 5½ in.
(p. 54)

39. Panel 1
Pen and ink, 4½ x 5½ in.
(p. 27)

40. Panel 5
Pen and ink, 4½ x 5½ in.
(p. 54)

41. Panel 13
Pen and ink, 4½ x 5½ in.
(p. 55)

42. Panel 17
Pen and ink, 4½ x 5½ in.
(p. 55)

43. Panel 22
Pen and ink, 4½ x 5½ in.
(p. 56)

44. Panel 27
Pen and ink, 4½ x 5½ in.
(p. 56)

45. Panel 29
Pen and ink, 4½ x 5½ in.
(p. 57)

46. Panel U
Pen and ink, 4½ x 5½ in.
(p. 57)

THE NURSERY FRIEZE
New York: The Fantod Press, 1964

47. Final manuscript for *The Nursery
Frieze*
Typescript on paper,
11 x 8½ in. (p. 32)

48. Study for *The Nursery Frieze*
Pen and ink, 11 x 8½ in.
(p. 59)

49. Study for *The Nursery Frieze*
Pen and ink, 11 x 8½ in.
(p. 59)

50. Study for *The Nursery Frieze*
Pen and ink, 11 x 8½ in.
(p. 59)

51. Finished drawing for *The Nursery Frieze*
Pen and ink, 2¾ x 13¼ in.
(p. 60)

52. Finished drawing for *The Nursery Frieze*
Pen and ink, 2¾ x 13½ in.
(p. 60)

THE REMEMBERED VISIT: A STORY TAKEN FROM LIFE
New York: Simon & Schuster, 1965

53. Sometimes she was made ill by curious dishes.
Pen and ink, 3⁹/₁₆ x 4¹⁵/₁₆ in.
(n.i.)

54. They were shown into a garden where the topiary was being neglected.
Pen and ink, 3⁹/₁₆ x 4¹⁵/₁₆ in.
(p. 58)

55. He and Miss Skrim-Pshaw mentioned a great many people who had done things in their conversation.
Pen and ink, 3⁹/₁₆ x 4¹⁵/₁₆ in.
(p. 58)

56. Months went by.
Pen and ink, 3⁹/₁₆ x 4¹⁵/₁₆ in.
(p. 17)

THE GILDED BAT
New York: Simon & Schuster, 1966

57. Eventually she was allowed to go up on point.
Pen and ink, 4 x 5½ in.
(p. 62)

58. Maud obtained a place in the corps of the Ballet Hochepot.
Pen and ink, 4 x 5½ in.
(p. 63)

59. After Federojenska did a grand jeté into the wings one matinee and was never seen again, Maud took over *Oiseau de Glace* to great acclaim.
Pen and ink, 4 x 5½ in.
(p. 63)

60. She had become the reigning ballerina of the age, and one of its symbols.
Pen and ink, 4 x 5½ in.
(p. 64)

61. Her life was really no different from what it had ever been.
Pen and ink, 4 x 5½ in.
(p. 64)

THE BLUE ASPIC
New York: Meredith Press, 1968

62. As Tsi-Nan-Fu Caviglia had her greatest triumph to date. (Working draft)
Pen and pencil on paper, 5¾ x 5¼ in. (p. 65)

63. While dressing, Gertrúdis Callosidad dipped into a box of candied violets from an unknown admirer.
Pen and ink, 4 x 5½ in.
(p. 66)

64. A statue fell on the Duke of Whaup during the second interval of *Amable Tastu*.
Pen and ink, 4 x 5½ in.
(p. 66)

65. Caviglia cruised the Adriatic with Basil Zaribaydjian, the financier, on his yacht, the *Maud*.
Pen and ink, 4 x 5½ in.
(p. 67)

66. Jasper's records got broken as he was escaping from the asylum.
Pen and ink, 4 x 5½ in.
(p. 67)

THE SECRETS: VOLUME ONE, THE OTHER STATUE
New York: Simon & Schuster, 1968

67. He was recognized at once by Lady Isobel Stringless, Lord Wherewithal's aunt, although they had last met seventeen years before on St Clot in the Maladroit Islands.
Pen and ink, 4½ x 5½ in.
(p. 68)

68. A clergyman staying at the Upturned Pig, the Rev. O. MacAbloo, wandered in a remote corner of the shrubbery.
Pen and ink, 4½ x 5½ in.
(p. 69)

69. Augustus woke up to find his stuffed twisby was missing.
Pen and ink, 4½ x 5½ in.
(p. 69)

70. A sudden gust of wind came up from nowhere and rushed through the trees.
Pen and ink, 4½ x 5½ in.
(p. 70)

71. After it had passed, Lord Wherewithal was found crushed beneath a statue blown down from the parapet.
Pen and ink, 4½ x 5½ in.
(p. 70)

72. Emily, helping her brother look for his twisby, saw a candlestick mounted on a horse's hoof thrown from a limousine as it drove away.
Pen and ink, 4½ x 5½ in.
(p. 71)

73. Lord Wherewithal had been murdered, said Dr Belgravius, to gain possession of it.
Pen and ink, 4½ x 5½ in.
(p. 71)

THE EPIPLECTIC BICYCLE
New York: Dodd, Mead, 1969

74. Page of studies for *The Epiplectic Bicycle*
Pen and ink, 11 x 8½ in.
(p. 72)

75. off which they rapidly ate a quantity of berries.
Pen and ink, 3½ x 7in.
(p. 73)

76. Embley and Yewbert were hitting one another with croquet mallets
Pen and ink, 2¼ x 4⅝ in.
(p. 73)

**THE IRON TONIC: OR, A WINTER
AFTERNOON IN LONELY VALLEY**
New York: Albondocani Press, 1969

77. The people at the grey hotel /
Are either aged or unwell.
Pen and ink, 4¼ x 8½ in.
(p. 74)

78. The monuments above the
dead / Are too eroded to be
read.
Pen and ink, 4¼ x 8½ in.
(p. 75)

79. They've gone and left it all
alone: / An absolutely useless
stone.
Pen and ink, 4¼ x 8½ in.
(p. 75)

**THE CHINESE OBELISKS:
FOURTH ALPHABET**
New York: The Fantod Press, 1970

80. A was an Author who went for
a walk
Pen and ink, 4 x 5 in. (p. 35)

THE OSBICK BIRD
New York: The Fantod Press, 1970

81. Page of studies for
The Osbick Bird
Pen and ink, 9⅞ x 7 in.
(p. 33)

82. Page of studies for
The Osbick Bird
Pen and ink, 11 x 8½ in.
(p. 76)

83. Page of studies for
The Osbick Bird
Pen and ink, 11 x 8½ in. (n.i.)

84. The top of the zagava tree /
Was frequently where they
had tea.
Pen and ink, 4 x 5 in. (p. 77)

85. In winter they were both
discreet / And wore galoshes
on their feet.
Pen and ink, 4 x 5 in. (p. 77)

86. And when at last poor Emblus
died / The osbick bird was by
his side.
Pen and ink, 4 x 5 in. (p. 78)

87. He was interred; the bird
alone / Was left to sit upon
his stone.
Pen and ink, 4 x 5 in. (p. 78)

88. But after several months, one
day / It changed its mind and
flew away.
Pen and ink, 4 x 5 in. (n.i.)

**THE DERANGED COUSINS;
OR, WHATEVER**
New York: The Fantod Press, 1971

89. They lived in a house covered
with roses on the edge of a
marsh.
Pen and ink, 4 x 5 in. (p. 79)

90. Mary struck Rose with a brown
china doorknob she had
already found and killed her.
Pen and ink, 4 x 5 in. (p. 20)

91. She had Marsh bury her in a
field known as the Rabbits'
Restroom.
Pen and ink, 4 x 5 in. (p. 79)

92. They must have been
contaminated, for he died in
agony during the night.
Pen and ink, 4 x 5 in. (p. 20)

[THE UNTITLED BOOK]
[Edward Pig, pseudo.]
New York: The Fantod Press, 1971

93. Draft of manuscript for *The
Untitled Book* with annotations
10⅞ x 8½ in. (p. 80)

94. Cover for *The Untitled Book*
Pen and ink, 4 x 5 in. (p. 80)

95. Ipsifendus
Pen and ink, 4 x 5 in. (p. 81)

96. Quoggenzocker
Pen and ink, 4 x 5 in. (p. 81)

97. hoo
Pen and ink, 4 x 5 in. (p. 25)

**THE LAVENDER LEOTARD; OR,
GOING A LOT TO THE NEW YORK
CITY BALLET**
New York: Gotham Book Mart, 1973

98. The author introduces two
small, distant, ageless, and
wholly imaginary relatives to
fifty seasons of the New York
City Ballet.
Pen and ink, 3¼ x 2¹/₁₆ in.
(p. 15)

A LIMERICK
Dennis, Mass.: Salt-Works Press,
1973

99. Little Zooks, of whom no one
was fond
Pen and ink, 4½ x 3½ in.
(p. 82)

100. They shot towards the roof and
beyond
Pen and ink, 4½ x 3½ in.
(p. 82)

101. The infant's trajectory passed
him over the rectory
Pen and ink, 4½ x 3½ in.
(p. 83)

102. And into a lily-choked pond
Pen and ink, 4½ x 3½ in.
(p. 83)

**THE LOST LIONS; OR, HAVING
OPENED THE WRONG ENVELOPE**
New York: The Fantod Press, 1973

103. With his sudden wealth he
bought a stylish house in
extensive grounds, and began
to raise lions.
Pen and ink, 4 x 5 in. (p. 84)

104. He devoted himself to raising
more lions and working at his
diaries.
Pen and ink, 4 x 5 in. (p. 84)

**THE GLORIOUS NOSEBLEED:
FIFTH ALPHABET**
New York: Dodd, Mead, 1975

105. She knitted mufflers Endlessly.
Pen and ink, 4 x 5 in. (p. 85)

106. They searched the cellars
Fruitlessly.
Pen and ink, 4 x 5 in. (p. 85)

107. She toyed with her beads
Jadedly.
Pen and ink, 4 x 5 in. (n.i.)

108. He ran through the hall
Maniacally.
Pen and ink, 4 x 5 in. (n.i.)

109. He wrote it all down Zealously.
Pen and ink, 4 x 5 in. (p. 36)

THE BROKEN SPOKE
New York: Dodd, Mead, 1976

110. Wrap-around cover for
The Broken Spoke
Pen, ink, and watercolor,
6¾ x 17 in. (p. 86)

*111. *Les Insectes Cyclistes*
Pen, ink, and watercolor,
15¾ x 13½ in. (p. 86)
Collection of Valerie and
Matthew Young

THE LOATHSOME COUPLE
New York: Dodd, Mead, 1977

112. That year Mona Gritch was
born to a pair of drunkards.
Pen and ink, 4½ x 5½ in.
(p. 88)

113. By the time he was twelve
Harold had caught the cold
that afterwards never left him.
Pen and ink, 4½ x 5½ in.
(n.i.)

114. As a child Mona already had
thick ankles and thin hair.
Pen and ink, 4½ x 5½ in.
(p. 88)

115. They went to the local cinema
whenever there was a crime
film playing.
Pen and ink, 4½ x 5½ in.
(p. 89)

116. Following one particularly
exciting one, they fumbled
with each other in a cold
woodshed.
Pen and ink, 4½ x 5½ in.
(p. 89)

LES URNES UTILES
Cambridge, Mass.: Haltry-Ferguson
Publishing, 1980

117. Vapours
Pen and ink, 4 x 5 in. (p. 90)

THE RAGING TIDE; OR, THE BLACK DOLL'S IMBROGLIO
New York: Beaufort Book
Publishers, 1987

118. No. 12—Figbash emerged from
the woodwork before Naeelah
and Hooglyboo. If this does
not upset you unduly, turn to
16. If you wish to be morally
improved, turn to 18.
Pen and ink, 4 x 6⅜ in. (p. 91)

119. No. 18—There's no going to
town in a bathtub. If you want
to get back to the story, turn
to 16. If you would like to tour
the Villa Amnesia, turn to 23.
Pen and ink, 4 x 6⅜ in. (p. 23)

120. Sketches of Figbash, no date
Pen and ink, 5 x 3 in. (p. 91)

121. Sketches of characters
Pen and ink, each about 2 in.
tall (n.i.)

DOGEAR WRYDE POSTCARDS: TRAGÉDIES TOPIARES
One of a series from *The Betrayed
Confidence: Seven Series of Dogear
Wryde Postcards*
Orleans, Mass.: Parnassus Imprints,
1992

122. le Chien d'arrêt
Pen and ink, 4¼ x 6½ in.
(p. 92)

123. les Serpents
Pen and ink, 4¼ x 6½ in.
(p. 92)

124. l'Automobile
Pen and ink, 4¼ x 6½ in.
(p. 93)

125. l'Ours
Pen and ink, 4¼ x 6½ in.
(p. 93)

THE TUNING FORK
New York: The Fantod Press, 1990

126. A monster of alarming size /
Was peering at her in surprise
Pen and ink, 4 x 5 in. (p. 28)

VERSE ADVICE
Published in *Amphigorey Again*,
New York: Harcourt Brace, 2006

127. It's possible to pick up crumbs /
By pressing on them with the
thumbs.
Pen and ink, 3⅝ x 3¼ in. (p. 94)

128. The helpful thought for
which you look / Is written
somewhere in a book.
Pen and ink, 3⅝ x 3¼ in.
([p. 1])

129. At twilight objects often start /
To make odd sounds and fall
apart.
Pen and ink, 3⅝ x 3¼ in. (p. 94)

130. One cannot hope to end one's
life / With nothing but a butter
knife.
Pen and ink, 3⅝ x 3¼ in. (p. 94)

131. The seaweed on the shore cries
out / But only it knows what
about.
Pen and ink, 3⅝ x 3¼ in. (p. 94)

THE HAUNTED TEA-COSY: A DISPIRITED AND DISTASTEFUL DIVERSION FOR CHRISTMAS
Published in *Amphigorey Again*,
New York: Harcourt Brace, 2006

132. 'I am the Bahhum Bug,' it
declared; 'I am here to diffuse
the interests of didacticism.'
Pen and ink, 2½ x 3⅛ in. (p. 30)

133. Albinia Fennel reclined on a
chaise longue and waited for a
letter from her brother in far-
off Hokkaido, Japan.
Pen and ink, 2½ x 3⅛ in. (p. 31)

BOOKS BY OTHER AUTHORS

THE JUMBLIES
by Edward Lear
New York: Young Scott Books, 1968

134. The water it soon came in, it
did, / The water it soon came
in; / So to keep them dry, they
wrapped their feet / In a pinky
paper all folded neat / And they
fastened it down with a pin.
Pen and ink, 3¾ x 6¾ in. (p. 14)

135. And they passed the night in a crockery-jar, / And each of them said, 'How wise we are! / Though the sky be dark, and the voyage be long, / Yet we never can think we were rash or wrong, / While round in our Sieve we spin!'
Pen and ink, 3¾ x 6¾ in.
(p. 95)

136. They sailed to the Western Sea, they did, / To a land all covered with trees, / And they bought an Owl, and a useful Cart, / And a pound of Rice, and a Cranberry Tart, / And a hive of silvery Bees.
Pen and ink, 3¾ x 6¾ in.
(p. 96)

137. And they bought a Pig, and some green Jack-daws, / And a lovely Monkey with lollipop paws, / And forty bottles of Ring-Bo-Ree, / And no end of Stilton Cheese.
Pen and ink, 3¾ x 6¾ in.
(p. 96)

THE DONG WITH A LUMINOUS NOSE
by Edward Lear
New York: Young Scott Books, 1969

138. When awful darkness and silence reign / Over the great Gromboolian plain, / Through the long, long wintry nights;— / When the angry breakers roar / As they beat on the rocky shore;— / When Storm-clouds brood on the towering heights / Of the Hills of the Chankly Bore:—
Pen and ink, 3¾ x 6¾ in.
(p. 14)

139. Slowly it wanders,—pauses,—creeps,— / Anon it sparkles,—flashes and leaps; / And ever as onward it gleaming goes / A light on the Bong-tree stems it throws.
Pen and ink, 3¾ x 6¾ in.
(p. 97)

140. And those who watch at that midnight hour / From Hall or Terrace, or lofty Tower, / Cry, as the wild light passes along,— / 'The Dong!—the Dong! / 'The wandering Dong through the forest goes! / 'The Dong! the Dong! / 'The Dong with a luminous Nose!'
Pen and ink, 3¾ x 6¾ in.
(p. 97)

141. For the Jumblies came in a sieve, they did,— / Landing at eve near the Zemmery Fidd / Where the Oblong Oysters grow, / And the rocks are smooth and gray. / And all the woods and the valleys rang / With the Chorus they daily and nightly sang,—
Pen and ink, 3¾ x 6¾ in.
(p. 98)

142. Happily, happily passed those days! / While the cheerful Jumblies staid; / They danced in circlets all night long, / To the plaintive pipe of the lively Dong, / In moonlight, shine, or shade. / For day and night he was always there / By the side of the Jumbly Girl so fair, / With her sky-blue hands, and her sea-green hair.
Pen and ink, 3¾ x 6¾ in.
(p. 98)

143. 'Far and few, far and few, / Are the lands where the Jumblies live; / Their heads are green, and their hands are blue, / And they went to sea in a sieve.'
Pen and ink, 3¾ x 6¾ in.
(p. 99)

144. And all who watch at the midnight hour, / From Hall or Terrace, or lofty Tower, / Cry, as they trace the Meteor bright, / Moving along through the dreary night,—
Pen and ink, 3¾ x 6¾ in.
(p. 99)

OLD POSSUM'S BOOK OF PRACTICAL CATS
by T. S. Eliot
New York: Harcourt Brace Jovanovich, 1982

145. Cover for *Old Possum's Book of Practical Cats*
Pen and ink, 7¾ x 5 in.
(p. 29)

146. The Naming of Cats
Pen and ink, 6½ x 4½ in.
(p. 100)

147. Macavity: The Mystery Cat
Pen and ink, 6½ x 4½ in.
(p. 100)

CAUTIONARY TALES FOR CHILDREN
by Hilaire Belloc
New York: Harcourt, 2002
Published posthumously.

148. Front and back covers for *Cautionary Tales for Children*
Pen, ink, and watercolor, 12⅞ x 9⅜ in. (p. 101)

149. Algernon, / Who played with a Loaded Gun, / and, on missing his Sister, was / reprimanded by his Father
Pen and ink, 7 x 3¾ in.
(p. 102)

150. Young Algernon, the Doctor's Son, / Was playing with a Loaded Gun. / He pointed it towards his sister, / Aimed very carefully, but Missed her!
Pen and ink, 5⁵⁄₁₆ x 3¾ in.
(p. 103)

151. His Father, who was standing near, / The Loud Explosion chanced to Hear, / And reprimanded Algernon / For playing with a Loaded Gun.
Pen and ink, 5⁵⁄₁₆ x 3¾ in.
(p. 103)

152. Jim, / Who ran away from his Nurse, / and was eaten by a Lion
Pen and ink, 7 x 4¼ in.
(p. 102)

MISCELLANEOUS ARTWORKS

153. Illustrated envelope (birds on trapezes), March 1948
Pen, ink, and watercolor, 4⅛ x 9½ in. (p. 104)

154. Illustrated envelope (angels watering vines), April 1948
Pen, ink, and watercolor, 4⅛ x 9½ in. (p. 105)

155. Illustrated envelope (angel with banner), April 1948
Pen, ink, and watercolor, 4⅛ x 9½ in. (p. 105)

156. Illustrated envelope (man on trapeze), May 1948
Pen, ink, and watercolor, 4⅛ x 9½ in. (p. 105)

157. Illustrated envelope (man in cannon), May 1948
Pen, ink, and watercolor, 4⅛ x 9½ in. (p. 106)

158. Illustrated envelope (man climbing ladder in the clouds), May 1948
Pen, ink, and watercolor, 4⅛ x 9½ in. (p. 106)

159. Illustrated envelope (man about to be garroted), May 1948
Pen, ink, and watercolor, 4⅛ x 9½ in. (p. 106)

160. Dragon and Man Exchange Gifts, circa 1950
Pen and ink, 6⅛ x 4⅛ in. (p. 108)

161. Cover for *Lafcadio's Adventures* by André Gide, New York: Doubleday, 1953
Pen and ink, 7⅜ x 4⅞ in. (p. 34)

162. Cover for *Redburn: His First Voyage* by Herman Melville, New York, Doubleday, 1957
Pen and ink, 7⅜ x 5 in. (p. 34)

163. Study for the cover for *Amphigorey*, New York: G. P. Putnam's Sons, 1972
Pen and ink, 11 x 8½ in. (p. 107)

*164. Insect on Unicycle, 1976
Etching and aquatint, 4⅞ x 1⅞ in. (p. 124)
Collection of Frances Massey Dulaney

*165. Drop curtain design for *Dracula*, 1977
Pen, ink, and watercolor, 20½ x 27 in. (p. 109)
Collection of Frances Massey Dulaney

166. Self-Portrait with Flying Dog, 1978
Pen and ink, 5½ x 3½ in. (p. 6)

——

The Mikado, by W. S. Gilbert and Sir Arthur Sullivan
Costume and set designs created by Edward Gorey for the Carnegie Mellon University drama department, 1983

167. Set design for *The Mikado*
Watercolor, 8¼ x 12 in. (p. 110)

168. Set design for *The Mikado*
Watercolor, 6¼ x 12 in. (n.i.)

169. Costume design for the Mikado
Pen, ink, and watercolor, 5½ x 4½ in. (p. 110)

170. Costume design for Pishtush
Pen, ink, and watercolor, 4⅞ x 3½ in. (p. 110)

171. Costume design for Koko
Pen, ink, and watercolor, 4¾ x 3½ in. (p. 111)

172. Costume design for Poohbah
Pen, ink, and watercolor, 5½ x 3¼ in. (p. 111)

173. Costume design for Nankipoo
Pen, ink, and watercolor, 4¾ x 4½ in. (p. 111)

174. Costume design for Katisha
Pen, ink, and watercolor, 4½ x 4¾ in. (p. 112)

175. Costume design for men's chorus
Pen, ink, and watercolor, 4½ x 3½ in. (p. 112)

176. Costume design for women's chorus
Pen, ink, and watercolor, 4½ x 2⅞ in. (p. 112)

177. Drop curtain design for *The Mikado*
Pen, ink, and watercolor, 7½ x 9¾ in. (p. 13)

——

178. Set design for *Giselle*, Act II, Eglevsky Ballet, 1994
Ink on paper, 5 x 10 in. (p. 113)

179. The Galoshes of Remorse, frontispiece for *Amphigorey Again*, New York: Harcourt Brace, 2006
Pen, ink, and watercolor, 9¾ x 7¼ in. (p. 114)

180. Creativity, published in *Amphigorey Again*, New York: Harcourt Brace, 2006
Tear sheet, 8½ x 6¼ in. (p. 115)

181. *Gazebo*, no date
Pen and ink, 6 x 10 in. (p. 116)

182. Untitled, no date
Pen and ink, 10 x 8 in. (p. 8)

183. Self-Portrait with Floating Cats, no date
Pen, ink, and watercolor, 4⅝ x 3¾ in. (p. 37)

184. Sketchbook, no date
Pen and pencil on paper (n.i.)

185. Sketchbook, no date
Pen and pencil on paper (n.i.)

*186. Fur Coat (**Brandywine River Museum Only**), no date
Sheared beaver skin (n.i.)
Collection of Frances Massey Dulaney

*187. Figbash doll, no date
Cotton and rice, 11 x 12 in. (n.i.)
Collection of Frances Massey Dulaney

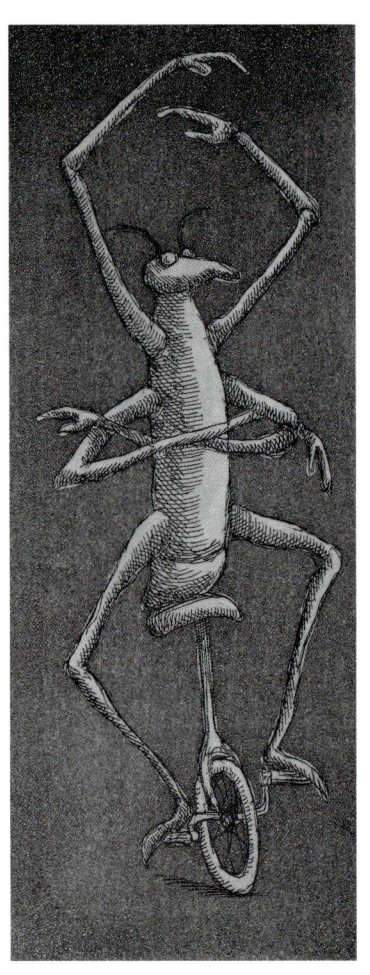

164. *Insect on Unicycle*, 1976

Author **KAREN WILKIN**, a curator and critic specializing in twentieth-century modernism, is the co-author of *The World of Edward Gorey* (Abrams, 1996) and the author of *Ascending Peculiarity: Edward Gorey on Edward Gorey* (Harcourt, 2001), as well as monographs on Anthony Caro, Stuart Davis, Hans Hofmann, Helen Frankenthaler, Giorgio Morandi, and David Smith. She is a regular contributor to *The New Criterion, Art in America,* and *The Wall Street Journal,* and a contributing editor for art for *The Hudson Review.*

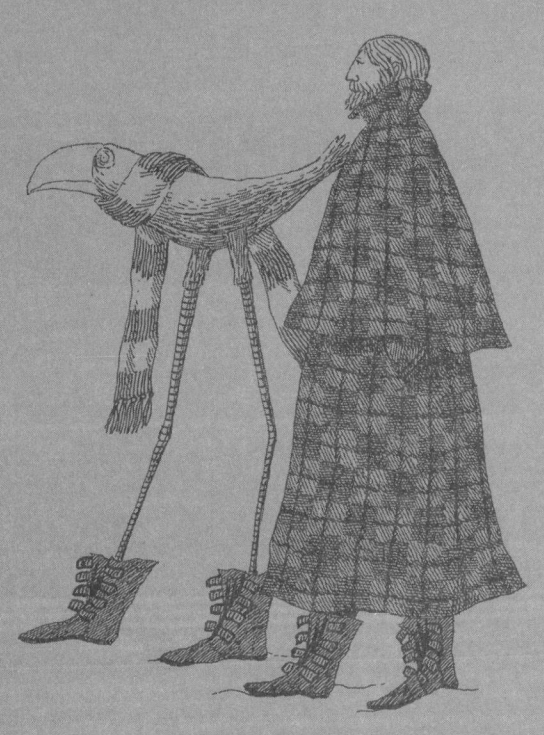